Web Application Design and Implementation

THE WILEY BICENTENNIAL—KNOWLEDGE FOR GENERATIONS

*E*ach generation has its unique needs and aspirations. When Charles Wiley first opened his small printing shop in lower Manhattan in 1807, it was a generation of boundless potential searching for an identity. And we were there, helping to define a new American literary tradition. Over half a century later, in the midst of the Second Industrial Revolution, it was a generation focused on building the future. Once again, we were there, supplying the critical scientific, technical, and engineering knowledge that helped frame the world. Throughout the 20th Century, and into the new millennium, nations began to reach out beyond their own borders and a new international community was born. Wiley was there, expanding its operations around the world to enable a global exchange of ideas, opinions, and know-how.

For 200 years, Wiley has been an integral part of each generation's journey, enabling the flow of information and understanding necessary to meet their needs and fulfill their aspirations. Today, bold new technologies are changing the way we live and learn. Wiley will be there, providing you the must-have knowledge you need to imagine new worlds, new possibilities, and new opportunities.

Generations come and go, but you can always count on Wiley to provide you the knowledge you need, when and where you need it!

WILLIAM J. PESCE
PRESIDENT AND CHIEF EXECUTIVE OFFICER

PETER BOOTH WILEY
CHAIRMAN OF THE BOARD

Web Application Design and Implementation

Apache 2, PHP5, MySQL, JavaScript, and Linux/UNIX

Steven A. Gabarró

Stevens Institute of Technology
Hoboken, New Jersey

WILEY-INTERSCIENCE
A John Wiley & Sons, Inc., Publication

Library of Congress Cataloging-in-Publication Data:
Gabarró, Steven A., 1979–
    Web application design and implementation: Apache 2, PHP5, MySQL,
JavaScript, and Linux/Unix / by Steven A. Gabarró.
        p.   cm.
    Includes index.
    ISBN-13: 978-0-471-77391-7 (cloth)
    ISBN-10: 0-471-77391-3 (cloth)
    1. Web site development.   2. Web sites–Design.   3. Application
software–Development.   I. Title.
    TK5105.8883.G33 2007
    006.7–dc22
                                                            2006014999

Printed in the United States of America.

10 9 8 7 6 5 4 3 2 1

Contents

Preface

ABOUT THE AUTHOR

Steven Gabarró was born in 1979 and raised in Alicante, Spain. He started programming early, learning BASIC (Beginner's All-purpose Symbolic Instruction Code) at age 9. Later on, in high school, he learned Turbo Pascal and C. At that point it was pretty obvious that he was going to end up as a computer scientist. He ended up studying for a master's degree in computer science in the Ecole Pour l'Informatique et les Techniques Avancées, where he specialized in advanced multimedia and Web technologies, graduating with honors, finishing third in his class. He went to the United States in January 2002, enrolling in the Masters of Science in Information Systems at the Stevens Institute of Technology, in Hoboken, New Jersey. There he quickly advanced from teaching assistant to full-time instructor. On his appointment as full-time faculty, he created the first Web programming course at Stevens, based on his personal experiences. This book is the result of that course, and is a close reflection of what Steven teaches his students.

BEFORE WE GET STARTED

In my years of programming, I have learned tons of different programming languages, ranging from Basic to Java, and including C, PHP, JavaScript, Visual Basic, C++, Assembly 68k, and many others. Because of this variety I have always been obsessed with utilizing the tools I had available to combine the best aspects of each programming language.

With this mentality I decided to create a Web programming course that would teach the ins and outs of the most commonly used free Web technologies. I have always supported free software, and as the big UNIX fan that I am, I had to teach open-source technologies. This book is the result of the work I did on the course, with added content to take it a step further.

WHO SHOULD READ THIS BOOK?

The way this book is organized, it should be ideal for anyone trying to learn how to create complete Websites with no previous knowledge of any of the languages presented. It does require some minimum knowledge of programming in general, as well as object-oriented programming basics to understand Chapter 8.

It is also a good read for Web designers that know about making pages look nice, but have no knowledge of how to create dynamic pages built through a database or anyone who would like to pick up on the art of programming pages. Realize that I have never been a good graphic designer, so this book will not tell you how to do things like making decisions regarding the proper colors, fonts, or sizes to use, or other cosmetic details. I will deal with how to set those features up, but will not tell you how to pick your layout or color schemes, because I am definitely not good at it. Instead, I will concentrate on how to actually program useful pages with loads of functionality.

ABOUT THE EXAMPLES

All the examples have been tested, and if any are not compatible with a specific browser, this will be stated in the text. You can find all the example files, as well as an example solution for the mini exercises and the indexer/searcher case study at ftp://ftp.wiley.com/public/sci_tech_med/web_application. I will also work on extra examples that I will make available to illustrate other areas of the book that did not get a full example. I would have included many more examples, but then you would need two or three volumes this size. Instead, I will just put everything in a Website for you to download and test. I hope you enjoy it all!

HOW TO READ THIS BOOK

The book is organized to be read front to back, but you may skip chapters as you see fit, or use the book as a reference. The Introduction is a summary of Chapter 19 and should be used by people already experienced in Web development. It is basically meant as a guide to using this book as a "Web programming cookbook." You may read this Introduction for brief guidelines or go straight to Chapter 19 if you need an in-depth explanation with a practical example.

Acknowledgments

I'd like to express great thanks to my family first for always being there for me. I wouldn't be where I am without them, and I'll never manage to thank them enough for that. To my very close (and special, a.k.a. N.B.) friends, I thank you for your support and patience over the years; it is not easy putting up with me for so long, but you have always given me some of the best times I could hope for. Quick "howdy" to my online friends at COTW and BF2C for helping me steam off when I had too much work and needed a break. Thanks to Larry Bernstein for allowing me the opportunity to write this book, and of course thanks to the people at John Wiley & Sons for getting my first book published even though I'm still "a kid." Special thanks to Whitney, Paul and Melissa for all of their help and patience; and to Ben for the cover image. ☺

Introduction

Web Application Recipe

OVERVIEW

You might be wondering why you are reading an "Introduction" chapter and why this chapter is called "Web Application Recipe." Well, this chapter is your quick guide to professional Web application design and implementation. It is in essence a summary of the last chapter of the book (Chapter 19), created mainly for people with enough experience in Web programming to skip some of the chapters presented. This chapter will give you the rundown of the major steps in the lifecycle of a Web project, and will refer to the chapters where you might find more in-depth information on the topics covered. I call it the "recipe" because it gives you the general layout of what needs to be done, before getting into the specific details that each individual chapter will cover. For a more in-depth guideline with a practical example, be sure to read Chapter 19.

PROCEDURE

Step 1—Understanding the Problem and Finding the Solution

The first step in Web development (and any type of project, to be honest) is to understand what the problem is, as well as what input will be used and

Web Application Design and Implementation: Apache 2, PHP5, MySQL, JavaScript, and Linux/UNIX, by Steven A. Gabarró
Copyright © 2007 by John Wiley & Sons, Inc.

what output should be produced. This phase is usually done in meetings between the project manager and the project sponsor (the person paying for the project). This is a crucial phase as it defines the scope of the project, such as the features that need to be implemented, and the feel that the page should have. The main area of discussion in this step is *what* the project will do, without concentrating on the "how."

Step 2—Designing the Database

When creating web applications, chances are your program will need to store data; hence the use of databases. Many developers create the database as they implement the program, but this can cause serious troubles as they realize well into the project that the initial design of the database is flawed and all the work needs to be redone. This is why you should *always* start by designing the database, keeping in mind what the project needs are. Chapters 11 and 12 will show you how to design and create a database. In a database-driven project the database is the heart of the project.

Step 3—Major Functionalities

Once the database is created, it is time to program the major functionalities of your application. Many programmers tend to spend a lot of time making sure that the pages they create look good, without worrying about whether they actually do something. Webpage appearance is obviously important, but you will get more out of an ugly functional Web application than with a pretty-looking useless page. Most of the work needed in this phase will require accessing the database. To find out more about how to do so, check Chapter 13. This step is basically like programming the brain of your application, ensuring that its core runs perfectly well.

Step 4—Backside

Once the core of the project is up and running, you need to implement the back end of the project. This is the section of the project that will be used by administrators to manage the Website after it has been published, and it is a good idea to have it up and running before the regular users start meddling with the Web application. If you need some information on writing scripts in PHP, check out Chapters 5–9.

Step 5—Improvements on Functionality

This is the phase where you start having fun with the project and improve its functionalities. It is the opportunity to begin improving the client-side functionalities by adding some JavaScript scripts to your pages, such as form verifications. Check Chapters 14–18 for more information on how to program in JavaScript. Just make sure that the improvements you decide to work on are within the scope of the project, to avoid what is known as "scope creep" (see Chapter 19).

Step 6—Improvements on Looks

Once your project is working, you may start working on the esthetics. Start by using style sheets (Chapter 10), and do not hesitate to ask your favorite Web designer for help. In case you wonder about the difference between a web developer and a Web designer, in essence, a Web designer takes care of the looks (appearance) of Websites and Web developers write the scripts that make the pages work. This is the step that adds the skin to the project.

Step 7—Thorough Testing, Hacking Attempts

This is probably one of the most important phases in the project. The goal of this phase is to ensure that the project is flawless and that you have made it hackerproof. The best asset in this phase is imagination and a bit of paranoia. Never assume that your users will be friendly, using your application for what it was meant to be. The true secret to a hacker-safe program is to think like a hacker. Try to think of any security hole that you might not have fixed yet and *fix it*! This step is the equivalent of getting some immunizations for your project. The more time you spend here, the less time you will spend dealing with attacks.

Step 8—Presentation

Assuming that you are not writing the application for yourself and there is money involved, you will need to present your final project to your project sponsor. The key here is to be relaxed and be confident that your project is rock-solid. If you follow the guidelines in this book, this should not be a problem. If you are presenting to a nontechnical person, start by showing the general features of the project, getting into details only when asked to do so. If you are presenting to a fellow developer, go straight to the functionalities.

Step 9—Publication

When the project has been approved, it is time to release it. Place it in your desired host and make sure that everything is set up properly so that users worldwide can access it. This phase should be fairly fast.

Step 10—Celebration (and Maintenance)

Once the project is published, this is your chance for a small break. Enjoy your favorite brew, have a good night's sleep, and get back to work! Once a project is published, you need to maintain it, updating the database as needed or fixing bugs that users might have found.

1

Fundamentals

THE ORIGINS OF THE INTERNET

Not that long ago, in a galaxy pretty close by, men and women used to live without practical means of communication. Paper was the main medium used for information sharing and horses the main carrier for that medium. But science kept working, and in 1831 Joseph Henry invented the first electric telegraph. Four years later, Samuel Morse invented the Morse code, and worked on the very first long-distance electric telegraph line, which he finished in 1843. A bigger leap in communication progress was made by Alexander Graham Bell, who patented the electric telephone in 1876. Long-distance communication was finally a reality, but still archaic compared to what was to be achieved. With the arrival of computers in the midtwentieth century, people realized the potential of storing and processing data in those amazing new machines. Furthermore, the United States and the Soviet Union were deep in the Cold War, and the fear of a possible strike was constantly present in the military's mind. One of the main concerns was the possibility that all communication between remote locations could be interrupted by an attack. Telephone and telegraph lines were out in the open, and could be easily damaged, so the National Security Agency (NSA) thought of a way to preserve communications. Emulating the principles of telephone communication, in the 1960s, the NSA thought of connecting computers through

Web Application Design and Implementation: Apache 2, PHP5, MySQL, JavaScript, and Linux/UNIX, by Steven A. Gabarró
Copyright © 2007 by John Wiley & Sons, Inc.

wide-area networks (WANs), so that if the phone lines went down, they would still be able to send orders to detachments across the country, through the use of computers. In order to make this idea a reality, the Advanced Research Project Agency (ARPA) created the first computer network in 1969, and named it the ARPANET. It was composed of only four computers, located in the University of California at Los Angeles (UCLA), the University of California at Santa Barbara (UCSB), the University of Utah, and the Stanford Research Institute (SRI). Three years later, in 1972, the use of routers allowed the ARPANET to have 20 nodes and 50 host computers, which could all communicate through tools such as the telnet and FTP (File Transfer Protocol). In 1974 Vincent Cerf, from the SRI, and Robert Kahn, from the Defense Advanced Research Project Agency (DARPA), presented the Transmission Control Protocol/Internet Protocol (TCP/IP) basics, forever changing the way computers would communicate. In 1983 the Defense Communication Agency (DCA) took control of the ARPANET and separated the military section to form the MILNET, which would be used for military purposes only. In the mid-1980s the two main existing networks, the ARPANET and the NSFNET (created by the National Science Foundation), merged to create a massive computer network. That merge motivated a trend that brought more and more computers to the network, and this network of networks was then named "the Internet." By 1990 the Internet had 3000 subnets and over 200,000 host computers. The estimated number of host computers in the year 2004 was approximately 234 million, and growing.

THE WORLD WIDE WEB

After creation of the Internet, great potential could be seen way beyond the actual work that was being done. Computers were destined to do more than utilize telnets and FTP; it was great to be able to link one computer to another in order to send files, but the problem of communication was not yet totally solved. Scientists doing research had to connect to a remote computer and send their research results one at the time through FTP. This was faster than sending manuscripts through "snail mail," but it was still not the best option, so in 1989 Tim Berners-Lee presented the World Wide Web project to the Conseil Européen de Recherche Nucléaire (CERN; European Organization for Nuclear Research, based in Switzerland). The idea was to come up with a set of standards for information sharing that scientists around the world would be able to use. The goal was to be able to have all research documents in a format and location accessible to all interested regardless of the platform being used. In 1994 the World Wide Web Consortium (W3C) was created to lead the World Wide Web (WWW) to its full potential by developing common protocols that would promote its evolution and ensure its operability. You can find out more about the W3C visiting their Website, www.w3c.org.

THE WEB BROWSERS

Right at this point we have seen what lead to the creation of the computer network known as "the Internet," and the reasoning behind the apparition of the World Wide Web. But we still have a main problem that we haven't answered yet—how do we use all this to communicate? First the Internet brought us the media through which the information would flow, then the WWW provided a standard format for information formatting, but there was still the problem of *how* to read that information. To solve that problem, some tool had to be created that would use the current standards and decode Web documents and format them in such a way that would be intelligible to the user. The Web browsers came to the rescue and solved that problem. The first graphical user interface (GUI) with the WWW to appear was Mosaic, created by the National Center of Supercomputer Applications (NCSA) at the University of Illinois in 1993. In 1994 Norway entered in the pages of Internet history by creating the still-used Opera. Soon afterward Netscape appeared, followed by Microsoft's Internet Explorer, which appeared along Windows 95. From that point on, the browsing market has done nothing but evolve and—Fortunately for us, the users—improve. Nowadays the two main browsers used are Internet Explorer and Mozilla Firefox.

THE WEB SERVERS

Now that we know what the Internet is, the purpose of the World Wide Web, and why we use Web browsers, another question may arise: "Where are all these data stored?" It is definitely enlightening to know how we access all the information that the World Wide Web has to offer, but where *is* all that information? Well, the answer is pretty simple; it is in all the computers that form the Internet. Some people become alarmed, believing that any computer connected to the Internet will automatically make all of its files accessible to the entire world. Not to worry, that is not how it works. In order to share information in a specific computer, some software has to be installed on the computer, making it a "Web server." The server creates a list of folders that will be shared when someone attempts to connect to the computer using standard Web protocols. There are two main competitors in the Web server market. The first one, my personal favorite and the one used throughout this book, is Apache, developed by the Apache Software Foundation (www.apache.org). Apache has the great advantage of being totally free of charge and works on every platform. It is an open-source program, which means that you can actually see the code behind the server and even participate in the improvement of Apache. It is reliable and vastly used around the world, and pretty much the only reliable option on UNIX/Linux. The other main server is Microsoft's Internet Information Services (IIS, www.microsoft.com/iis). IIS is *not* open-source and works only on Windows operating systems, although a simplified free version is available with Windows XP Professional. The latest versions of IIS run on Windows Server 2003, which obviously is not free. Some of the differences between IIS and Apache reside in their user interface. Apache, as most UNIX-based software, is configured entirely through a simple text file that is loaded when the server starts up, whereas IIS has a GUI that is meant to be much more user-friendly. Choosing which server to use is based mainly on knowing which technologies will be used as well as the budget available. Users on a low budget will probably prefer the use of open-source technology and free development platforms; hence the use of Apache. If, on the other hand, you wish to use Microsoft's .NET and you have the money to afford it, IIS is the best option.

TCP/IP BASICS

As mentioned earlier, the Internet was strongly enhanced by the creation of TCP/IP by Cerf and Kahn, but how exactly did TCP/IP help in this new era of communications? When studying network communications, we learn about the Open Systems Interconnection (OSI) layer model. This model breaks down all computer networking into seven distinct layers. Computers can communicate at the same level through a set of protocols adapted to that particular layer. The seven layers are as follows (in ascending order):

1. *Physical layer*—responsible for sending raw bits over the communication channel. It is specific to the medium [twisted-pair or fiberoptic cable, wifi (wireless fidelity), etc.].

2. *Data link layer*—takes a raw transmission and transforms it into a line free of undetected transmission errors. It also breaks the input data into data frames and transmits them sequentially. Finally it attaches special bit patterns at the beginning and end of the frame like the *starting frame delimiter* (SFD), *cyclic redundancy check* (CRC), or the preamble. This is the layer responsible for flow control and error control.

3. *Network layer*—concerned with addressing and routing of messages to their respective final destinations.

4. *Transport layer*—provides services that support reliable end-to-end communications, such as generating the final address of the destination, establishing the connection, error recovery, and termination of the session.

5. *Session layer*—responsible for the dialog between two cooperating applications or processes. Remote login and spooling operations use the session layer to ensure successful login and to control the flow of data to the remote printer. The token management in a token ring configuration is handled by the session layer.

6. *Presentation layer*—concerned with the syntax and semantics of the information transmitted from end to end. For example, X Windows is considered a level 6 service.

7. *Application layer*—provides the utilities and tools for application programs and users, like telnet, FTP, DNS, and HTTP.

TCP/IP is basically a simplification of the OSI layer model that concentrates on only four layers: network access layer (Ethernet, FDDI, or ISDN), Internet layer (IP), transport layer (TCP, UDP), and application layer (FTP, telnet, SMTP, HTTP).

The Internet Layer

The Internet layer is the equivalent of the network layer in the OSI model. It contains the Internet Protocol (IP), which provides addressing, datagram services, data package segmentation, and transmission parameter selection. In order to function properly, TCP/IP relies on IP addresses, which are assigned to each computer. An IP address is composed of 4 bytes, and is usually shown as four numbers separated by dots. Each of these numbers can range between 0 and 255, since it represents only one of the bytes of the IP address (and, as you should know, you can represent 256 numbers with only 8 bits). Each IP address is composed of two parts, the network address and the computer address. To understand how the address is broken down, you need to know your subnet mask. The way it works is through a basic binary AND operation between your address and your subnet mask. The result of that operation represents the network address. For example, let's assume that your IP is 192.168.1.20, and your subnet mask is 255.255.255.0. Let us see how we get the network address:

If you are not sure about how to use the binary AND with nonbinary numbers, start by transforming each number to binary. 192.168.1.20 becomes 11000000.10101000.00000001.00010100, and 255.255.255.0 is 11111111.11111 111.11111111.00000000. Performing the AND operation between those two numbers gives us 11000000.10101000.00000001.00000000, which is no other than 192.168.1.0. You can achieve this result faster by realizing that 255 in binary is written 11111111, and since an AND operation between a 1 and any other bit will leave the bit unchanged, we can basically keep the numbers of the IP address that correspond to the 255s of the subnet mask. Then we know that a binary AND between 0 and anything will always be 0, so where our subnet mask is 0, we can directly write 0. So, if we have an IP of 155.180.24.45 and a subnet mask of 255.255.0.0, our network address will be 155.180.0.0.

This network address lets us know which computers we will be able to communicate with directly. Only computers that are in the same network can "see" each other, so a computer in a 192.168.1.0 network and another one in a network 155.180.0.0 will not be able to communicate with one another even if they are directly linked to each other. The rest of the IP address (20 in the first example, 24.45 in the second) corresponds to the particular computer address. Choosing a network appropriately is important since it will decide the amount of computers that you can connect. For instance, a network with a subnet mask of 255.255.255.0 will be able to accommodate only 254 distinct IP addresses. This type of network is said to be of class C. A network with subnet of 255.255.0.0 is said to be of class B, and finally 255.0.0.0 will be subnet of a network of class A. One of the most important things when choosing your computer's IP address is making sure that it is a valid address. You are not allowed to have an IP that is the same than your network address; for example, if your network is 192.168.1.0, you cannot have 192.168.1.0 as a computer's IP address. The other restriction is that your computer address cannot be all ones in binary; for instance, in the same network as in the previous example, the address 192.168.1.255 is not authorized (as 255 is 11111111 in binary). This type of address is used by TCP/IP to send broadcast messages to all computers within the network.

Now that we know how the IP address work, you might be wondering how you can be in a class C network (with a maximum of 254 computers) and still be able to access millions of computers worldwide, even though they are not in the same local network as you are. Well, the answer to that is basically the use of routers. Routers are small machines that act as a bridge between two separate networks. To function, they have two network cards in two separate networks. For example, you could have a router with one of its IP addresses as 192.168.1.254 in a class C network, and the other IP as 155.180.255.254 in a class B network. If a computer connected to the class C network attempts to access an IP that is not part of the 192.168.1.0 network, it sends the IP requested to the router, which will then try to find that address using its second branch. The whole principle of the Internet is based on millions of networks connected through routers. Now, because of the amount of routers in the world, there is a virtually infinite amount of ways to submit data between two computers. To avoid taking the wrong path, several protocols can be used.

Remembering the IP addresses of all the possible computers we would like to access is pretty difficult, so symbolic addresses were created. Those addresses work as a set of aliases of real IP addresses, such as .com, .gov, .net, .es, and .co.uk. To make it even easier, it is possible to assign a name to a specific address, such as google.com, for example. In order to retrieve the corresponding IP, the computer accesses something called a *Domain Name Service* (DNS), which contains a table with all equivalences between names and IPs. Every time you see a dot in a name, this means that you are accessing a subdomain; for example, if you visit the page http://steven.bewchy.com/, you are looking within all companies (.com) for the one called "bewchy," and once you find it, you look for the subdomain called "steven" within "bewchy." The "http://" section allows the computer to know that you wish to access that domain using the HTTP protocol. DNS is another protocol residing in the Internet layer.

The Transport Layer

The transport layer is home to two main protocols: the User Datagram Protocol (UDP) and the Transmission Control Protocol (TCP). UDP is a connectionless protocol, meaning that the order in which messages are sent by the emitting computer is not necessarily the order in which they will be received in the destination computer. This protocol is not of interest in this book, so we will not go any further in the explanation of UDP. TCP, on the other hand, is very important for Web access; it is a connection-centered protocol. TCP handles the connection, disconnection, data flow control and transfer, sequencing, and many other tasks required to establish a proper communication between two computers. It receives the data flow that needs to be sent by the user and breaks it down into packets of usually 64 kB (kilobytes; i.e., 65,536 bytes), which are then sent through the IP protocol. In order to send those packets, TCP needs to open something called a "socket," which is a couple of the type <IP address, port> which can be used by programs to access files. Sockets can be opened or closed, and allow both reading and writing. For example, a character in a TV show who asks the computer technician to "open a socket on a computer" is actually requesting access to the computer through its IP address on a specific port. You can imagine "ports" as electronic gates that reside within your computer and that are needed to send or receive information. For example, when you access a Webpage, the information contained in the page is sent to you via your port 80 (generally). If you access an FTP server, you are using your port 21; if you are connecting through SSH (Secure SHell; used to connect to remote computers), you're probably using port 22.

The Application Layer

This layer is responsible for the protocols that most users know or at least have heard about. The first and uttermost important for this book is the HyperText Transfer Protocol (HTTP). HTTP was created for the exchange of HTML documents; it is based on TCP/IP and is the protocol responsible for the communication between Web server and Web client (you and your browser!). This protocol is meant to be multiplatform, so everything is sent in ASCII (American Standard Code for Information Interchange) format, as plain characters. We shall talk more about HTML documents in the next chapter.

Many other protocols in the application layer are important in the everyday life of an Internet user, such as the following ones:

- *File Transfer Protocol* (FTP)—responsible for transferring files.
- *Simple Mail Transfer Protocol* (SMTP)—responsible for sending emails.
- *Post Office Protocol* (POP)—usually seen as POP3 by email clients, this protocol allows you to retrieve email messages from your mail server.
- *Internet Message Access Protocol* (IMAP)—another protocol used for email transfers.

- *Telnet*—widely used in the early days of the Internet but fortunately is now loosing importance. It allows you to remotely connect to a computer, but the *major* disadvantage is that it does not encrypt any of the data sent through this protocol (and that includes your passwords).
- *Common Gateway Interface* (CGI)—discussed further in the next chapter; in a nutshell, it allows you to use the output of external applications in any Webpage. It is *not* a programming language!!

THE TOOLBOX

To conclude this chapter, I will list some programs that I believe all Web developers should know about. All opinions are entirely personal, and you are more than free to disagree with me.

Browsers

As mentioned earlier, browsers are essential in the use of the Internet and choosing the right one for you is an important decision to make. Throughout this book we will discuss some of the differences between these browsers, especially during the JavaScript coverage. The most commonly used by Microsoft Windows users is obviously Internet Explorer (http://www.micro-soft.com/ie/), since it comes with the operating system. MSIE is a very user-friendly browser, and perfect for Mr. or Mrs. Anybody that just wants to browse the web. As a developer you must know that it is a dangerous tool, since no matter how disgusting your HTML code might be, MSIE will manage to make the output look decent, especially when using tables or frames. So do not assume your page is perfectly written just because MSIE displays it nicely. One of the advantages of MSIE is that JavaScript works perfectly well with it, so you will probably love it when we are working on that language. It also contains many plug-in that are required in many websites, so you might actually be required to use it to fully appreciate some websites. The major flaw it has as far as I'm concerned, and a reason why I stopped using it, is the number of security holes it contains. Granted, in most cases no one will ever attack your computer using those security holes, but as a computer scientist, I like being protected.

Another browser that had great influence in the world of browsing is Netscape (http://browser.netscape.com/ns8/), which had a great growth in the late 90s. Unfortunately for Netscape, it has been going downhill for few years now, and personally it will never cross my mind to use it again until they improve it greatly. I actually stopped using NS when they released their version 6, mostly due to JavaScript incompatibilities that will be mentioned in further chapters. But basically Netscape had a set of Netscape-specific HTML tags that were both useful and necessary for the use of JavaScript on that browser, but they decided to wipe those out on version 6, which pretty much was like forcing programmers to reprogram every single JavaScript code programmed for version 5. When I discovered that, I decided to stop using Netscape.

Another browser that was quite "cute" for lack of better words was Neo-Planet (www.neoplanet.com). It was not really a full fledged browser but more like an add-on for MSIE. Unfortunately it is no longer available for download in their official website. The fun thing about NeoPlanet was the use of skins and sounds, which would allow you to have for example a "shaggadelic" skin based on the movie *Austin Powers* with nice flashy colors, peace signs instead of the regular buttons, and the voice of Mike Myers saying "Oh Behave", "Yeah Baby!" and other catchy phrases from the movie every time you clicked on a link. There were skins for all tastes, and was definitely the funniest browser I ever used in my life. It did get boring and repetitive after a while though.

UNIX lovers have been using a browser called Mozilla for quite some time. It is like a dream come true for UNIX lovers due to its small size, basic appearance and good functionality. Mozilla evolved and created the Mozilla Firefox browser (www.getfirefox.com), which I have to say, is my current browser. It is probably the most secure browser available for free right now, and has great features like the use of tabs, which allow you to have as many open websites as you wish on a single browser window. It also has an extensive set of skins, though I've never really used them. There are many other features but I'll let you look into it.

Maybe some of you use things like America Online and its built-in browser, but I'd rather not say what I think about AOL to make sure that I don't offend anyone. To phrase it very politely, "I, Steven Gabarró, do *not* like AOL."

FTP

If you are trying to install an FTP server on a Windows machine, I would have to recommend Serv-U FTP (www.serv-u.com). It is a great server software that will probably allow you to do anything you want to with it. If you are looking for an FTP server for UNIX, there are so many good, and free, ones that I won't even bother mentioning them (there was probably one included in your UNIX/Linux distribution).

If you are trying to get a nice FTP client, one of the most commonly used (or at least it was when I discovered FTP) is Cute-FTP (www.cuteftp.com). There are many others free and not free, but my favorite would have to be LeechFTP, which allows the use of multiple threads, which speeds up the transfer of multiple files. Unfortunately, the development of LeechFTP has not been continued for over a year, so there are no really recent (as of 2006) versions. I still like my old version, though, since it never gave me any problems. It would seem (at the time of this writing) that the people working on LeechFTP are now working on a new client called BitBeamer (www.bit-beamer.com). I have never tried that software, so I cannot vouch for it, but it is supposed to have all the features that LeechFTP had.

Email Clients

One of the most widely used email clients is Outlook Express, which comes standard with every copy of Windows (since Windows 95). It is simple and works well, and is preinstalled with Windows, so no need to add extra software if that is your platform. There is also the more complicated version called Outlook, which does all Outlook Express does but adds in a calendar, nicer agenda, but also heavier software to run. Personally I prefer the Express version.

Another survivor of the old ages, and the first email client I ever used in my life, is Eudora (www.eudora.com). I haven't used it since 1997 or so, so I am not really in a position to tell you how good the latest versions are.

Many users simply like using the clients that come with their browsers, such as Netscape mail, or directly with Web-based email clients like Hotmail (www.hotmail.com), or Yahoo (http://mail.yahoo.com), which allow you to view emails directly on a browser. Personally I'd recommend you use Gmail (www.gmail.com) created by the people from Google. It is by far the *best* Web-based email tool I have used in over 10 years of Internet use, and it is still in its Beta version, so Google can still improve it. The only problem is that you can create an account only if you are invited to do so by a current user.

If what you use is UNIX or Linux, the two main email clients I know and have used are "Pine" (Program for Internet News & Mail) and "Elm" (Electronic Mail), but I would have to vouch for Elm. It is a very small simple application that runs straight from your shell and lets you choose your text editor. They are both usually included with the major UNIX/Linux distributions.

Programming Tools

Whenever you start programming Webpages, you will have to choose which software to use, and you might think you need a lot of money for licenses and so on. Well, think again, because you have excellent tools that will be more than enough to program Websites (and I strongly recommend that you use these when working with this book). On Windows platform you have two great tools called Notepad and Wordpad. I personally prefer the first one because it is much simpler and does not have all the unnecessary things that Wordpad has. On UNIX you have "vi" and "emacs," which is pretty much like choosing between Red Sox and Yankees (or between Real Madrid and FC Barcelona), since in most cases people that like one hate the other. In my case it is true: I love emacs and hate vi. But it is only a question of taste.

If you think those tools are too basic for you and you would like to see some colors in your code when you type it, you might want to choose something like HomeSite by Macromedia (www.macromedia.com/software/home-site). It is a simple text editor adapted to Web development, so it recognizes the syntax and highlights special words and tags. It also allows you to preview the page and comes with a great tool for the creation of style sheets. Similar to HomeSite but a bit simpler is UltraEdit (www.ultraedit.com), which allows you to import or create your own set of syntax rules and colors associated with those rules.

Another well-known editing tool is Macromedia's DreamWeaver (www. macromedia.com/software/dreamweaver). The basic way to use Dream-Weaver is to simply drag and drop the elements you wish to have in the page. You can also type directly in a "preview" of the page, having DreamWeaver take care of all the actual coding. Because of this feature, I do not recommend it for this course, since it promotes laziness, and adds too much useless code. If you *really* want to use it, please use the split view and type in the code directly. (The split view will allow you to see both the preview and code at the same time).

Finally, we have Microsoft's FrontPage (www.microsoft.com/frontpage), which is definitely not my favorite tool for Web programming. It creates a large amount of unnecessary folders and files when you are just trying to create a simple Website, and adds useless code in the pages that you create. It might be a great option for people wanting to create a Webpage without having to understand any of the code, like web designers, for example. If you are a Web developer, code should be your number one priority, making Front-Page my last choice. Last, and least, is Microsoft's Word "Export to HTML" feature, which should be used only by non-Web-savvy people to quickly create pages from Word documents. It is very problematic, and I discourage its use.

Other Useful Tools

Finally, there are some tools that are useful for the "cosmetic" part of Web programming, such as Adobe's PhotoShop and ImageReady (www.adobe. com/photoshop), probably some of the best image editing software in the market. They both come as a single bundle, with PhotoShop used mainly for pictures and ImageReady focused mainly on images for the Web.

Macromedia also offers an array of tools to create animations and facilitate the design of a Website such as Flash, Fireworks, FreeHand, or Director.

2

The Different Approaches of Web Programming

BEFORE WE GET STARTED

Before I head on and start explaining the different languages available in the Web programming market, let me stress that all the opinions stated are exclusively my personal views. I tend to be very opinionated, but I will try to justify both my criticism and praises of the different languages presented.

THE BASICS—HTML

The very first programming language that must be mentioned when discussing Web programming is obviously HTML. The WWW could not be what it is today if it weren't for this language. The HTML (HyperText Markup Language) is, as the name indicates, a "markup" language, which generally means that it is based on the use of tags to provide functionality. The "code" in an HTML file is simply text containing those tags that provide functionality and different looks to the page. It is an interpreted client-side language, meaning that for an HTML page to be viewed, a browser must first download it from a server into a client machine and then execute the code line by line.

HTML relies strongly on the use of Universal Resource Identifiers (URI). Each URI represents a way to refer to a page, an image, or even an email

Web Application Design and Implementation: Apache 2, PHP5, MySQL, JavaScript, and Linux/UNIX, by Steven A. Gabarró
Copyright © 2007 by John Wiley & Sons, Inc.

address. The location of a page is a URI commonly called URL (Universal Resource Location). For example, an email address URI would look like mailto:myname@mydomain.com, a normal URL could be http://www.mydomain.com/myfolder/mypage.html#section2. Usually a URL can be of two types: absolute or relative. An *absolute* URL is basically a URL that includes the information on the full path of a file or folder, like domain, subdomain, file, section, ... A *relative* URL is one in which you can see not the entire path of the file, but how to reach it from the current working directory. For example, if you had the tree structure shown below in your "mydomain.com," and you were viewing the page "foobar.html," the image mypic.jpg could be accessed by using either http://www.mydomain.com/images/mypic.jpg (absolute URL) or ../images/mypic.jpg (URL relative to the folder *files*):

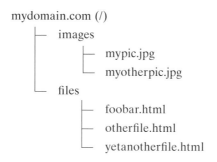

As you noticed, relative paths usually start with "../", which means "go to parent directory" or "./", which means "current directory." Relative paths are an easy way to make a Website more portable since they are independent of the domain that the pages are in. It is especially useful if, like me, you test all your pages in a local computer before uploading the files to your host.

The use of URIs is pretty much a necessity in HTML because they allow you to embed images to a page, send information from a form to a processing script, create an image map, link to an external style sheet, create frame documents, cite an external reference, or also refer to metadata conventions to describe the page.

THE CREATOR—SGML

SGML, or Standard Generalized Markup Language, is a system for defining markup languages, like HTML. It is a descendant of IBM's Generalized Markup Language (GML) developed in the 1960s. It relies strongly on the use of DTDs (Document Type Definitions) to define the syntax of markup constructs. SGML is not really used on the Web in its full version, but smaller subsets of SGML are becoming increasingly prevalent in many information exchange standards.

OTHER SGML-BASED LANGUAGES—XML AND XSL

The eXtensible Markup Language (XML) is a simplification of SGML that relies on the use of tags to organize information in any format that its writer deems the best. It is a very common language that is at the base of platforms like .NET. It is used mostly to exchange information through the Web in an organized manner, making it easy to retrieve information from its files. XML files are actually interpreted by most browsers nowadays, showing its contents in a tree format, such as you would see on a file explorer.

Here is an example of an XML file containing information of some games that I like:

```
<?xml version="1.0" encoding="ISO-8859-1"?>
<GAMESLIST>
  <GAME>
    <NAME>Star Wars Galaxies</NAME>
    <DEVELOPER>Sony Online Entertainment / Lucas
Arts</DEVELOPER>
    <CATEGORY>MMORPG</CATEGORY>
    <RELEASED>Summer 2003</RELEASED>
    <CLAN>Clan of The Wroshyr</CLAN>
    <CHARACTER>Elder Bewchabbacc The Black</CHARACTER>
  </GAME>
  <GAME>
    <NAME>Battlefield 2</NAME>
    <DEVELOPER>Electronic Arts / Dice Software</DEVELOPER>
    <CATEGORY>FPS</CATEGORY>
    <RELEASED>Summer 2005</RELEASED>
    <CLAN>101st Airborne Division - 160th Special
Operations Aviation Regiment "Night Stalkers"</CLAN>
    <CHARACTER>Captain Bewchy</CHARACTER>
  </GAME>
  <GAME>
    <NAME>Pac man - aka Puck-Man</NAME>
    <DEVELOPER>Namco</DEVELOPER>
    <CATEGORY>Oldie</CATEGORY>
    <RELEASED>1980</RELEASED>
    <CLAN>Nbuns Team</CLAN>
    <CHARACTER>Nica</CHARACTER>
  </GAME>
</GAMESLIST>
```

Because the output produced by browsers when opening a basic XML file tends to provide too much information, and it does not have a flexible appearance, XSL was created. The eXtensible Style sheet Language is used as a perfect complement of XML files, by specifying the appearance that each section of an XML file should have. It relies on the XSLT (XSL Transformations), which through a single link of the XSL file on the XML file, will produce any type of output that the programmer decides to use. It allows a really quick presentation of the contents of the XML file, with a much nicer appearance. Note that the XSL file is dependent on the XML file as far as tags are concerned, but if you have well-formatted XML and XSL files, any added element to the XML file will still be properly formatted by the XSL. Here is an example of an XSL file that will allow us to format the previous XML file:

```
<?xml version="1.0" encoding="ISO-8859-1" ?>
<html xsl:version="1.0" xmlns:xsl="http://www.w3.org/1999/
XSL/Transform" xmlns="http://www.w3.org/1999/xhtml">
  <BODY style="font-family:Arial,helvetica,
sans-serif;font-size:12pt;background-color:#EEEEEE">
    <xsl:for-each select="GAMESLIST/GAME">
      <div style="background-color:grey;color:
white;padding:4px">
        <span style="font-weight:bold"><xsl:value-of
select="NAME"/></span>
        by <xsl:value-of select="DEVELOPER"/>
      </div>
      <div style="margin-left:20px;margin-bottom:1em;font-
size:10pt">
        <xsl:value-of select="CATEGORY"/> game released in
        <xsl:value-of select="RELEASED"/>. I play it with the
        <xsl:value-of select="CLAN"/> as
        <xsl:value-of select="CHARACTER"/>.
      </div>
    </xsl:for-each>
  </BODY>
</html>
```

In order to link our XML file to the XSL file, you would simply add the following line right after the *<?xml. . . . ?>* line of the XML file:

<?xml-stylesheet type="text/xsl" href="videogames.xsl" ?>

THE GOOD OLD Java

A language that must be mentioned when studying virtually any programming area is Java. Because of its multiplatform characteristics, this object-oriented language has been chosen by many developers in the past. The rise of technologies such as J2EE (Java 2 Enterprise Edition) or J2ME made the use of Java a necessity. One problem in using Java in the Web is mostly that Java applications run as applets embedded in Webpages, not as a working part of the page itself. Basically, your Java-based Webpages are not really pages, whose appearance changes depending on the Java code. Instead, the page itself is like a frame for a full Java application. This means that the code must be compiled first into "byte codes," which will have to be downloaded by the client and will start running only after the client has received the entire program.

Java is currently undergoing some changes and improvements that will supposedly make it a very strong choice for Web programming, but in my opinion, it is far from the best option out there. The fact that applets need to be fully downloaded and then interpreted by a Java virtual machine in the client's computer makes it slow, and speed is usually a major factor in the Web. It is also quite complex to use, since it is a full object-oriented programming language, and not really the fastest way to write a scripting page.

I personally do not recommend the use of Java for Web applications unless you will be working with J2EE or J2ME. If you are attempting any other project on the Web, I recommend a scripting language instead.

SOMETHING DIFFERENT—JavaScript

Here comes one of the greater sources of confusion among young developers. Despite the name "JavaScript," this programming language is very different from Java. First, it is a compact, object-based scripting language, generally used to develop client-side scripting pages, and sometimes server Internet applications. In many cases, JavaScript is code that is embedded directly in the HTML code of a page, to be executed by the client. This means that the code is downloaded at the same time as is the rest of the page, making it entirely visible. It is then interpreted line by line at the same time as are the HTML tags. Again, it is different from Java; some of the major differences are listed in Table 2.1.

TABLE 2.1 Differences between Java and JavaScript

Java	JavaScript
Compiled byte codes are downloaded from server to the client prior to execution	Interpreted by the client as it gets downloaded
Object-oriented; applets consisting of classes with inheritance	Object-based; uses built-in extensible objects, but there are no classes or inheritance
Applets distinct from HTML	Code integrated with HTML
Variables data types MUST be declared	Variables data types are not declared
Static binding; object references must exist at compile time	Dynamic binding; object references checked at runtime

THE SAVIOR—PHP

Well, you are probably wondering about the title I gave this section, but let me explain my logic behind it. I am one of those old-school developers who believe that C language is one of the best programming languages ever, because of its flexibility and how easy it is to learn. C is a language that, with a small toolset, can allow you to achieve pretty much anything you wish to achieve. Well, for me, PHP is pretty much "C for the Web." The syntax is very similar, with less syntax restrictions, as we will see little by little, but follows the two concepts of C that I like the most: flexibility and ease of use. It is really easy to learn; an experienced programmer can pick it up in a couple of days. Another great asset of PHP is the fact that it runs server-side, meaning that the code is executed before the client has access to it, but we shall discuss this later on. Let us talk about the basics.

PHP is a recursive acronym of Hypertext PreProcessor and, as the name indicates, works like many preprocessors found in other languages. This means that the code is read line by line and interpreted as it goes, or at least that was how PHP started. It is an open-source scripting language, so you will be able to find many sites enhancing its development. It also means that the PHP project is created and maintained by developers who wish to invest their free time in making the product better, yet free.

PHP was designed to work for the Web, and its code is embedded directly in HTML pages, although, as we shall see later, it is possible to separate HTML and PHP through the use of templates. Interestingly, PHP is not limited to work on the Web, and can actually be used to create command-line scripts that you could run from a shell, or even GUI (Graphical User Interface) applications through the use of the PHP-GTK library.

PHP is also designed to work closely with a wide variety of databases, including Oracle, MySQL, PostgreSQL, ODBC, and Sybase among others, making it an excellent choice for database-driven Websites, regardless of the database you wish to use. It also includes an extensive set of libraries that allows developers to interact with a wide range of other technologies. PHP developers can write applications that will generate images, PDF documents, work LDAP authentication servers, communicate with flash animations, and many other things that unfortunately we will not be able to discuss, since it would probably take several volumes.

THE RIVAL—ASP.NET

Active Server Pages (ASP) and now ASP.NET are probably among the major sources of confusion among developers. ASP used to be an actual programming language developed by Microsoft that worked similarly to PHP; it was a server-side scripting language, hence the title "the rival." With the arrival of the .NET platform, ASP.NET received an entirely new meaning, referring to a development platform, rather than an actual programming language; that is why you will probably see in the markets that teach how to "program in ASP.net *with* another programming language." There are many to choose from, including, for example, Visual Basic.Net. The whole idea is that you can develop ASP.NET applications in your desired language. It is all based on the use of the Common Language Runtime (CLR) designed for .NET. It is widely used with Web services; it is highly efficient and very popular in big corporations. One main difference from PHP is the fact that it is not open source, and its development depends exclusively on Microsoft's developer team. This also means that using it might become quite expensive if you are to work on the "official" professional version of the developer. I personally like to call this the "PHP for high class."

THE MYTH—CGI

Now, here is a good source of laughter among recruiters who know about Web programming. Many people think that CGI (Common Gateway Interface) is an actual programming language and tend to "beef up" their resumes, adding it to their list of known programming languages, without really understanding what CGI is. CGI is a common gateway interface, and is definitely not a programming language. It is a standard for interfacing external applications with information servers, or, if you prefer, a "magical door" that will allow you to run your normal executable files in a Webpage. CGI applications are executed in real time, allowing a dynamic output, such as, for example, generating a Webpage adapted to a set of received inputs. The way it works is simple; you first write an application in your favorite language and compile it to an executable rename it to "file.cgi" (note that this is technically optional, and many developers leave script names as "file.exe"; I personally discourage this). Some of the most common allowed programming languages are C/C++, FORTRAN, Perl, TCL, UNIX Shell script, Visual Basic, and Apple script. Of course, to make your application more useful for the Web, it is usually written to receive a set of parameters and produce HTML code that will be displayed as the page's output on the browser.

ANOTHER BIG OPTION—Perl

Even though I used Perl only when I was a computer science student, and considering that it is never in my list of languages to use, I have nothing negative to say about it. Perl is a very powerful programming language, and also very flexible, if anything, it is more complicated to learn and use than PHP. It is also open-source, and one of the best options if your application is meant to work extensively with text manipulation. Some of the most powerful regular expression tools were created for Perl, and then exported to other languages, as we will see when we study PCRE functions in PHP. Websites such as Amazon.com are partly built in Perl, so you can see that it is not just a little programming language for small applications. It also has the ability to interface with external C/C++ libraries through the use of XS and SWIG.

THE FUTURE?—C#

C# was a language created to work with .NET as a simple yet powerful object-oriented programming language, mixing a programming interface similar to the old Visual Basic, yet having the object-oriented features you could find in C++. It is Microsoft's answer to Sun's Java. Java became increasingly popular through J2EE, so Microsoft decided to create a language following the same principles on their version of the three-tier architecture programming platform, .NET. It strongly relies on XML as information exchange format, and it is gaining popularity for programming Web services. As do other .NET languages, it requires code to be compiled, yet it follows the principle of Java's byte codes, by compiling into a platform-free language, that will be interpreted by clients.

The reason behind the question mark is that even though C# is a fairly recent language it is meant to be the flagship in the .NET revolution—or at least that is what Microsoft representatives were announcing when they presented .NET. The reality is that its acceptance is still growing, but many .NET developers prefer relying on older programming languages that they are more familiar with. .NET is still gaining importance, and who knows, maybe it will be the most predominant platform for Web services, not only on Microsoft applications and Websites, but as a more global solution. If that happens, surely C# will become increasingly popular and will be the first choice of programming language for new developers.

CLIENT-SIDE VERSUS SERVER-SIDE—WHICH SIDE TO PICK?

As we have seen, most scripting languages are defined as either client-side or server-side. A *client-side* program is basically a program that needs to be fully downloaded by the browser to use it. The code in many cases is embedded in HTML code, which results in full disclosure of how your program works, since all users can read it by choosing the "view page source" option in their browsers. In many cases the code is interpreted by plugins in the client, which brings us to another problem of client-side applications—they are browser-dependent. As we will see when studying JavaScript, many features are not cross-browser, meaning that they can be used only in a specific browser, sometimes even in a specific version of it. The positive side of client-side scripting, and the reason for its continued use, is that once the code is downloaded, the server has nothing else to do. The client is solely responsible for any calculations or actions that might take place, which allows programmers to create Webpages that will change dynamically as the code is executed.

Server-side applications run in the server, as the term indicates. This means that when a client attempts to access a script programmed that way, the query is sent to the server along with any input that the script might need. The script then runs on the server, utilizing server resources only, and then sends the final output to the client, who can see only that result, and has no access to the source code itself. This obviously is a great asset since it protects the code, which is very important for security reasons. Another great advantage of having scripts run directly on the server is that you need to worry only whether the server knows how to run it properly. Unlike the scenario in client-side applications, the script will run exactly the same way, producing the same output regardless of the client's platform or browser. On the negative side, each time you wish to do something dynamic, you must communicate back and forth between client and server.

Now that we know the differences between both sides, it is generally the time to choose your preference, by selecting the language to use. Most developers, and therefore most books out there, tend to choose only one side, but not me. Even though it is possible to create Websites based on just one technology, taking advantage of server-side and client-side programming simultaneously gives much more flexibility and allows a greater set of functionalities. Some features run better in client-side, some in server-side, so restricting yourself to only one will potentially limit your final project. Throughout this book we will learn when it is better to use a client-side language such as JavaScript, or a server-side language like PHP.

MY CHOICES—PHP, MySQL, JavaScript

Now that we have seen some of the most common options that programmers face when engaging in Web programming, we must choose which technologies to use. In our case, the choices are obviously known. One question you might ask is why those choices and not others.

First, we have PHP. It is one of the most powerful and flexible programming languages for the Web. It is free, is easy to learn (making it ideal for a one-semester course), and simplifies any database access you might want to use.

JavaScript, although I do not like it as much as a language itself as it is much more restrictive syntaxwise than PHP, is a really useful programming language. As we will see, it is important to have a client-side language to couple with PHP to make our pages more lifelike, dynamically changing without having to constantly communicate with the server, and JavaScript will help us fulfill that need.

MySQL, even though we have not discussed it yet, is a free database that can be installed in any platform, providing a reliable solution for information handling. It is also extremely easy to use MySQL databases with PHP, which will make our job so much easier. My "second best" option for databases would be PostgreSQL, similar to MySQL with even some extra features, but again, we shall follow the path of simplicity for this book.

Finally, and pretty much most importantly, these are the languages that I have been using for years, and I never had any problems with them. Knowing how to properly mix these three programming languages should allow you to create any professional database-driven Website you would like to. Also, although you might use different technologies in the future, mastering these three will give you the mindset needed for Web development. It is like learning how to play soccer; you must learn how to kick the ball, regardless of the shoes you will wear or the team you will support. Web programming is much the same; if you know how to properly design a Website, the language choice will be only secondary.

3

Introduction to HTML

WHAT DO YOU NEED TO GET STARTED?

Before we start discussing HTML, let me give you a checklist of things you should have with you when programming. First, you need a basic text editor like Notepad or emacs. You can also use more advanced tools, like the ones mentioned in Chapter 1, but if you really wish to learn the ins and outs of HTML, you are better off with a basic editor. The next needed thing is a browser, which will be used to test the pages and make sure that they look the way you want. Third, you need, obviously, some basic HTML knowledge. Last but not least, you need good music. People usually think I'm kidding when I mention music as a necessity, but from my experience, the right music can activate the brain to work more efficiently. The right music will depend on your own personal taste, but I would recommend either classical if you work better in a calm environment or hard rock, punk, and other fast-paced music if, like me, you prefer the music tempo to drive your fingers into a typing frenzy. This chapter will try to make sure you have element number three: basic HTML knowledge.

Web Application Design and Implementation: Apache 2, PHP5, MySQL, JavaScript, and Linux/UNIX, by Steven A. Gabarró
Copyright © 2007 by John Wiley & Sons, Inc.

HOW DOES HTML WORK?

Syntax Basics

HTML is a markup language and, as such, works entirely through the use of tags. Each tag is used to define different parts of the file, different styles, links, images, embedded elements, forms, and so on. Each tag starts with the character "<" and finishes with ">". Keep this in mind because those characters are restricted for tags, meaning that your page might behave in a strange way if you attempt to use it in a normal string. If you wish to use that character, refer to the special characters table shown in Appendix A. Now, some tags require an opening and a closing tag in order to show the area of effect of the tag. In those cases the closing tag will always start with "</", followed by the name of the tag it is closing (without the attributes list) and ">".

For example, to have some text appearing in white, you could use the *FONT* tag, with the attribute *color* set to "white." To do so, your opening tag would be *<FONT color="white">* and your closing tag would be *</FONT>*. Your final portion of code would look like this:

<FONT color="white"> This text will show up in white</FONT>

Note that HTML is not case-sensitive, so you can mix uppercase and lowercase letters. Nevertheless, I strongly advise everyone to capitalize all tags since it makes code reading much easier.

Finally, remember to name your files with either .html or .htm as their extension.

File Structure

It is very important to understand the basic structure of an HTML file, knowing exactly where each part of your code must be written in. It is something fairly easy to remember, but unfortunately there are still people who claim to be Web programmers but who misuse the file's main areas. Good Web design and programming demands efficient and effective use of the available tools. This book is designed to avoid these pitfalls.

The first thing is the full file, which must always start with the tag *<HTML>* and finish with *</HTML>*. You should never have HTML tags before the opening tag, nor after the closing one. One of the reasons for this occasional error is the fact that most browsers can now ignore major errors like this one and still manage to create a proper-looking output, but please always start your files by setting up these two tags.

The next section to know is the header, limited by the tags *<HEAD>* and *</HEAD>*. This section holds all information related to the file, including its author, its keywords, its title, and sometimes even some JavaScript functions that will be used in the page. Most basic pages use the header only to specify the title that will appear on the browser window. To do so, use the *<TITLE>* . . . *</TITLE>* tags. Any text written between the opening and closing tags will appear in the title bar of the browser.

The final area is the body, starting with *<BODY>* and finishing with *</BODY>*. The body of a page is the actual content of the page, meaning that the data that will appear inside the browser window. The body tag can accept a set of properties that allow you to set up a background image (*background*) or color (*bgcolor*); specify font colors for text (*color)*, links (*link*), visited links (*vlink*), active links (*alink*), and even action scripts to run on load or unload of the page. There should always be a body section in a Webpage, unless you are using the page as a frameset definition page (see discussion later).

Here is an example of what a "Hello world" HTML page should look like:

```
<HTML>
  <HEAD>
    <TITLE>Hello World Page</TITLE>
  </HEAD>
  <BODY>
   HELLO WORLD!!!<BR>
   And have a nice day!
  </BODY>
</HTML>
```

Note the indentation I have used. This is not required, but will improve the readability of your code. You will also note the use of the tag *
*, which forces a break of line. It is important to realize that any group of white spaces (whether it is a tab, a new line, or basic spaces) is always translated on the screen as a single white space. This is important to know since the appearance your code has will not necessarily be the same as in the output. Check the following example:

```
<HTML>
  <HEAD>
    <TITLE>Hello World Page</TITLE>
  </HEAD>
  <BODY>
   HELLO WORLD!!!
   And have a nice day!
  </BODY>
</HTML>
```

You probably noticed that this code is almost exactly the same as the previous one except that there is no *
* tag after "Hello World!!!." In this example, the text "And have a nice day!" would show on the same line as "HELLO

WORLD!!!," even though it is written a line below it, because the "new line" will be translated into a single white space.

As a teacher I enforce the use of the basic six tags needed for an HTML proper structure, so I would recommend everyone to make it a habit to write them all as soon as a page is created, and then fill in the blanks.

Tag Parameters

As we saw previously with the *FONT* and *BODY* tags, it is possible to add attributes to an opening HTML tag to make it more effective. Each attribute will affect the area after the opening tag and will finish with the closing tag. Remember that there is no need to write the attributes in the closing tag. Checking the W3C website (www.w3c.org) can get you an exhaustive list of all the attributes that tags can use, but I will give you the ones I consider most important for the tags that I will teach you at the end of this chapter.

BASIC TEXT FORMATTING

There are many ways to format text in HTML, but we will discuss only the real basics right now. There will be more details on styles in Chapter 10. The tags I am about to show you are considered to be deprecated and should be replaced with the use of style sheets, but as much as this is true, you probably want to get started without having to learn advanced formatting features. In that case, the following tags are ideal.

The first basic tool commonly used for formatting text is the *<P> . . . </P>* tag, which stands for "paragraph." As the name indicates, it defines an area that works as a single block, and most browsers will automatically break a new line at the end of a paragraph. I try not to use this tag when writing normal text since the output on the screen might be different depending on the browser, so I prefer to handle my paragraphs manually. On the other hand, paragraphs are really useful when using style sheets, as we will see in Chapter 10.

A very useful tool in HTML is the different heading styles that can be used. There are six basic levels of headings that can be used to easily write titles, chapters, or sections. Each heading is treated as a paragraph, so a new line is added automatically when the tag is closed. To use a heading, simply wrap your title with *<Hn> . . . </Hn>*, where "*n*" is the level of title you wish to use from 1 to 6 (with H1 the biggest heading and H6 the smallest). If you wish to add extra linebreaks you can use, as seen earlier, the *
* tag.

To change the appearance of text, you can use *<I> . . . </I>* to italicize a text, *<B> . . . </B>* to make it bold, or *<U> . . . </U>* to underline it. As always, these tags affect the text only between opening and closing tags. It is also possible to use the *<FONT>* tag to specify colors, fonts, sizes, and background colors, for example, but it is considered poor programming practice to use these in your HTML code since it makes it much more difficult to read. Instead, you should use styles, which, again, we will see in Chapter 10.

Most tags, including *<P>*, accept an attribute called *ALIGN* that allows setting of the horizontal alignment of a block by setting it to "left," "center," "right," or "justify." It is also possible to center an area of the page by using the *<CENTER> . . . </CENTER>* tag. The advantage of the *<CENTER>* tag is that it will act on anything between opening and closing tags, regardless of the type of element (form input, image, paragraph, button, etc.).

To do a basic enhancement on your page's look, you can use horizontal rules. These are horizontal lines used mostly to separate sections and paragraphs. To use it, just write *<HR>* with any of the following attributes: *ALIGN* (left, center, or right), *NOSHADE* to remove the shade under the line, *SIZE* (in pixels) to specify the height of the line, and *WIDTH* (length in either pixels or percentage of the page) to specify the linewidth. An example of a nice-looking rule could be *<HR ALIGN=center SIZE=1 WIDTH=75%>*, which would create a line of 75% of the page's width, centered in the page, and with 1 pixel height. Note that this tag does not need to be closed.

Finally, to conclude this set of basic formatting tools, I would have to add the *<BLOCKQUOTE> . . . </BLOCKQUOTE>* tag. This tag was created to be used to quote other people in a text, but it has a nice property. Any text inside a *<BLOCKQUOTE>* tag is automatically indented, which is great for a really fast indentation solution. I personally have used it in the past to force a blank margin at the beginning of my pages, making the output cleaner.

Here is an example using all these tags:

```
<HTML>
  <HEAD>
    <TITLE>Formatting example</TITLE>
  </HEAD>
  <BODY>
    <BLOCKQUOTE>
     All my text will show up with an indentation!
     <P ALIGN=right>This is a first paragraph with right
alignment</P>
     <P ALIGN=left>And this is a separate left-aligned
paragraph with things written in <I>italic</I>, <B>bold</B>,
<U>underlined</U> and even <U><B><I>all mixed up</I></B></U></P>
     <CENTER>
       <HR size=1 width=75%>
       <H1>Heading1</H1>
       <H2>Heading2</H2>
       <H6>Heading6, and like the others I'm centered!</H6>
     </CENTER>
    </BLOCKQUOTE>
  </BODY>
</HTML>
```

EXTERNAL REFERENCES

Two of the most common features in Webpages are links and images. They are two ways of referring to an external file. One places an image in the middle of the page, while the other sets up a clickable area that will open any type of file, or even open your default email client to send an email.

Links

Let us start with the links. Any text or image can be turned into a link by wrapping it with the *<A>...</A>* tag. The attributes for the *<A>* tag are essential for its proper functioning. The first attribute to set should be *HREF*, which will hold the URL that the link will refer to. The address could be an absolute or relative URI, or a call to a mail client by entering <u>mailto:any-email@address.here</u>. You can also select a target for the link, which specifies where the link should be open. This is done by using *TARGET* followed by the name of the window or frame where you wish the link to open. If the name has been set to a window or frame, it will work without complications, but if it has not been set yet, the link will pop up a new window that will receive the name written in the target parameter. From this point on, any link targeting the same name will open on that new window. Instead of providing a name, it is also possible to enter *_blank* to always open the link in a new popup window, *_self* to open the link in the current window or frame, *_parent* to open the link in the parent frame (see the section on frames), or *_top* to open the link in the parent of all parents (top frame). Here is a link example:

<A HREF="page.html" TARGET=_blank>This is the clickable area</A>

Another interesting use of the *<A>* tag is to create linking points in the page. This means creating a point in the page that can be linked to, allowing fast scrolling of long pages. To use this feature, write *<A NAME="anyname">* *...</A>*. To then link to that area, just add *#anyname* at the end of the address of the file you are linking to, or directly enter *#anyname* as the *HREF* if you wish to move inside the current file. Here is an example:

```
<HTML>
  <HEAD><TITLE>Link Examples</TITLE></HEAD>
  <BODY>
    <A NAME="top">This</A> is the top of the page!<BR>
    Here is a normal <A HREF="http://www.google.com"
target="_blank">link</A><BR>
    Now I'm going to add loads of BRs to make this page
really long!<BR><BR><BR><BR><BR><BR><BR><BR><BR><BR>
```

```
<BR><BR><BR><BR><BR><BR><BR><BR><BR><BR><BR><BR><BR><BR>
<BR><BR><BR><BR><BR><BR><BR><BR><BR><BR><BR><BR><BR><BR>
<BR><BR><BR><BR><BR><BR><BR><BR><BR><BR><BR><BR><BR><BR>
<BR><BR><BR><BR><BR><BR><BR><BR><BR><BR><BR><BR><BR><BR>
<BR><BR><BR><BR><BR><BR><BR><BR><BR><BR><BR><BR><BR><BR>
<BR><BR><BR><BR><BR><BR><BR><BR><BR><BR><BR><BR><BR><BR>
<BR><BR><BR><BR><BR><BR><BR><BR><BR><BR><BR><BR><BR><BR>
   This should be pretty low on the page so take me <A
HREF="#top">to the top!</A>
   </BODY>
</HTML>
```

Images

Using images in Websites is like using table salt when cooking. Without it, the site is too bland, but include too many images, and it becomes hard to enjoy. I must say, as most people discovering animated GIF images for the first time, my first HTML page was an array of ridiculous images, including the "all-star" work-in-progress animation, email-me image, and other classics found in virtually all "I'm learning HTML" Websites. In retrospect, I can say that that page was certainly the ugliest page I ever wrote in my life, but people learn from past mistakes. So here is my advice to all of you—keep it simple and don't overdo images!

Another important thing about images is size and format. People seldom realize that the bigger the image, the longer it will take to load, especially for those people out there who still use dialup connections. Generally images should be kept under 100 kB. Another important factor is the format. Most browsers accept a vast variety of image formats; however, for example including a BMP image is *strongly* discouraged, simply because as in all noncompressed formats, the images will tend to be unnecessarily huge. The most commonly used formats are GIF, JPG, and PNG, and you should try to limit your images' formats to either one of these three. Keep in mind that GIF images allow animations, but are limited to 256 colors. Generally, use JPG for images that require higher quality and GIF for icons and such. Also keep in mind that even though you can add an image as a background for the page, you do not necessarily need an image as big as the contents of the page. A technique I regularly use when creating my background images is to utilize the fact that background images are shown as a mosaic, filling the entire page with as many copies of the image as needed. For example, if there is a color you really want to use but it cannot be defined with the standard hexadecimal red-green-blue notation, you can create a picture of 1 pixel by 1 pixel (1×1 pixel) filled with the color you wish to use. When using it as a background, that pixel will be used all over the page to fill in the background, but will need to be downloaded only once to the client. Another nice technique is to include images of just a few pixels in height and very large width (I usually make the format 1600 pixels wide and 1–10 pixels tall depending on the effect I wish to achieve). The idea is to create a pattern that will be repeated line by line on the left side of your page. A nice image I created was for a school example where I decided to elicit that "bluebook" feeling. To do so I had an image that was all white, with a blue horizontal line and a red vertical line to create the margin. Just by selecting that image as the *BACKGROUND* property of my *<BODY>* tag created the desired effect, with an image that was less than 1 kB.

To include an image in the middle of a page, simply use the *<IMG>* tag, which does not need to be closed. The parameters to use include first *SRC*, which defines the URI of the image to be shown. It is also possible to specify the size of the image through *WIDTH* and *HEIGHT*. Note that if you do not set the size of the image, it will be displayed in its original size, but if you set both attributes your image might be distorted if you do not respect the image's aspect ratio. The best way to set a new size for an image that you wish to portray as either bigger or smaller is to simply set up one of the parameters as a number of pixels or a percentage of the original size. By writing only one of the attributes and omitting the other, you will be able to preserve the aspect ratio while changing the size of the image. The last but not least attribute is *ALT*, which takes a string, usually describing the image. This is extremely important if you wish to make your Website compatible with nongraphical browsers like Links, for example. When an image cannot be displayed by a browser, only the name will appear where the image should be. If you write the description of the image in the *ALT* attribute, instead of the picture's name, you will see that description. A good example of why this is useful would be Websites that are mainly picture-based, meaning that all menu options are actually pictures with text inside them. In these cases, the *ALT* should be whatever text the image holds. For example, if menu1.gif is a picture that says "register," the *ALT* for that picture should be "register" also. That way, a person visiting the Website will still be able to use it even though the images won't show up, as "register" will be much clearer to understand than "menu1.gif."

ORGANIZING DATA

When creating a Webpage, something very important to keep in mind is organizing the contents to ensure that the page is not cluttered or disorganized. This is especially important when adding pictures in the middle of paragraphs while attempting to keep a professional look. The main techniques used to organize information in a page are lists, tables, and frames. The first, as we will see right now, is not really useful with images but is a great way to create topic lists or any set of small text that needs some ordering.

Lists

Lists are a tool rarely used by developers on Webpages for reasons that I do not fully understand. I have often seen students creating paragraphs after paragraphs starting with a number or series of numbers to create a topic list for example, when HTML provides the tools to do so automatically.

There are two main types of lists: ordered and unordered. An *ordered* list will always include the position of the current element in front of the text itself, whereas *unordered* lists pretty much are the same as adding bullets in front of the text. An ordered list is created with the tag *<OL> . . . </OL>* and should always include *TYPE* as a parameter, with either one of the following values:

1—for decimal numbers (1, 2, 3, 4, . . .)

a—for lowercase alphabetical characters (a, b, c, d, . . .)

A—for uppercase alphabetical characters (A, B, C, D, . . .)

i—for lowercase roman numerals (i, ii, iii, iv, v, vi, . . .)

I—for uppercase roman numerals (I, II, III, IV, V, VI, . . .)

Another optional parameter is *START*, which takes a number that will be considered the position of the first element in the list. For example, a list defined as *<OL TYPE=I START=19> . . . </OL>* would have its elements numbered as XIX for the first one, XX for the second, XXI for the third, and so on.

Unordered lists are created with *<UL> . . . </UL>*, and, as you probably guessed, also require a *TYPE* parameter that will define the aspect of the bullets:

disk—for a filled-in circle

square—for a square outline

circle—for a circle outline

Once you have defined an area to work as a list, you can add a new element by starting its line with the tag *<LI>*. Think of this tag as a bullet or number that you place in front of text, since it does not need to be closed. Each *<LI>* will either add a bullet or put the next number or letter following the last *<LI>* used in the same list. Note than you can use nested lists if you wish to by simply using *<UL> . . . </UL>* or *<OL> . . . </OL>* instead of a new *<LI>* tag. Each new nested list will be automatically indented, along with all its contents, keeping the lists clean.

Here is an example of nested lists:

```
<HTML>
  <HEAD><TITLE>Nested Lists</TITLE></HEAD>
  <BODY>
    <OL TYPE=I START=19>
      <LI>I'm the first element, yet I show up as 19!!
      <LI>Second line
      <LI>And now something different!
      <UL TYPE=circle>
        <LI>Aren't circles pretty?
        <LI>Just wait until you try the other types!
      </UL>
      <LI>Where was I again?
    </OL>
  </BODY>
</HTML>
```

Tables

Tables are probably one of the most widely used systems for organizing pictures and text. A table is a very efficient tool when used properly but can cause painful results if not handled with care. Many programmers actually base their entire Websites on really complex tables, which gives a consistent look to their pages. Generally speaking, table fanatics tend to hate frames (next section) and vice versa. I personally think they are both needed. I use frames for the general layout of the site (header, menus, body, etc.), and I use tables to organize individual pages. The reason for this is that, whereas many people have pages that all start with the exact same several dozen lines only for menus and headings that need to be loaded in every single page that is opened, I just use a frame that loads it once, and stays open. Each page will open only the new content, without necessitating reloading of the page's entire layout. But anyway, let us see how to use tables!

The very first thing is to define an area that will be treated as a table. It is very important to close it if you wish your page to have the desired look regardless of the version of the browser. In the mid-1990s browsers would go crazy when a table was not closed properly; nowadays browsers tend to solve the problem and output the right aspect. Regardless, make sure that you close the tags! This is also important when starting new rows and cells, as we shall see. The official HTML syntax states that it is not necessary to close a row or cell definition, but I would strongly recommend everyone to do so, since it will make tables much easier to understand. To create a table, the tag used is *<TABLE>...</TABLE>*. This tag can take, among others, the following parameters:

WIDTH—specifies in pixels or percentage the width of the table

HEIGHT—specifies in pixels or percentage the height of the table

BORDER—defines the size in pixels of the table's border

CELLSPACING—defines in pixels the spacing between cells

CELLPADDING—defines in pixels the padding around each cell

ALIGN—"left," "right," or "center"; specifies where the table will be aligned on the page

BGCOLOR—background color for the page, in either letters or hexadecimal RGB values

Note that *WIDTH* and *HEIGHT* can be omitted if you want the table to adapt to the size of the cells. Many graphic designers use these settings to create restricted pages that appear to be a single box, allowing the page to look exactly the same regardless of the resolution used by the client. The *BORDER* parameter has to be used wisely; make it too big, and the page will look goofy. I generally set it to 0 or 1 for either no border at all or just a small one. A border of 0 is extremely useful when, for example, using images as menu options. By having images of the exact same size placed in a table, you can give many fancy effects to your pages, such as, for example, tabs in a folder, or a set of buttons in a futuristic interface. It is all up to your imagination and your skills with image editors. Personally I am definitely not a graphic designer, so I tend to keep it simple, or use text for my menus.

Once you have defined the general rules for your table, you must specify the cells left to right and row by row. This means that the very first thing is to define a row with the tags *<TR> . . . </TR>*. Each new row must start and finish with these tags, which seldom take parameters (except maybe styles or heights). Once you are inside a row, you must write the cells one by one, in the order in which they will appear with either *<TD> . . . </TD>* for standard cells or *<TH> . . . </TH>* for header cells. The header cells are usually in the first row, and will automatically center and render the text they contain in boldface. Regardless of the cell type selected, you can use the following parameters:

HEIGHT, WIDTH, BGCOLOR—do the same as with *<TABLE>* but for the current cell only

ALIGN—"left," "center," "justify," "right," or "char"; specifies the text alignment inside the cell

VALIGN—"top," "middle," "bottom," or "baseline"; specifies the vertical alignment of the text inside the cell

ROWSPAN and *COLSPAN*—take the number of rows or columns that the cell should use

ROWSPAN and *COLSPAN* are probably two of the major sources of error in tables among HTML developers. They are not complicated, but it is easy to mess up if you do not watch out. The number they accept represents the span that the cell should take rowwise or columnwise. For example, a *ROWSPAN=2* would mean that the current cell will use two rows. Obviously, setting either parameter to 1 will do nothing to the cell. The dangerous thing about these is that you must remember where you expanded a new row or column in order to avoid extra cells popping out of the table. Note that expanded cells use room on the following rows and columns, never the previous ones.

Check this *bad* example:

```
<HTML>
  <HEAD><TITLE>Bad Tables</TITLE></HEAD>
  <BODY>
    <TABLE BORDER=2 WIDTH=500>
      <TR>
        <TD>Let's make a 3x3 table!</TD>
        <TD COLSPAN=2>I'm going to expand this cell!</TD>
        <TD>So should I add a third cell?</TD>
      </TR>
      <TR>
        <TD ROWSPAN=3>What happens with a rowspan of 3?
I'm on second row and there's only supposed to be one
more!</TD>
        <TD>This table is going to look horrible!</TD>
        <TD>Let's just be done with it...</TD>
      </TR>
      <TR>
        <TD>Last row! and the first cell I type in the
code</TD>
        <TD>Wait a second...Didn't I rowspan? So even
though I'm the second set of TDs I appear third!!! Let
us avoid adding a new cell then</TD>
      </TR>
    </TABLE>
  </BODY>
</HTML>
```

Obviously this example was an array of horrible mistakes. Let us fix it by doing a proper 3×3 table with good rowspans and colspans. The aspect we wish to create is shown in Table 3.1.

TABLE 3.1   Desired Separation between Cells

1	2 and 3	
4 and 7	5	6
	8	9

Here is the code to achieve the format shown Table 3.1:

```
<HTML>
  <HEAD><TITLE>Good Tables</TITLE></HEAD>
  <BODY>
    <TABLE BORDER=2 WIDTH=600>
      <TR>
        <TH WIDTH=200>1</TH>
        <TH COLSPAN=2>2 and 3</TH>
      </TR>
      <TR>
        <TD ROWSPAN=2 VALIGN="bottom">4 and 7</TD>
        <TD>5</TD>
        <TD ALIGN=center>6</TD>
      </TR>
      <TR>
        <TD>8</TD>
        <TD>9</TD>
      </TR>
    </TABLE>
  </BODY>
</HTML>
```

My last little tip with tables is to always start drawing a normal table with no expanded cells, and then figure out which ones need to be expanded. When creating Webpages, paper and pen are still your biggest ally!

Frames

Here is another source of syntax errors, and widely hated by *<TABLE>* users. Personally, as stated in the tables section, I tend to use frames on a regular basis, since it allows me to have some sets of data to load to the client once and only once, to then remain open. By doing so instead of systematically creating my entire layout with tables, I can have content pages that are much lighter and faster to load for the client. The idea behind a frame is to break down your main window into several miniwindows, called "frames." Each frame can independently open a separate Webpage, yet it is possible to communicate between them. Some important things to know about frames is that you need a page to hold the frameset, which will define the aspect of each frame, and then the files you will load in each one of those frames. Frameset definitions replace the *<BODY>...</BODY>* tag, but some old browsers cannot use frames, so you might want to create a "noframes" section.

Let's start with the basics. The very first thing to do, as stated above, is to write the frameset right after the *<HEAD>...</HEAD>* in the page that will be loaded. This page will have nothing displayed except the title, but is extremely important. To create a frameset, use the tag *<FRAMESET>...*

</FRAMESET> with either *ROWS* or *COLS* as parameter. You can technically use both at the same time, creating a frameset working like tables with no rowspan or colspan, but it is recommended to restrict the use to only one type. The type of data you should put in those attributes are called "multi-length" since they provide the sizes of all frames that the frameset will hold. If, for example, your frameset needs to have five rows, you will have a *ROWS* attribute with five lengths in order, separated by commas. Lengths can be a number of pixels, a percentage of the screen, or an asterisk (*), meaning "whatever is left on the screen." Suppose that you wish to break up the window into three rows: the first one 100 pixels tall, the last one representing 10% of the screen, and the middle one using the rest of the window. You would write *<FRAMESET ROWS="100, *, 10%>...</FRAMESET>*. It is also possible to specify the attribute *BORDER*, which sets the border size between frames in that frameset.

Once the frameset is defined, you need to define each frame that will be included, filling the rows or columns you created with the *<FRAMESET>* tag. Note that these frames must be in the order in which you want them to appear, and note also that you can use a new frameset instead of a frame in an available slot. The basic frames are created with the tag *<FRAME>*, which does not need to be closed. There are two parameters that should always be set, and few optional ones. First there is *NAME*, which is essential since it provides the name that will define the frame itself, and which will be used in the *TARGET* attribute of a link wanting to open a page in that frame. Then we have *SRC*, which is used to specify the URL of the file that will be loaded in that frame when the frameset is created. Other parameters include *NORESIZE*, which takes no values, needs only to be added or omitted, and prevents the frame from being resized. *SCROLLING* can be set to "yes," always allowing a scrollbar in that frame; "no," to never allow scrollbars; or "auto," to include a scrollbar only when needed. By default, *SCROLLING* is set to auto.

Here is an example of a frameset page that will open some of the examples we saw in this chapter in four different frames. You will note that the top frame loads *about:blank*, which is simply a standard name understood by browsers as a blank page:

```
<HTML>
  <HEAD><TITLE>Frames example</TITLE></HEAD>
  <FRAMESET ROWS="100,*,100" BORDER=2>
    <FRAME NAME="title" SRC="about:blank">
    <FRAMESET COLS="25%, *" BORDER=0>
      <FRAME NAME="menu" SRC="links.html" SCROLLING=NO>
      <FRAME NAME="body" SRC="goodtables.html" NORESIZE>
    </FRAMESET>
    <FRAME NAME="footer" SRC="nestedlists.html">
  </FRAMESET>
</HTML>
```

As stated earlier, some browsers are not capable of working with frames, usually because the browser was of an older date than the addition of frames in the HTML standards. The general behavior of a browser that is reading an unknown tag is to ignore that tag. Obviously a browser that cannot process frames will ignore our entire frameset and frame definitions, as it does not recognize the tags. We can take advantage of that behavior and use another frame-related tag to create an alternate version of our page that would not employ frames, but instead would use tables, for example. To do so, you can use the *<NOFRAMES>...</NOFRAMES>* tag, and put a normal *<BODY>...</BODY>* block inside it. This new block should be included right before the last *</FRAMESET>* tag. The way it will be processed is simple. If the browser knows frames, it will ignore anything between *<NOFRAMES>* and *</NOFRAMES>* and therefore skip the body you added. If the browser does not understand frames, it will not understand the *<NOFRAMES>* tag and ignore both opening and closing tags, but will still parse what is between them. At that point it will find a *<BODY>* that will be considered the normal beginning of the body section of a standard page. You should always have a noframes section when working with frames, to at least ask the user to get a browser supporting frames. Here is an improved version of our previous example:

```
<HTML>
  <HEAD><TITLE>Frames example</TITLE></HEAD>
  <FRAMESET ROWS="100,*,100" BORDER=2>
    <FRAME NAME="title" SRC="about:blank">
    <FRAMESET COLS="25%, *" BORDER=0>
      <FRAME NAME="menu" SRC="links.html" SCROLLING=NO>
      <FRAME NAME="body" SRC="goodtables.html" NORESIZE>
    </FRAMESET>
    <FRAME NAME="footer" SRC="nestedlists.html">
    <NOFRAMES>
      <BODY>
       Please get yourself a good browser like <A
HREF="http://www.getfirefox.com">Firefox</A>
      </BODY>
    </NOFRAMES>
  </FRAMESET>
</HTML>
```

There is another very curious type of frame called the "inline frame" (or "iframe"), which is basically a frame that can be used as an image. It has the advantage of being usable inside a normal body of a page, and does not require any frameset definition. You can utilize this asset to, for example, include it in a table, surrounding it by images of a TV frame to create a TV effect. The TV screen would basically be the inline frame that would be used to display the contents. You can top it off with a remote-looking menu that will have links targeting that iframe. To create an iframe, use the tag *<IFRAME>...</IFRAME>*, where the space between the opening and closing tags is used to enter the "alternate" version, in case the browser does not support iframes (it is similar to the "noframes" section). The *<IFRAME>* tag needs the following attributes:

SRC—the URI to be loaded in the frame

NAME—name of the frame enabling you to link to it

WIDTH—frame width

HEIGHT—frame height

ALIGN—"top," "middle," "bottom," "left," or "right" for frame alignment

FRAMEBORDER—1 or 0 to have or not have a frame border

MARGINWIDTH—size in pixels for the margin width

MARGINHEIGHT—size in pixels for the margin height

SCROLLING—"yes," "no," or the default "auto" to allow scrollbars

Here is an example of a page having an iframe inside a table:

```
<HTML>
  <HEAD><TITLE>IFRAME in TABLE</TITLE></HEAD>
  <BODY>
    <CENTER>
      <TABLE BORDER=0>
        <TR>
          <TD ROWSPAN=3>I want <A HREF="http://www.
getfirefox.com" target="coolframe">Firefox</A>!</TD>
          <TH> INLINE FRAME</TH>
          <TD ROWSPAN=3> I want to look for <A
HREF="http://www.google.com"
target="coolframe">something</A>!</TD>
        </TR>
        <TR>
          <TD><IFRAME SRC="http://www.google.com"
NAME="coolframe" WIDTH=400 HEIGHT=300 ALIGN=middle
FRAMEBORDER=0>The Iframe is NOT WORKING!!</IFRAME></TD>
        </TR>
        <TR>
          <TD align=center>This was cool</TD>
        </TR>
      </TABLE>
    </CENTER>
  </BODY>
</HTML>
```

SPECIAL CHARACTERS

The last piece of information necessary for now in order to start creating Websites is how to use special characters. As mentioned at the beginning of this chapter, you are not allowed to use the characters < and > except for tags, but what if you wanted to use that symbol for a mathematical comparison? Here is where special characters come in handy. Other typical example is white spaces; as stated earlier, any large group of white spaces is translated into a single white space by browsers, so what if you wanted to force five white spaces between two words? Another final crucial example, at least for me, is my last name, "Gabarró." As you noticed, it contains an accent on the o, which few keyboards around the world have, and that, depending on the regional settings, might not show up on the screen if I just use the character "ó." Many people would just ignore this and write "Gabarro," but as a proud Spaniard, I need my accent, and luckily enough I can get it in HTML in a way that will be printed in any computer, regardless of its settings.

All special characters in HTML start with an ampersand (&) and finish with a semicolon (;). For example, the character "ó" is written *ó*, meaning that when writing my last name on a Webpage I have to spell it *Gabarró*. White spaces are done with * *, < is *<*, and > is *>*.

You can find a large reference table such as that in Appendix A.

4

Work Environment

INTRODUCTION

In this chapter we will see step-by-step how to install all the software that we will need for our Websites to run. This includes an Apache Web server, the PHP engine, and a MySQL database. We will also see how to install and use two powerful PHP-based applications: phpMyAdmin to manipulate databases, and phpBB, a free bulletin board tool.

The installation guidelines are for Microsoft Windows based computers. These tools also work on UNIX, but chances are you already have a Web server and PHP installed as part of the UNIX/Linux distribution of your choice. You can find more information on UNIX/Linux installation guidelines in Appendix B.

DOWNLOADING THE SOFTWARE

The first obvious thing to do is download all the necessary software that we will use. The Apache Web server can be found at www.apache.org. Once there, click on "HTTP server," find the latest stable release (the current version at the time of this writing is 2.0.55 with a Windows installer and 2.2.0 as a UNIX source package), click on "download," and find the "Win32 binary

Web Application Design and Implementation: Apache 2, PHP5, MySQL, JavaScript, and Linux/UNIX, by Steven A. Gabarró
Copyright © 2007 by John Wiley & Sons, Inc.

(MSI Installer)," which will simplify the installation process. Download the file somewhere safe along with all the files that we will download next.

To download PHP, go to www.php.net, click on "downloads," and choose the newest stable Windows zip package (version 5.1.2 as of right now), choose the download mirror closest to your geographic location, and save the file with the Apache installer.

The MySQL server can be found at www.mysql.com. Click on "developer zone," and find the "MySQL server download" (current version is 5.0). Find the Windows downloads sections and the file for "Windows (×86)" by picking a mirror. At that point you may enter some personal information, although this is optional.

The two last tools are phpMyAdmin and phpBB. The former can be found at www.phpmyadmin.net. In the main page you should be able to see all the different available versions; just download the latest stable version (2.7.0, p. l2, as of the time of this writing). Pick your favorite compression format, choose a mirror, and download. PhpBB can be found at www.phpbb.com; go to "download" and download the full package in zip, gzip or bz2 format, depending on your favorite compressing tool. If you are unsure, just pick zip. Choose the mirror again and save the file on your drive.

INSTALLING THE Apache SERVER

Installation Steps

To avoid problems, the first thing to do is stop any service that might use the port 80, such as, for example, instant messaging tools like AIM or Skype. It might also be a good idea to temporarily disable your computer's firewall while you install this application.

Start by double-clicking on the installer file that you downloaded. Click on "next," read and accept the terms in the license agreement, click "next" again, read the description if you wish to, and then get to the "server informa- tion" configuration page. All these settings can be modified later on, but you might want to set them up right away. First you will see the "network domain." If your computer is in a domain, enter that information there. If you are unsure of your network domain, simply type "localhost". The next field is "server name," which represents your computer name in the domain written right before. For example, if your domain was *in.home.net*, and your com- puter name is *mycomp*, you would enter *in.home.net* in the first field and *mycomp.in.home.net* in the second. As before, if you are unsure, just type "localhost". Finally enter the email address to which users should send ques- tions in case they encounter a problem accessing your sites.

You must then choose whether to install the application as a service for all users on port 80, or just for the current user on port 8080. The main differ- ence between the two is that a service installation will basically start up your server when the computer does, and will be working on the standard port used by Web applications. The other option is to have the server running only when you decide to launch it manually on a nondefault port. I recommend the first option. Choose the "typical" installation, and select the folder in which to install it (I will assume that you used the default folder in further steps). Click "next" and then "finish."

Checking the Installation

At this point the application should automatically install and start running. It is time to check the installation. Your systray (that area with little icons, on the bottom right of your desktop, where the clock is) should have a new icon: a red feather with a green "play" symbol. If you see this feather, Apache is installed. If you see the green play symbol, Apache is running, but if you see a red "stop" symbol, this means that the server could not start. Double-clicking on the icon will bring up the Apache service monitor, which will allow you to start, stop, or restart the Web server. Keep in mind that you will need to restart the server each time you modify its configuration, so get familiar with the tool. When you are done with it, click on "OK."

Possible Errors

If for some reason Apache is not running at this point, chances are you will see an error message saying "Service not installed." This is usually due to other services running on port 80, which will prevent installation of other services on the same port. Luckily, we can change Apache's standard port. To do so, open a command console (click "start," then "run," and type "cmd"), in the console access your Apache installation folder (C:/Program Files/Apache Group/Apache2/bin), and type "*apache –k install*". That should install the service, but you may still get an error saying "could not bind to address 0.0.0.0:80". Note that ":" means "using the port." In that case, find the file located in [. . .]/Apache2/conf/httpd.conf and open it. This is the most important file for Apache; it is its configuration file and is loaded automatically each time the server is started. Find the line that says "*Listen 80*" and replace it with "*Listen 127.0.0.1:80*", save the file, and again try to run the "*apache –k install*" on your console. If that still does not work, again replace that same line with "*Listen 127.0.0.1:8080*". The reasons for these different errors are all related to Windows' services, and the way you access the server. The line "Listen 80" means that Apache tries to accept incoming requests through port 80 on the local computer. Sometimes the server is incorrectly installed, and there is no reference to what constitutes the "local" computer. To force this binding, we add the 127.0.0.1 IP address, which always represents the local computer. We are basically telling Apache which socket to use to accept all communications. If there is another service running on port 80, this will still not work; hence the need to change Apache's port to something else. The port 8080 is the standard "Alternative" for Web servers.

Configuring Apache

By now your basic Apache server should be running. You can check it by opening a browser and accessing http://localhost/ (or http://localhost:8080/ if you changed the port that Apache uses). This should open a page telling you that your installation was a success. Now it is time to set up your preferences. My first recommendation is to create a folder called "Web" on a secondary hard disk or partition of your choice. This will be the folder in which all your Web applications will run. I will assume that your folder is "D:/Web". Open [...]/Apache2/conf/httpd.conf and leave it open as we will be modifying it when we install PHP.

The first thing to do is find the line that starts with *"DocumentRoot"* followed by a path. Change the path to the one you will use; for example, change the line to *DocumentRoot "D:/Web."* If you are afraid of messing up the configuration file, you can comment out the existing line by placing the character # in front of the line, and typing a new line with your chosen Document Root. Note that Apache uses forward slashes (/) instead of backslashes (\). This allows your Apache to know which folder in your computer to go to when trying to find Webpages. The next thing to do is set up the rights for that folder; you may again use the basic settings, by finding the line that starts as *<Directory* followed by the same path that was initially set as "DocumentRoot." Replace that path with the same one you used for your "DocumentRoot." Your new line should be *<Directory "D:/Web">*. This line represents the opening tag for a set of rules that will be applied to that folder. It is important to remember to set the rights to the folders you want to access, or you may get a "forbidden" error message when trying to access it.

The next thing to set up is the list of files that will be opened by default when trying to access a folder. This information can be found in the line that starts as *"DirectoryIndex index.html index.html.var."* Here you may set up any file that you would like to use as a directory index. I recommend adding at least the following: index.php and index.htm, but you might want to add index.php3 index.php4 index.php5 index.phtml if you are planning on running old PHP applications.

Save the file and restart your Apache. Remember to keep your httpd.conf file opened as we will be using it in a few minutes. If you did not make any syntax errors, Apache should restart easily. In case of a typo, Apache should inform you of the line with the problem. Find it and correct the typo. Access your localhost through your browser once more. You should now see the contents of your "Web" folder or one of the directory index files if there is one.

INSTALLING PHP5

Find the zip file you downloaded and extract it to C:\PHP\. Add C:\PHP to your Windows PATH. To do so, open your "system properties" window by either right-clicking on "My Computer" and selecting "properties," or by selecting the option through your control panel. Click on "advanced" and then "environment variables." In "system variables" you should see one called "PATH"; select it, click on "Edit," go to end of the "Variable value:" field, and add ";C:\PHP\" (without the double quotes). *Do not delete any of the other information in that field*!!! Adding the PHP folder to the PATH will help Windows find any file inside that folder. Accept all windows by clicking on "Accept" or "OK" until they are closed.

Now go to your C:\PHP\ folder and rename the file "php.ini-recommended" as "php.ini." You can also do a copy of that file and rename the copy. Open the file and find the line that says ";*extension=php_mysql.dll*" and remove the semicolon in front of the line. Do the same with the line containing ";*extension=php_mbstring.dll*." This will tell PHP to start up with the MySQL and MBString extensions. The first is obviously needed to run MySQL; the second one is needed for phpMyAdmin. Now look for the line *extension_dir = "./"* and replace it with *extension_dir = c:/php/ext*.

One last thing you might want to do for development purposes is turn on the error display on pages. By default, any script error is logged into a file but does not show up on the screen. Find the section on error reporting and make sure that you have the following lines:

error_reporting = E_ALL
; Print out errors (as a part of the output). For production web sites,
; you're strongly encouraged to turn this feature off, and use error logging
; instead (see below). Keeping display_errors enabled on a production
web site
; may reveal security information to end users, such as file paths on your
Web
; server, your database schema or other information.
display_errors = on

Changing *display_errors* to on will allow you to view any script error when you attempt to run them. As you can read in the php.ini file, it is recommended to turn this feature off for pages that will be publicly available, as it may show information that should remain hidden to the user. For development purposes, it's much easier if you can see all errors and notices so that you can correct them before publishing your page.

Save the file and open your Apache's httpd.conf. Go to the end of the file and add the following lines:

LoadModule php5_module "c:/php/php5apache2.dll"
AddType application/x-httpd-php .php .phtml .php3 .php4 .php5
PHPIniDir "C:/PHP"

The first line tells Apache to load the PHP module when Apache starts, which will allow PHP files to be executed. The second line adds a new type of application, namely, PHP applications, which should be identified through the files extensions listed in the line. You may add any file extension that you would like to run through the PHP processor. The final line tells Apache where to find the php.ini file.

Now copy the file C:\PHP\libmysql.dll to your C:\Windows\System32\ folder and restart Apache. This step should not really be necessary, but I have seen many cases in which not doing so resulted in some problems in loading the MySQL extension. If you reload your http://localhost/ on your browser, assuming that there are no directory index files in your Web folder, you should see at the end of the page a line that says "*Apache/2.0.55 (Win32) PHP/5.1.2 Server at localhost Port 80*," assuming that you installed the same versions as I did.

Testing PHP

Go to your "document root" folder (D:\Web in our example) and create a new folder called *phpwork* or something similar. This folder will be the one in which all your PHP work should be saved. Inside that new folder, create a file called index.php containing the following code:

<?PHP phpinfo(); ?>

Try to access http://localhost/phpwork/; this should show a huge table with all the PHP configuration information.

INSTALLING MySQL

Locate the file you downloaded, decompress it, and launch Setup.exe. Choose "typical" installation, let it copy all files, and skip signup. Make sure that the option "configure the MySQL server now" is selected, and click on "finish." Click "next" and choose "detailed configuration." Now through all the windows, select "developer machine," "nontransactional database only" (unless you are planning on using MyISAM, which I will not explain in this book), "decision support" (assuming that the installation is for your work computer and will be used only by a few programmers. If you are configuring a Web server that will be accessed by many users, you might want to choose one of the other options). Make sure that you enable TCP/IP networking, and remember the port number (3306 by default), "enable strict mode," choose your character set, and "install as window service." You may even choose "include bin directory in Windows PATH" to make it easier for you to change settings later on. Select a "root" password; this is very important, and *never* forget that information. Choose whether you want to enable root access from remote machines or not (I recommend "not" if you are going to be physically working on the computer to prevent possible security breaches). Click on "execute," which will configure your MySQL.

Adding a MySQL User

I strongly recommend that everyone create a new user that will have the right to use the MySQL database other than the root. This will be the user that we will use in our PHP scripts. Open a command console (as we did when solving Apache problems) and type "*mysql --user=root --password=your_pass mysql*", replacing "your_pass" with the password you selected for the root during the installation of MySQL. This will open the MySQL console. Now type "*GRANT ALL PRIVILEGES ON *.* TO 'newuser'@'localhost' IDENTIFIED BY 'newpass' WITH GRANT OPTION;*", replacing "newuser" and "newpass" with the username and password you wish to use with PHP. Press "enter," then type "\quit" and "enter" again.

How Do I Know if MySQL is Running?

If you managed to open the MySQL console and added a user, MySQL is running, so we can move to the next step: testing whether PHP can connect to MySQL, and in no way better than using phpMyAdmin.

INSTALLING PhpMyAdmin

Decompress the zip file you downloaded inside your document root, and rename the folder to something easy for you to remember but hard for someone to guess. This will prevent people from trying to access your administration tool. Go to the folder and locate the file *config.default.php*. Either rename it to *config.inc.php* or copy the file and rename the copy. Open the file (Wordpad will probably output the text in a nicer way than Notepad), locate the line *$cfg['PmaAbsoluteUri'] = ";"* and enter the absolute URI of your phpMy-Admin folder. For example, if you called the folder "mysqlAdmin" and you placed it in your document root, you should type "*$cfg[PmaAbsoluteUri'] = 'http://localhost/mysqlAdmin';*". Next find the first line that says "*$cfg ['Servers'][$i]['user'] = 'root'; // MySQL user*" and replace "root" with the user you created with MySQL. In the following line enter the password for that user and save the file. If you created a user "newuser" with "newpass" as a password, your two lines should look like this:

$cfg['Servers'][$i]['user'] = 'newuser'; // MySQL user

$cfg['Servers'][$i]['password'] = 'newpass'; // MySQL password (only needed

   Save the file and access the folder through your browser (e.g., http://localhost/mysqlAdmin/). This should open up phpMyAdmin's interface. If there is any error, it would show up in this window. Typical errors include bad user/passwords and wrong absolute URIs.

We will see how to use phpMyAdmin in Chapter 12, but for now let us create a new database that will be used by phpBB. In the main page type the name of the database you want to create (I will choose "forum") and click on "create." If you look on the dropdown menu on the left menu, you should see a new database called "forum" with 0 tables. Congratulations! This means that your phpMyAdmin is working perfectly well.

INSTALLING A BULLETIN BOARD: phpBB

Bulletin boards are spreading over the Internet to connect people with the same interests in a discussion area. PHPBB is one of the most popular PHP bulletin board solutions, mostly because of its simplicity. We will see how to install this application and how to set it up. You will find more detailed information in Appendix C.

Installation Steps

Start by decompressing the zip file inside your document root and rename the folder, for example, as "forum," and access http://localhost/forum/install/install.php. This is an automated PHP script that will configure your boards to work with your database. Make sure that you select MySQL 4.x/5.x as your database type (unless your host has a different database), method "install." Your database configuration should be "localhost" for hostname and "forum" for database name (or the name you chose when creating a test database in the previous steps). Use the user and password you created when installing MySQL (and the same that you used for phpMyAdmin). You should leave the prefix with the default "phpbb_" as it will help you recognize the tables used by phpBB. Enter your email address (for users to mail you about any problem), enter your domain (localhost if running only locally, your computer's name if you plan on using it on a local-area network only, or the domain in which you are installing phpBB if phpBB will be used over the Internet), your server port (80 by default), the folder in which you installed the forums, and a user and password that you will use in the boards. It is preferable to use a user/password different from the one in your database settings. Each message you will write in the boards will have your username attached to it, so you might want to use your favorite nickname.

Finish the installation by clicking on the "install" buttons until you see a message telling you to delete two directories. Delete those two directories in your forum/folder to prevent malicious attempts to reconfigure your boards.

Try to access http://localhost/forum/; this should open up the boards' main page, which should include one forum called "test forum 1." Using phpBB is very intuitive; clicking on a forum name will open the list of messages in that category. Each message is a "thread" in which all users can discuss whatever they feel like. Let us configure our boards and add new forums.

Start by logging in with the user/password you entered during the install, either by entering it at the bottom of the page or clicking on "log in." I do not recommend selecting the "remember me" option if you are the administrator, to avoid having someone log in as an admin through your computer and change the forum settings. Now that you are logged in, you will notice that at the bottom of the page there is a new link that says "go to administration panel." Click on it, and reenter your user/password information (this is a double-check for security reasons). The way this application works is through the menus on the left. The main area shows the current configuration page. When entering the administration panel, you can see the forum's statistics, as well as who is online. PhpBB will also let you know if you have the latest version installed.

On the left menu click on "management" to enter the forum administration. Here you can create new forums and categories. Let us start by editing the existing one to make it look nicer. Next, to "test category 1," click on "edit" and change the name to "announcements." Do to same with "test forum 1" and rename it to "news," along with the description of your choice. Leave everything by default and click on "update." You can use the two text-boxes to create new forums and categories. Each forum will be attached to a category. The order in which you see categories and forums is the same one that the users will see.

The next menu ("permissions") allows you to change the rights of each forum. Select a forum and then the rights you want to use. I recommend selecting "advanced mode" for more flexibility. In advanced mode you can determine who can view, read, post, reply, edit, delete, turn a thread into a sticky thread (always remaining on top of a forum), turn a thread into an announcement (like sticky threads, but with a different icon), vote in polls, and create a poll. The options for each one of these categories are ALL to allow use for everybody, REG to allow it only for registered users who have created a user and a password, PRIVATE to only allow it for the users or groups of your choice, MOD to only allow it for moderators, and ADMIN to allow it only for administrators.

A little further down in the menu you will see "configuration." This is where you can set all the settings for your boards, and is pretty self-explanatory. While you are there, change the "site name" and "site description" to something more welcoming than "yourdomain.com" and "a_little_text to describe your forum." If you wish to force users to enter valid email addresses when creating a new account, select "user" in the "enable account activation" option. I recommend that you also enable the visual confirmation and disable user emails via the board. Change your system time zone [e.g., EST time is GMT (Greenwich Mean Time) −5].

Finally, at the end of the menu, you can see the "User Admin," where you can manage users individually, create ranks, and set individual permissions or moderator rights.

Check Appendix C for a full description of how to administrate a phpBB board.

BASIC SECURITY CONSIDERATIONS

Now that you have everything installed, keep everything safe!! Remember that PHP is a server-side language, so any PHP script runs on your server and can access any file on the server even if that file is not accessible through your http://localhost/. Take advantage of this to store files that may contain secret information in folders that are not in your document root if you are running Windows. For example, if you have a file required by PHP that contains your database information (user, password, domain, etc.), you can store it on C:\UltraSecretStuff\, and later, when PHP needs to access it, just enter the local path instead of an "http" address. This way, users will not be able to attempt opening the file.

If you are running on a UNIX/Linux machine, use tools like *chmod* and *chown* to your advantage. By default, PHP applications run with limited user permissions on UNIX/Linux servers, so that you can create folders and allow only yourself the right to enter them. This way anyone trying to access the folder through an "http://" will get a "forbidden" error page, whereas your PHP will still be able to access the folder and its files. For example, if your document root is located in ~/web/ and you create a folder ~/web/includes/ with important information needed by PHP, you might want to set that folder's rights to read and execute only for the owner.

A file's rights on a UNIX/Linux system is represented through a set of letters (that you can see if you type "ls –l" in the folder containing the files). The letter *r* stands for read, *w* for write, and *x* for execute. These letters appear in groups of three and are either present or replaced by a dash (-). There are three groups, the first for the owner of the file, the second for the people in the same group as the owner, and the last for the rest. If, for example, a file has –rwxr-xr–– before its name when doing "ls –l," this means the user can read, write, and execute the file or directory; people in the owner's group can read it and execute it; and the others can only read it. All folders inside the document root that need to be accessible by all users should have the rights –rwxr-xr-x or what we call "755." The number is basically the translation of the rights into octal. Each group of three characters (r, w, and x) represents a single bit set to 1 if the letter is present or 0 if there is a dash. For example, rwx would be binary 111, which equals to 7 in octal; r-x is 101, which equals to 5. To change a file's rights, you need to type *chmod rights file*, for example, *chmod 755 myfile*. When a folder contains secret information, you might want to set it with a *chmod 700 folder* to allow yourself to read, write, and execute, but forbid access to all others (except the root user, of course). PHP should still be able to access those folders, but no one else would from their computers.

You may also want to use *chown*, which allows you to change the owner of a file. For example, typing *chown myuser myfile* will change the owner of *myfile* to the user *myuser*.

CONCLUSION

If you have reached this step with no errors, *congratulations*!! You probably survived the hardest part of working with PHP. Now let us start using what we have installed and learn the PHP basics.

5

PHP—A Server-Side Scripting Language

HOW DOES IT WORK?

Some "New" Words on PHP

As you should already know, PHP is a server-side scripting language. PHP scripts are usually accessed through forms that send information using either the GET or POST methods (as we will discuss in Chapter 9). It was created in 1995 by Rasmus Lerdorf, and initially called PHP/FI.

For a long time there were two main versions that coexisted: PHP3 and PHP4, and now we have PHP5, which made PHP3 a thing of the past. PHP4 is still used by many PHP users, even after they install PHP5. The main difference between the versions is the way they operate. PHP3 was a pure interpreted language, which means that code was interpreted line by line on the server as the code was read. PHP4 introduced the script motor "Zend" that increased the treatment speed. PHP4 was a sort of object code compiler that was then sent to the Zend engine. The arrival PHP5 brought Zend2, and even faster script motor, as well as real object-oriented programming, as we will see in Chapter 8. Most PHP5 users actually don't take advantage of the object-oriented capabilities of PHP5, so they technically use PHP4 on a PHP5 installation.

This chapter covers the basics of PHP, so it could be considered a PHP4 tutorial. Chapter 8 will introduce you to using objects in PHP5.

Web Application Design and Implementation: Apache 2, PHP5, MySQL, JavaScript, and Linux/UNIX, by Steven A. Gabarró

Syntax Generalities

PHP code is usually inserted inside HTML code. This allows for small parts of an HTML page to be executed before the page is downloaded to the user's computer. To insert PHP code in any page, you must use *<?PHP*. For a long time it was fine to just write *<?*, but the newer versions of PHP encourage the use of the full *<?PHP* opening tag, to prevent all possible confusion in executing the scripts. Once the opening symbol has been written, you enter the "PHP zone." Anything that you type will be executed by your PHP engine before you send the final page to the user. When you are done writing your script, or portion of script, you must close the "PHP zone" with *?>*. You actually already saw an example of this when we wrote our index.php file containing *<?PHP phpinfo(); ?>*. This means that we start the PHP, and call the function *phpinfo()*. This is the function that outputs all the configuration settings of PHP. Each instruction in PHP must end with a semicolon, not doing so will make the page not work, so be careful!

You can create comments in PHP by using the same symbols as in C language. You can either select an area of comment, starting with */* and finishing with **/*, or you can use *//* to comment anything from there until the end of the line. Here is an example:

```
<?PHP/* --------- INDEX.PHP FILE --------
        ---- This file checks the phpinfo ----*/
     phpinfo(); //This is the line that will be executed
     // the rest are all comments
?>
```

INSTRUCTIONS

In PHP you may use instructions, functions calls, loops, and conditions (plus objects with PHP5), but never forget the semicolon at the end of each function call and every instruction.

A first easy function to use is *echo*, which allows printing on the page. Remember that when you run PHP code, it runs in the server, and any output that occurs will appear instead of the code where the instruction was called, so if you wish to make an "echo" in an HTML page containing all proper tags, you should place the PHP code between the opening and closing *body* tags. Here is a clean example:

```
<HTML>
  <HEAD>
    <TITLE>Script1</TITLE>
  </HEAD>
  <BODY>
  <?PHP echo "Hello World!"; ?>
  </BODY>
</HTML>
```

You could say that PHP4 is an "expression-oriented" programming language. An expression is basically a set of characters following a specific syntax. Expressions always have a value that can be a numeral or string, including 0 or the void string "". To know what a PHP code does, you simply need to locate and understand the expressions, as well as the information they hold.

The first type of expression available consists of elementary expressions, such as constants or variables. For example, the number *100* would be considered an expression with the value 100. Variables like *$a* would be expressed with a value equal to the content of the variable.

We have also composed expressions created by storing an elementary expression in a variable. Note that all variables in PHP start with the dollar sign ($). The following two lines would be considered as two expressions:

$$\$a = 100;$$
$$\$b = \$a;$$

This would store the elementary expression *100* into the variable *$a*. Then the elementary expression *$a* (containing the value 100) would be stored in *$b*. In the end both *$a* and *$b* would be equal to 100.

Another type of expression consists of functions. Assuming that we have a function called *test()* that returns the value of 100, doing *$result = test();* would use the function *test()* as an expression and store it in *$result* making that variable hold the number 100.

It is also possible to postincrement, postdecrease, preincrement, and predecrease a variable. This is still considered an expression. Check this code:

```
<?PHP
  $var = 100;
  echo $var++; //echoes $var and increments it by 1
  echo ++$var; //increments $var by 1 and echoes it
  echo $var--; //echoes $var and decreases it by 1
  echo --$var; //decreases $var and echoes it
?>
```

If you execute this code, you will note that it outputs 100102102100 with no spaces between the numbers. This is due to the fact that we are only outputting numbers, without inserting white spaces or breaks of line. We will see further on how to concatenate strings to variables.

PHP expressions can also be the values TRUE and FALSE. By default, these two constants are equal to 1 and 0, respectively. Note that if you write

```
<?PHP
  $var = TRUE;
  echo $var;
?>
```

the output will be the number *1* and not *TRUE*.

A comparison is also considered an expression, having a value of 1 for true and 0 for false. For example, *$a = $b < 0;* would store 1 inside *$a* if *$b* is lower than 0, and would store 0 if *$b* is greater than or equal to 0. The existing comparison operators are

>	Greater than
>=	Greater than or equal to
==	Equal to
!=	Different from
<=	Less than or equal to
<	Less than

Another type of expressions is the combination of operators with the affectation symbol (=). For example, *$a += 10;* will increase *$a* by 10. This works with any operator, and it has the following equivalence (we will assume that <op> is an operator): *$a <op> = $b* is the same as *$a = $a <op> $b*.

Here are a few examples:

$a -= ($b + $c);* will calculate *$a − ($b + $c) and store the result in *$a*
*$a *= $a;* will multiply *$a* by *$a* and store the result in *$a*
$a /= 2;* will divide *$a by 2 and store the result in *$a*

The last basic type of expression is the conditional operator. This allows us to check a Boolean value (*TRUE* or *FALSE*) and use an expression if the value is true, a different one if it is false. The basic syntax is *expression1 ? expression2 : expression3;*. In this example *expression1* will be checked as true or false. If it is true, then *expression2* will be evaluated. If it was false, expression 3 will be evaluated. For example

```
<?PHP
  $a = 100;
  $b = 50;
  $c = ($a < $b) ? 50: 25; // will compare $a to $b if
                           //$a is less than $b, 50
  //is evaluated. If $a is greater or equal than $b,
  //then 25 is evaluated.
  echo $c;
?>
```

This example would output 25. Remember than an expression can be a function or even an operation, so you could use this to calculate a positive difference as follows:

```
<?PHP
  $a = 100;
  $b = 12;
  $positive_difference = ($a >= $b) ? ($a - $b) : ($b - $a);
  echo $positive_difference;
?>
```

OPERATORS

You may use the following operators:

- *Arithmetic.* Use + to add, – to subtract, * to multiply, / to divide, % to calculate the remainder of a division (called the *modulo operator*).
- *Affectation.* Use = to store the value of the expression on the right to the variable on the left of the sign.
- *Affectation with Operation.* As we saw above, += –= *= /= %= .= (the operator "." allows us to concatenate strings.
- *Reference Affectation.* Using $a = &$b; causes $a to point to the same memory location as $b is. It is pretty much the same as making $a an alias of $b. Note that unlike in C language, this operation does *not* copy the address of $b in the variable $a. It just makes $a and $b refer to the same location. Changing $a will also have an effect on $b.
- *Bit Operations.* Use & (binary *AND*), | (binary *OR*), ^ (binary exclusive *OR*, "*XOR*"), ~ (binary *NOT*), << (logical shift to the left), >> (logical shift to the right).
- *Other Comparison Operators.* Use === for "identical," meaning that both expressions around the operator have the same value and are of the same type (see example further down). Use !== for not identical.
- *Increments and Decrements.* Same as before ($a++, ++$a, --$a, and $a--)
- *Logical Operators.* The following can be used:

    "*and*" or "*&&*" for *AND*

    "*or*" or "*||*" for *OR*

    "*xor*" for exclusive *OR* (*XOR*)

    ! for *NOT*

    These operators are used for logical operations, such as mixing several comparisons in one big expression. Do not mix logical and binary operators which do bit-by-bit operations with the expressions around them.

MATHEMATICAL FUNCTIONS

There are many mathematical functions at the disposition of PHP developers. Here are the most important ones and some basic explanations on how they work:

- *abs*—calculates the absolute value of a number. For example, *abs(–10)* will return 10

- *acos, asin, atan, atan2*—calculates the arc cosine, arc sine, arc tangent, and tanget of two variables. For example, *atan($x)* calculates the arc tangent of *$x*.

- *acosh, asinh, atanh*—calculates the inverse hyperbolic cosine, inverse hyperbolic sine, and inverse hyperbolic tangent.

- *cos, sin, tan*—calculates the cosine, sine, and tangent of a variable. For example, *cos(acos($x))* will return *$x*.

- *base_convert*—converts the first parameter from the base given in the second parameter to the base given as third parameter. For example, *base_convert(1110,2,10)* will convert 1110 from base 2 to base 10, hence returning the number 14.

- *bindec, decbin, dechex, hexdec, decoct, octdec*—converts a number from binary to decimal; from decimal to binary; from decimal to hexadecimal; from hex to decimal; from decimal to octal; and from octal to decimal. For example, *bindec(1001)* returns 9; *decbin(3)* returns 11; *dechex(16)* returns 10; *hexdec(FF)* returns 255; *decoct(256)* returns 400; and *octdec(400)* returns 256.

- *round, floor, ceil*—does a regular rounding of a number, rounds down, and rounds up. For example, *round(1.6)* returns 2; *floor(1.9)* returns 1; and *ceil(1.1)* returns 2.

- *exp*—returns the exponent of the Neperian (or e). For example, *exp(5.7)* returns 298.87.

- *sqrt*—calculates the square root of a number. For example, *sqrt(16)* returns 4.

- *log, log10*—calculates the natural logarithm and the base 10 logarithm of a number. For example, *log(2.7)* returns 0.99 and *log10(100)* returns 2.

- *min, max*—calculates the minimum and maximum of a series of numbers. For example, *max(23,54,12,53,62,24)* would return 62. Both functions can accept any amount of parameters.

- *pi*—returns the value of Π. Just type *pi()* to use it.

- *pow*—calculates the power of a number. For example, *pow(2,3)* calculates 2 to the power of 3, so it would return 8.

- *number_format*—reformats a number into a string. The first parameter is the number, the second is the number of numbers to show after the decimal point, the third is the symbol used as a decimal point, and the last parameter is the symbol used to separate groups of three digits. For example, *number_format(123456.7, '2', '.', ',')* would return the string "*123,456.70.*"

- *rand, mt_rand*—generates a random number and a random number using the Mersenne Twister algorithm. Just type either *mt_rand()* or *rand()*.

- *srand, mt_srand*—allows you to seed the random-number generator, whether standard or using the Mersenne Twister. For example, you could use *mt_srand(123)* followed by *mt_rand()* to get a random number seeded with the number 123. Whenever you need to generate a random number, it is preferable for better results to combine *mt_srand* with a seed that will change constantly. For example, you can do "*mt_rand(crc32 (microtime()));*" *microtime* gets the current timestamp (exact date and time in microseconds), and *crc2* gets a string to return a number, namely, the polynomial of a string. This little method can be found at <u>www.php. net</u>, where it is explained in detail.
- *getrandmax(), mt_getrandmax()*—returns the highest number that the random function can generate, in either normal or Mersenne Twister version.

DATA TYPES

In PHP it is not necessary to specify the type of a variable. All variables do have a type, but that type can change depending on what information is stored in the variable. For example, doing *$a = 10;* will make the variable *$a* an integer, but if a few lines later we do *$a = "Hello";*, that same variable *$a* will become a string.

The basic data types in PHP are integer (int), double (or real, or float), string, array, object, and Boolean. It is possible to check the type of a variable by either calling *gettype($a),* which returns a string with the type of *$a,* or by calling one of the many "is_" functions that return true if the variable is of the type that makes up the function name, and false otherwise. The functions are *is_long(), is_double(), is_string(), is_array(), is_object(), is_bool(), is_float(), is_int(), is_integer(), is_real(),* and *is_numeric().* Naturally, *is_ numeric* will check whether the variable passed as a parameter is of any numerical type.

As already mentioned, it is possible to change a variable's type simply by storing a different type of value in that same variable. It is also possible to modify a variable's type without changing its contents. This process is called *casting*, and it can be done either permanently, or just for one instance. To change a type permanently, use the *settype* function. For example, *settype($a, "double");* would change the type of the variable *$a* to a double. If you wish to change the type of a variable only when reading it once, without having to permanently change its type, you can simply precede the variable name with the new type surrounded by parentheses. In the following example we will store an integer contained in the variable *$a*, into *$b*, which will be holding that same number as a double:

$a = 5;
$b = (double)$a;

Remember that when using the "identical" (===) comparison, the types of the compared variables must be the same!!

Here is an example code illustrating types:

```
<?PHP
 $a = 5;
 echo gettype($a)." ";
 $b = (double)$a;
 echo gettype($b)." ";
 if ($a == $b)
   echo "$a and $b are the same!!";
 else
   echo "$a and $b are different!!";
 if ($a === $b)
   echo " And they are identical!";
 else
   echo " But they are NOT identical!!";
?>
```

This code will output *integer double 5 and 5 are the same!! But they are NOT identical!!*

CONSTANTS

It is possible (and sometimes recommended) to use constants in PHP. These should always be used whenever you have a piece of information that you will use throughout your code but that might have to be modified in future versions. For example, if you are writing a script to handle data in an array, and you decide the maximum size will be 100, you should create a constant called *MAX_SIZE* and set it to 100. Throughout your code you will write *MAX_SIZE* instead of 100 each time you need to do an operation related to the size of the array. By doing so you will add a good level of modifiability to your program; for example, if you decided to expand the array to 500 items, you would need to change only the constant definition, and not each use you made of the constant. This approach applies to any programming language that allows the use of constants.

To create a constant in PHP, simply type *define(name, value)*. For example, *define("MAX_SIZE", 100);* or *define("DB", "C:/DataBase/");*. From that moment on, doing *echo MAX_SIZE;* would output 100.

There are also a set of predefined constants that can be used in any PHP code. These are part of the language and need not to be declared.

NULL:	Same as 0
__FILE__:	Name of the current running PHP file
__LINE__:	Current line of PHP code being executed

PHP_VERSION: Shows the current running version of PHP
PHP_OS: Shows the operating system version
TRUE: Boolean value 1
FALSE: Boolean value 0

Other constants exist, but these would be considered the most important ones to remember.

VARIABLES

As we have seen, we can use variables in PHP. There is no need to define a variable, nor declare it, before its use. But I would recommend that you initialize a variable if you are planning to use it for concatenations or operations that will modify the variable inside a loop, such as iterators, for example. A typical source of notices (type of errors) is when you have a variable that will be used to store a total inside a loop. If the loop body is the first place where that variable is used, and the code looks like *$var += $somedata;*, you will get a notice. This is due to the fact that the first time the code runs, the server has no idea what *$var* holds. By default it will assume 0, so the code will produce the desired result, but the notice will be there. Simply avoid that by initializing *$var* before the loop (doing *$var = 0;* or *$var =* " "; if the variable will hold a string).

Variable names are case-sensitive, meaning that *$Var* and *$var* are considered two different variables. Variables should *always* start with the dollar sign ($) followed by a letter and any series of letters, numbers, or the underscore (_) sign. For example, *$var1_hooah* is a valid name, but *$1var* is not.

You can check at anytime whether a variable has been set by using the *isset* command. This is really useful in pages that are meant to be open through an HTML form. In those cases, information has to be sent to the script, so by simply checking at the beginning of the script if the variable is set you can avoid many problems and notices. For example, if you were receiving a variable called "name" through a POST method (as we will see in later chapters), you should start your code with something similar to the following:

```
<?PHP
  if (!isset($_POST["name"])) // If the variable "name"
sent through
    {                         //the POST method is not set
    echo "You did not arrive here through the form!";
    exit();
  }
  else
  { // regular code goes here
  }
?>
```

It is possible to check whether a variable is empty through the *empty* function. This function will simply check if the variable contains either 0 or the empty string "". It returns true when the variable is empty, false otherwise.

To unset a variable, you can use *unset*. For example, you can use this technique in code requiring a flag by combining it with the *isset* method as follows:

```
<?PHP
  $a = 0;
  while (isset($a))
  {
    // do something and at one point do the next line
    unset($a); // this will unset the variable, so the while
          // condition will no longer be true
  }
?>
```

This is just an example; it would actually be simpler to have *$a* change its value from TRUE to FALSE, and change our condition to *while ($a)*. Unsetting a variable is usually a good choice when you want to enhance the security in your script, prevent loopholes, and make sure that everything that is supposed to be gone does not exist anymore.

A variable in PHP is local to the function that it belongs to. This means that a variable defined inside the implementation of a function has a meaning only inside that function and will not be recognized outside it. The opposite is also true. A variable defined in the main area of your code will not be accessible inside a function unless it is sent as a parameter to that function. Note that, unlike many other programming languages, PHP does not need a "main" function. Instead, any code written in your PHP code file is considered to be part of the "main" unless it is a function definition. Therefore it is possible, although not recommended, to have function declarations and implementations right in the middle of regular "main" code. Doing this would make your code pretty messy, so I would advise you to write all functions at the end of your file, or even better, on an external include file.

It is possible to create global variables in PHP, although many programmers will advise you to avoid using global variables when possible. To indicate inside a function that a variable is global, simply type *global* followed by the name of variable you want to use as global. For example, if your "main" contained a variable $Gl_DBserver that you wish to access in a function as a global variable, simply write *global $Gl_DBserver;* in the first line of your function implementation.

Functions can also use static variables. A static variable is a variable that has meaning only inside the function in which it was defined, but that doesn't get erased when the function is finished working. Instead, the value of a static variable is remembered for the next call of that function. The initialization of a static variable should always happen in the line that declares it as static; this way the initialization will occur only the first time the function is called, without overwriting its value in each successive call. Check this example:

```php
<?PHP
  function static_example()
  {
    static $count = 0;
    echo "You have called the function ".++$count." times";
  }
?>
```

The first time the function is called, a variable *$count* is created as static, and set to 0. This will only happen the first time the function is called; the next time, the program will understand that *$count* already exists. When we echo the string "You have called the function," note that right after this string we have placed a dot (.), allowing the concatenation of anything to the previous string. We concatenate ++*$count*, which will then be concatenated with "times." Our total string will tell us how many times we accessed the function. The preincrement is due to our initialization to 0 of the static variable. The first time the function is called, the preincrement will modify *$count* from 0 to 1. Next time the function is called, *$count* will still be holding 1, and will be incremented to 2 before echoing the message.

6

PHP Arrays and Flow of Control

ARRAYS

Basic Arrays

Arrays are sets of data stored as a single variable. You could imagine a set as a cabinet with multiple drawers. Each drawer holds an element, and the position of the element is called its "index." Unlike most programming languages, where arrays hold values of the same type, arrays in PHP can hold any type of data in each one of its elements. This makes PHP arrays much more flexible but can potentially create many problems if you don't remember the types used for each index. In order to store values inside an array, you need to place the index to access between square brackets, right after the variable name holding the entire array. For example, if $myArray is an array, you could access the element at index 3 by writing *$myArray[3]*. Note that indices start at 0, but you are not required to use consecutive indices. In other programming languages you *must* use index 0, then 1, 2, 3, and so forth. In PHP you may have an array with three elements positioned at indices 12, 42, and 51, for example. It is not recommended but it causes no issues. Here is an example that stores an integer, a string, and a double in the same array and then will echo the types of those elements:

Web Application Design and Implementation: Apache 2, PHP5, MySQL, JavaScript, and Linux/UNIX, by Steven A. Gabarró

```
<?PHP
  $var[0]  =  1;
  $var[1]  =  "Two";
  $var[2]  =  3.00;
  $i  =  0;
  while  ($i  <  count($var))  {
    echo  gettype($var[$i])."<BR>";
    $i++;
  }
?>
```

Don't worry about the *while* section, as we will discuss this a few sections later. Note the use of the function *count* that returns the number of elements inside an array. Also, doing *$var[$i]* simply reads the element at the index *$i*.

It is also possible to define an array as a single line using the function *array*. Check this example:

```
<?PHP
  $ var = array();  //creates  an  empty  array,  useful  to
                    //avoid  some  notices
  $var2 = array(1,  "Two",  3.00);  //same  array  as  we  had
                                    //before
?>
```

Associative Arrays

It is also possible to create associative arrays. An associative array is basically an array in which the index can be a word. It is important to realize that an element in an associative array will actually have two indices. First you will have the real index of the element, as indicated during its creation. This "real index" is generally called the "key" of the element. The other index is a numbered index that is known internally by PHP, which basically holds the order in which the elements are held in the array. Check this example:

```
<?PHP
  $var["number"]  =  1;
  $var["string"]  =  "Two";
  $var["secondnum"]  =  3.00;
?>
```

In this example we have created an associative array with three elements. The keys of these elements will be "number," "string," and "secondnum," but you will still be able to refer to the elements through the indices 0, 1, and 2, respectively. The numbered indices will always respect the order in which the elements are in memory.

Another way to create an associative is through the *array* method, as we used with regular arrays. The difference is that in this case you are to write the entries using the format *"key"=>element*. For example, the previous associative array would be written

```
$var = array("number"=>1, "string"=>"Two",
"secondnum"=>3.0);
```

Multidimensional Arrays

One final type of array is the multidimensional array. This basically represents an array that contains an array as one or more of its elements. This could be used, for example, to hold information on different contacts for an address book. Check this code:

```
<?PHP
  for ($i=0; $i < 10; $i++)
    $contacts[$i] = array(
      "Name"=>"Name" .$i,
      "Surname"=>"Surname" .$i,
      "Tel"=>$i);
  foreach ($contacts as $c=>$details) // loop 1
    foreach ($details as $key=>$elem) // loop2
      echo $c.":" .$key."".$elem."<BR>"; // instruction
?>
```

This code would produce the following output

> 0: Name Name 0
> 0: Surname Surname 0
> 0: Tel 0
> 1: Name Name 1
> 1: Surname Surname 1
> 1: Tel 1
> 2: Name Name 2
> 2: Surname Surname 2
> 2: Tel 2
> [. . .]

and so on until number 9.

Let us see how the script works. First we use a "for" loop (which we will study after a few pages) to create 10 entries in a regular array. Each entry contains an associative array containing a name, a surname, and a telephone number. To make it simple, each name is the concatenation (thanks to the period symbol) of the word "name" and the current index. We follow a similar procedure with the surname. The telephone number is simply the current number. Then we use a tool called *foreach*, which allows us to go through every single entry in the *$contacts* array. Each entry in that array is obviously another array, so we use another *foreach* to extract all the details inside it and display them. The loop *foreach* allows really fast access to every entry in an array regardless of whether it is an associative array. There are two main ways of using foreach:

foreach ($arrayName as $variable)

or

foreach ($arrayName as $key=>$element)

Regardless of the case, *$arrayName* has to be an array. In the first case, *$variable* is a variable name that doesn't need to exist yet. The *foreach* loop will store every entry in the array in that variable, one at the time. As in all the other types of loops, the *foreach* will run the next line after the *foreach* as long as there are elements in the array. For example, you could display all elements in an array *$arr* as follows:

```
foreach($arr as $elem)
  echo $elem;
```

Each execution of the code under the *foreach* is called an *iteration* of the loop. In the first iteration, *$elem* will hold *$arr[0];* in the second iteration, *$elem* will be the same as *$arr[1];* and so on until there are no more elements in the array, in which case the program will skip directly to the instruction after the iterating statement. It is important to realize that your *$elem* holds an actual copy of the element in the array, not the element itself. Note that it is possible to group several instructions in a same loop by simply surrounding all the statements with curly braces. For example, the following code will run two instructions in each iteration:

```
foreach ($arr as $e)
{   echo $e." ";
    echo "<BR>";
}
```

The second version of *foreach* allows the creation of two variables, one for the current key, and one for the element associated with that key. Obviously this is useful mostly with associative arrays, but you may still use it with regular arrays, in which case your keys will be the indices of each element.

In our contacts example, the first *foreach* loop will check the $contacts array. Each entry in this array is an array, and the keys are simply numbers. The *foreach* will fill the variable $c with the current index, and the variable $details with the current entry, corresponding to the associative array with all the information on the contact. Since $details is an array, we may check its contents with another *foreach*. Our second *foreach* will parse the current $details array and fill $key with the current key and $elem with the entry associated to that key. Here is how the program runs:

    After the $contacts array is filled up and we enter the first loop:
        $c == 0; $details == $contacts[0];
        We enter the loop 2, checking the contents of $details
            $key == "Name"; $elem == "Name 0";
            We execute the instruction.
        Iteration 2 of the loop2
            $key == "Surname"; $elem == "Surname 0";
            We execute the instruction.
          Iteration 3 of loop 2
              $key == "Tel"; $elem == 0;
              We execute the instruction.
          There are no more entries in $details so loop 2 is done
        Iteration 2 of loop 1 starts
            $c == 1; $details == $contacts[1];
            We start a new loop 2, checking the new contents of $details
              $key == "Name"; $elem == "Name 1";
        [...] *Similar execution for all the middle entries...*
        Iteration 10 of loop 1 starts
            $c == 9; $details == $contacts[9];
            We enter the loop 2, checking the new contents of $details
              $key == "Name"; $elem == "Name 9";
              We execute the instruction.
        Iteration 2 of the loop2
            $key == "Surname"; $elem == "Surname 9";
            We execute the instruction.
        Iteration 3 of loop 2
            $key == "Tel"; $elem == 9;
            We execute the instruction.
          There are no more entries in $details so loop 2 is done
       There are no more entries in $contacts so loop 1 is done
     Our program finishes its execution.

It is also possible to access a particular element in an array by using multiple brackets. In our previous example $contacts is an array of arrays; therefore $contacts[0] is the first one of those arrays. Since $contacts[0] is an array, we can check its first entry by adding a new set of brackets. So, for example,

$contacts[0][1] would be the entry indexed at 1 in the entry 0 of $contacts. It would show up as *Surname 0*. Remember that indices start at 0, so something of the type $arr[3][6] would actually access the seventh entry in the fourth element of $arr.

The only limit to multidimensional arrays is your imagination! You can have any number of dimensions applied to an array, and not all entries need to hold an array. You could, for example, have an array of your friends. Each entry would hold an array containing the name of that friend along with an array of the relatives of that friend as in this example:

```
<?PHP
  $friends[0][0]  =  "Steven";
  $friends[0][1]["father"]  =  "Peter";
  $friends[0][1]["mother"]  =  "Jackie";
  $friends[0][1]["sister"]  =  "Romina";
  $friends[1][0]  =  "Christian";
  $friends[1][1]["brother"]  =  "Daniel";
  // and so on
?>
```

As you can see, we can utilize the flexibility of PHP to create entries that do not necessarily hold the same information. The only common thing is that for each friend indexed at *$i*, *$friends[$i][0]* will always be a name and *$friends[$i][1]* will be an array holding an associative array with the relatives. If you wanted to show the entire list of friends and their relatives you could use the following code:

```
<?PHP
  // we assume that we have a filled $friends array as
in the previous example
    foreach ($friends as $oneFriend)
    {   echo "Name: " .$oneFriend[0]. "<BR>";
        foreach ($oneFriend[1] as $relation=>$name)
          echo $relation. ": " .$name. "<BR>";
        echo "<BR>";
    }
?>
```

Array Functions

Here are some important functions useful for arrays manipulations. Realize that each time you have an array there is an internal pointer that informs you of the current position in the array. It basically refers to the current element's index.

- *array_walk*—allows you to run a specific function with each one of the elements in the array and returns TRUE or FALSE depending on wether it managed to run the function flawlessly. For example, typing *array_walk($arr, 'myfunction');* is the same as typing

    foreach($arr as $e)
        myfunction($e);

Always make sure that your "*myfunction*" accepts the type of data that your array is holding.
- *count*—for example, *$size = count($arr).* Returns the number of elements in the array.
- *current*—for example, *current($arr).* Returns the element at the current position, as given by the internal pointer.
- *each*—for example, *each($arr).* Returns the element at the current position, and moves to the next one.
- *end*—for example, *end($arr).* Places the internal pointer at the end of the array.
- *key*—for example, *key($arr).* Returns the key of the current element.
- *next*—for example, *next($arr).* Moves the internal pointer to the next element.
- *pos*—for example, *pos($arr).* Returns the current position of the internal pointer.
- *prev*—for example, *prev($arr).* Moves the internal pointer to the previous element.
- *reset*—for example, *reset($arr).* Places the internal pointer at the first element of the array.
- *sizeof*—same as *count.*
- *asort* and *arsort*—sorts the array associatively in either normal or reverse order (respectively). Sorting associatively means that the association between keys and elements will be respected. For example, if you have an entry *$arr["NJ"] = "New Jersey";* initially located at index 4 that is later moved to index 12, doing *$arr[12]* will still return *"New Jersey"*, and the key of that entry will still be *"NJ"*. Sorting is done by checking the elements.
- *ksort* and *krsort*—sorts the array associatively, in normal or reverse order, by looking at the key. It operates under the same principle as does *asort* or *arsort*, but instead of comparing the entries in the array to choose the order, the function will check the keys.
- *sort* and *rsort*—sorts the array in normal or reverse order, by checking the entries in the array. This sorting is nonassociative, so all keys are lost, and replaced with basic number indices.
- *uasort, uksort, usort*—for example, *usort($arr, "function");.* This will run a key sort, associative sort, or regular sort using your own function

as a comparison method. Your function should be adapted to the case you wish to use. For example, *usort* and *uasort* will need a function that accepts two elements of whatever type the array holds; *uksort* will need a function that accepts two strings. The function should return 0 if the values are identical, a positive number if the first parameter is greater than the second, or a negative number if the first parameter is less than the second. Check the example at the end of this list of functions.

- *list*—for example, *list($a, $b, $c) = $arr;*. This will copy the elements of the array into the variables listed. In this case *$a* will hold *$arr[0]*, *$b* will hold *$arr[1]*, and *$c* will hold *$arr[2]*. Note that you may use one or more variables in the list method.
- *range*—for example, *$arr = range($min, $max);*. Creates an array with the integer numbers between *$min* and *$max*.
- *shuffle*—for example, shuffle($arr); Shuffles the elements of the array.
- *array_count_values*—for example, *$arr1 = array_count_values($arr);*. Will check the contents of *$arr* and the number of times each element is repeated. The array returned contains the actual value counted as a key, and the number of times it appeared as an element.
- *array_keys*—for example, *$arr1 = array_keys($arr);*. Returns a nonassociative array containing the keys of *$arr*.
- *array_merge*—merges one or more arrays together and returns the resulting array. For example, *$arr = array_merge($arr1, $arr2, $arr3);* will merge the three arrays sent as parameters and return the merged array, which is stored in *$arr*. You may provide one or more arrays as parameters.
- *array_pad*—for example, *$arr1 = array_pad($arr, $n, $val);* will add *$n* times the value *$val* to the end of the array *$arr*. If *$n* is negative, the values are added at the beginning of the table. Returns the resulting array.
- *array_pop*—for example, *$elem = array_pop($arr);* will remove the last element of the *$arr* from the array and return it.
- *array_push*—pushes one or more elements at the end of an array. For example, *$n = array_push($arr, $a, $b, $c);* will add *$a, $b,* and *$c* at the end of *$arr*. The value returned is the new size of the array.
- *array_reverse*—for example, *array_reverse($arr);* returns a reversed version of *$arr*.
- *array_shift*—same as *array_pop* but removes the first element rather than the last.
- *array_unshift*—same as *array_push* but adds the elements at the beginning of the array rather than the end.
- *array_slice*—for example, *$arr2 = array_slice($arr, $pos, $n);* will return the *$n* elements from *$arr* starting at the position *$pos*. If *$n* is omitted, it returns all the elements from *$pos* to the end of the array. If *$n* is negative, the slice will stop *$n* elements before the end of the array.

- *array_splice*—for example, *$arr1 = array_splice ($arr, $pos, $n, $newarr);* will take out of *$arr $num* elements starting at *$pos* and replace them by the elements inside *$newarr*. The returned array holds the elements that were replaced.
- *array_values*—for example, *$values = array_values ($arr);* will return a nonassociative array holding just the values of *$arr*.
- *in_array*—for example, *in_array ($elem, $arr);* will check whether *$elem* is inside *$arr*. Returns TRUE if found, FALSE otherwise.

Here is an example using *usort*:

```php
<?PHP
// we are assuming we have an array $arr holding integers
// we sort using our compare function (which will
produce a reverse sort)
// and we print the results
  usort($arr, "compare");
  foreach ($arr as $key=>$elem)
    echo "$key=>$elem";
  function compare($a, $b) {
    if ($a==$b)
      return 0;
    elseif ($a < $b)
      return 1;
    else
      return -1;
  }
?>
```

PHP PROGRAM STRUCTURE AND FLOW OF CONTROL

A program in PHP is basically a set of instructions. It is possible to group instructions in a block using curly braces, as we saw in the *foreach* example. Grouping instructions in a single block allows treating the entire block as a single instruction. This behavior is especially useful in loops, as we saw earlier on.

Conditions

You can have your program select different paths in your program depending on your own conditions. You can do this using the *if . . . elseif . . . else* statements. The basic structure is

> *if (condition)*
> *instruction1;*
> *elseif (condition2)*
> *instruction2;*
> *else*
> *instruction3;*

Each condition should be a Boolean expression. If *condition* is true, then *instruction1* is executed and the program jumps to the instruction after *instruction3*. If it is false, *condition2* is tested; if true, *instruction2* is executed; if false, *instruction3* will run. Note that you may use any amount of *elseif* or you can even omit it. There should never be more than one *else* in each *if...elseif...else* block. Note that any *else* or *elseif* will refer to the last *if or elseif* created that did not have an *else/elseif* yet. To avoid getting lost with all the *if* and *else* statements, it is a good idea to write each else right under the *if* that it refers to. Check this example:

```
<?PHP
  if ($a < $b) // checks if $a is lower than $b
     echo $a. " is less than " .$b;
  elseif ($a > $b) // we get here only if $a was NOT
                   //less than $b
     echo $b. " is less than " .$a;
     else // $a is not lower nor greater than $b
        echo $a. " is equal to " .$b;
?>
```

Attention!! If you wish to compare for equality, make sure to use either the double or triple equal sign to check for equality or identical variables. Watch this example:

```
<?PHP
  if ($i = 34567)
     echo "This is always true!!!";
?>
```

Remember that FALSE is equal to 0, so a condition is considered to be FALSE only if the condition is equal to 0. Doing *if ($i = 34567)* will copy 34567 inside *$i* and check the value of *$i*. If *$i* is different from 0, it will be considered TRUE.

Each *if...elseif...else* group works as a single instruction. Check this example:

```
<?PHP
  if ($a < 100) // first condition
    if ($b < $100) // this if statement is the
                   //beginning of the
                   // block that will run if the first
                   //instruction is true
      echo "both numbers are less than 100";
    else // this else refers to the previous if, and is
         //still
         // part of the same block inside the first
         //condition
      echo "Only the first number is less than 100";
    elseif ($a == 100) // the previous else finished the
                       //second if
      // block, so this elseif refers to the first
      //condition
      echo "The first number was 100"
    else // this else refers to the elseif, and is part
         //of the
         // block started with the first condition
echo "The first number was greater than 100";
?>
```

You may avoid headaches and confusion by simply using curly braces for a better view of each block. The general structure would look like this:

```
if (condition)
{   statements if true
}
 elseif (condition2)
{   statements if condition is false and condition2 true
}
 elseif (condition3)
{   statements if condition and condition2 are false but condition3 is true
}
 else
{   statements if all conditions were false
}
```

It is generally considered poor programming practice to have too many nested *if* or *ifelse* statements. If you are trying to find a match to a variable, you may use a different alternative: the *switch . . . case*. The general syntax of a *switch . . . else* is as follows:

```
switch ($variableToCheck) {
    case value1:
        statements
        break;
    case value2:
        statements
        break;
    default:
        statements
}
```

The program will successively compare the $variableToCheck with all the different values written next to the *case* keyword. If a match is found, the program will run every instruction placed between the following colon symbol (:) and either the first *break* statement or the closing brace (whichever happens first). The case lines are not really considered instructions; you can think of them as little labels in front of the code lines. Therefore you can put several cases together, by listing many *case value*: lines before starting to write the code. Note that if you omit the *break* statements, the program will continue to execute the following instructions even if they were meant to be for a different case. The *default* case is run if no matches were found among the values. Here is a small example:

```
<?PHP
  $i = 2;
  switch ($i) {
    case 0:
    case 1:
      echo "i was either 0 or 1";
      break;
    case 2:
      echo "i was equal to 2";
      break;
    case 3:
      echo "i was 3";
      break;
    default:
      echo "I don't know what i was, because I can't
count to more than 3!";
  }
```

Loops

A loop is a way to repeat one or more statements a determined number of times. We already saw one type of loop adapted to arrays: the *foreach*.

The most basic loop is the *while* loop. It receives an expression that is tested before starting each iteration. The loop will keep on going until the expression becomes false. For example

```
<?PHP
  $i = 0;
while ($i < 10)
  {   echo $i++;
      echo " " ;
  }
?>
```

This loop will check whether i is less than 10. If it is, it prints i and increments it by one with the postincrement operator, prints a white space, and checks i again. The moment i is no longer less than 10 (i.e., when it reaches 10), the loop finishes. This code will show the numbers from 0 to 9 on the page. This type of loop is excellent in testing for a specific value change, but make sure that the statement can eventually be false, or you will enter an infinite loop!! Note that if the condition is false before the first iteration, the loop will never be entered and the body of the loop will never execute.

If you wish to make a loop that allows you to run its body at least once before checking the condition, you may use *do . . . while*. This type of loop works the in same way as a *while* but checks the condition after each iteration. It will always run the body at least once. The general syntax is

> do
> {   **statements**
> } while (**condition**);

If you wish to count a specific amount of numbers, you can use a *for* loop. This type of loop works similarly to a *while* but it allows you to run a set of expressions before the first check of the condition, and you can have a set of expressions to run after each iteration. The general syntax is

> for (**expr1, expr2 [, . . .]**; **condition**; **expr3, expr4 [, . . .]**)
> {   **statements**   }

All the expressions before the first semicolon are run only once, before entering the loop, the condition is tested before each iteration, and all the expressions after the second semicolon will run at the end of each iteration. Multiple expressions are separated by commas.

For example, the following loop would initialize i to 0 and would then check whether i is less than 10; if it is true, it will print the value followed by a white space and will increment i by one—this loop will finish when i reaches 10:

```
for ($i = 0; $i < 10; $i++)
        echo $i." ";
```

Regardless of the type of loop you are using, you may quit the loop by typing *break;*. It is also possible to force a new iteration without letting the loop finish the current one by typing *continue;*.

FUNCTIONS

You can create functions in PHP by simply writing

> *function **functionName(listofParameters)***
> *{*
> > ***body of function***
> *}*

Functions are usually written in include files or at the end of your program. They don't require specifying a return type, since you may store any type in any variable. The same goes for the parameters list. You do not need to specify their types. Note that variables defined in a function, as well as the names used for the parameters list, are local to the function. This means that they have meaning only inside the function. To return a value from a function, simply use *return* followed by the value to return. For example, you could write and use a function called *average* to calculate the average of two numbers with the following code:

```
<?PHP
 $a = average(12,76); //12 and 76 are called the
                      //arguments sent to average
function average($x, $y) // $x and $y are called the
                         //formal parameters
 { return ($x + $y) / 2;
 }
?>
```

You may send parameters by value or by reference. Sending a parameter by value means that the formal parameters receive a copy of the arguments, whereas sending a value by reference means that the formal parameters are an alias for the actual arguments. In the first case, any modifications done to the formal parameters will not affect the argument variables. If you send parameters by reference, any changes done to the formal parameters will also change the values of the arguments. To call a function sending parameters by value, simply write the name of the variable to be sent, for example, *average($a, $b);*. To send a parameter by reference, simply add the ampersand symbol in front of the argument, for example, *average(&$a, &$b);*

You may also force a function to work with parameters sent by reference by putting the ampersand only in front of the formal parameter rather than the argument. The following function will increment any parameter sent by one:

```PHP
<?PHP
  $x = 5;
  add_one($x);
  echo $x; //this will echo 6
  function add_one(&$a)
  {  $a++;  }
?>
```

7

Using Files, Folders, and Strings in PHP

USING FILES

The first useful thing to do in PHP with files is to use include files. These are files that are linked from any script through two possible techniques. Include files usually hold data such as user and password information for database connection, sets of functions commonly used, and headers and footers used in every page.

One way to link to an external file is to use *include(filename);*. Note that the filename could be a Web address of the type http://www.blabla.com/myfile.php, a relative path ./includes/include.php, or an absolute path /usr/home/sgabarro/includes/include.php. Note that PHP can access any file in the server (assuming that the proper permissions were set) even if those files are not accessible through the Web server. It is very important to exploit this ability when including files containing important information such as database settings, since it prevents malicious users from accessing those files through their browsers.

Doing an *include* will insert the external file inside the including script. If the called file has a return value, you may retrieve that value by storing the return value of the function *include*. Note that this function can be used inside loops.

The other method to link to files is *require(filename)*. This will execute the called file before inserting it in the script. It cannot use a return value,

Web Application Design and Implementation: Apache 2, PHP5, MySQL, JavaScript, and Linux/UNIX, by Steven A. Gabarró
Copyright © 2007 by John Wiley & Sons, Inc.

and it cannot be used in loops. I personally use *require* when I have sets of pages with the same header and footer, to make my code easier to read. The idea is to have a *header.php* file containing all initializations needed for your scripts, as well as all the needed HTML tags; and a *footer.php* file with all the closing instructions needed, as well as the closing HTML tags such as </body> or </html>. Your pages would then look like this:

```
<?PHP require("header.php"); ?>
I am inside my HTML body!!
<?PHP echo "And I can even create PHP code inside
it<BR>"; ?>
I am going to stop now
<?PHP    require("footer.php"); ?>
```

It is also possible to use files for things other than linking to include files. One thing to remember is that any file written, modified, created, or destroyed will be in the server since PHP is server-side. So it is a *very* bad idea to think of doing a malicious PHP script that will erase important files such as your windows.ini or php.ini files and putting the file in an accessible folder of your Web server. This would allow anyone to run the script erasing *your* files, as the script is in *your* server. So think carefully about what you are doing in your scripts before running them.

The first thing to do when you want to use a file for reading or writing purposes is to open it. To do so you may use the function *fopen*. This function returns a file descriptor that will be used by all other reading and writing methods. The function receives two parameters: the path to the file to open (URL, relative path, or local path) and a flag specifying the opening mode. The mode can be

"*r*"   Read only
"*r+*" Read and write
"*w*"   Write only
"*w+*" Read and write, erasing the file if it exists and creating it if it doesn't
"*a*"   Write-only but placing the internal pointer at the end of the file if it exists and creating it does not exist
"*a+*" Read/write, placing the internal pointer at the end or creating the file if it does not exist

In any case, you may add a *b* to indicate that you are using a binary file (e.g., "*ba*" will refer to a binary file opened as "append."

Realize that you may open a file for writing only if you have the proper permissions on that file. Assuming that you have the proper rights, you could create a new file for read/write doing

```
$fp = fopen("myNewFile", "w+");
```

Once your file is open, you may do the following:

- *fclose($fp)*—closes the file. You should always close a file when you are done with it.
- *feof($fp)*—checks whether the internal pointer is at the EOF (end of file).
- *fgetc($fp)*—reads the character at the current location and moves the internal pointer forward one character.
- *fgetcsv($fp, $len, $sep)*—reads a "comma-separated values" file and returns a single line of that file as an array containing the comma-separated values. *$len* and *$sep* are optional parameters. *$len* is the maximum length of a single line; *$sep* is a single character used as separator (set to "," by default).
- *fgets($fp, $len)*—reads a string of up to *$len*—1 bytes from the current location. Reading will also stop if there is a new line (\n) or the pointer reaches the EOF. Returns FALSE if you try to read beyond EOF.
- *fgetss($fp, $len)*—same as *fgets* but strips all HTML tags in the line.
- *fpassthru($fp)*—outputs all the bytes from the current position until the EOF.
- *fputs($fp, $str)* or *fwrite($fp, $str)*—writes the contents of *$str*.
- *fread($fp, $len)*—similar to *fgets* but stops only when up to *$len* have been read or EOF is reached.
- *fseek($fp, $offset, $whence)*—changes the location of the internal pointer. The new location is calculated through *$offset* (a number), depending of the value of *$whence* as follows. If *$whence == SEEK_SET*, set position equal to *$offset* bytes. If *$whence == SEEK_CUR*, set position to current position plus *$offset*. If *$whence == SEEK_END*, set position to EOF plus *$offset* (in this case you should make sure that *$offset* is negative). If omitted, *$whence* is set to *SEEK_SET*.
- *ftell($fp)*—returns the position of the file pointer.
- *rewind($fp)*—places the internal pointer at the beginning of the file. This is the same as doing *fseek($fp, 0, SEEK_SET);*.

Using only these functions, it is possible to combine them to gather information such as the size in bytes of a file, by simply doing the following (assuming that the file has been opened already):

```
fseek($fp, 0, SEEK_END);
$size = ftell($fp);
```

If you wanted to read all the lines in a file and output them with the line number in front of each of those lines, you could use the following code:

```
<?PHP
  $path = "./file.txt"; // our file path
  $i = 1; // our line counter
  If ($fp = fopen($path, "r")) //note that we can use the
                    // single = because fopen will return
                    // FALSE if there is a problem
  {  echo "File Opened<BR><BR>";
     while ($line = fgets($fp, 100)) // we assume that
                          //no line is
                          // longer than 100 characters
   {
     echo $i++.":  ".$str."<BR>";
   }
   fclose($fp); // DON'T FORGET TO CLOSE THE FILE!!!
  }
  else
    echo "Could not open file";
?>
```

Here are some file manipulation functions that can be used with a simple path rather than a file handler *$fp*:

- *copy($src, $dst)*—makes a copy of the file in the path *$src* into the file specified in the path *$dst*. Make sure that you have the proper rights to create files in the folder you are trying to copy to.
- *readfile($file)*—reads a entire file and ouputs its contents. This is the same as doing an *fopen* followed by a *fpassthru*.
- *rename($oldpath, $newpath)*—renames (or technically moves) a file from the oldpath to the newpath.
- *unlink($path)*—fun yet dangerous function. It deletes the file specified in *$path*.

It is also possible to retrieve information from the file system with the following functions (there are *many* functions, but I am going to list those that I consider the most useful ones):

- *basename($path)*—assuming that *$path* contains a full path with a filename, it will return the filename. For example, *basename("/usr/home/sgabarro/file.php")* would return "*file.php*."
- *diskfreespace($dir)*—returns the number of bytes available on the corresponding file system or disk partition.
- *file_exists($path)*—checks whether the file in the *$path* exists.
- *fileatime($file)*—returns the "last access" time for the file.
- *filectime($file)*—returns the "creation" time for the file.

- *filemtime($file)*—returns the "last modification" time for the file.
- *filegroup($file)*—returns the name of the group that owns the file on a UNIX/Linux file system.
- *fileowner($file)*—returns the name of the owner of the file on a UNIX/Linux file system.
- *fileperms($file)*—returns the permissions flags of the *$file* on a UNIX/Linux file system.
- *filesize($file)*—returns the size of the file.
- *filetype($file)*—returns the type of the file. A file could be a directory, an executable, a link, or a file. Note that on a Windows file system, a *$file* will always be either a directory or a file. Only UNIX/Linux has meaning for "executable" and "link."
- *is_dir($file), is_executable($file), is_file($file), is_link($file)*—returns TRUE if *$file* is a directory, an executable, a regular file, or a link (respectively).
- *readlink($link)*—reads the destination of a UNIX/Linux link.

When testing these methods, you may realize that sometimes your PHP code perceives a file as a directory or a directory as a file. This might happen when trying to check the type of a file or directory that is not in the current working directory. The current working directory is the location in your hard drive from where the script is running (basically, wherever your PHP file is stored). It is possible to change the current working directory in PHP by using the method *chdir($dir)*. This will continue executing whatever script you are in, but will consider *$dir* the actual current working directory. When checking files or directories in PHP it is *highly* recommended that you do a *chdir* to the containing folder before checking the types or even reading the contents of that folder.

FOLDER MANIPULATION

Assuming that you have used *chdir* to access a folder that you want to explore, it is possible to retrieve information on that folder through the following methods:

- *$folder = opendir($dir)*—opens the directory *$dir* in order to read its contents. Doing so will create an internal pointer that will allow you to parse its contents. The returned value is the handler needed in the following methods.
- *readdir($folder)*—assuming that the directory has been opened, this reads the current entry (which could be of any type) and moves the internal pointer to the next item in the folder.

- *rewinddir($folder)*—places the internal parsing pointer of an opened directory back to the first item in the folder.
- *closedir($folder)*—as when opening files, it is important to close an opened directory as soon as you have finished reading from it.

Here is an example of how you could open a directory, check the free space available, and display the directory's contents:

```
<?PHP
  $path="D:/Web/";
  chdir($path);
  $folder = opendir($path);
  $free = diskfreespace($path);
  echo "Let's check".$path."contents<BR>";
  echo $free." bytes free<BR>";
  while($file=readdir($folder)) {
    echo $file."<BR>";
  }
  closedir($folder);
?>
```

To finish with file/folders manipulation methods, here are some final functions that can be used with a string containing the needed path:

- *dirname($path)*—returns the directory portion of a path. If your path is a full local path, you can use *basename($path)* to get the filename, and *dirname($path)* to get to the directory in which the file is located.
- *mkdir($dir, $mode)*—creates the directory specified in *$path*. The *$mode* is ignored on Windows and is actually optional. It is used to set UNIX/Linux permissions. For example, to create a */usr/home/sgabarro/ newfolder/* that would be accessible only by the owner of the folder, I could do *mkdir("/usr/home/sgabarro/newfolder/", 0700);*.
- *rmdir($dir)*—deletes a directory. The directory must be empty for this to work.

BASIC STRING MANIPULATION

Changing a String

When manipulating strings received through forms, it is a common problem to have many extra white spaces before and after the actual string. Another common problem is special characters, such as single or double quotes or the backslash character. These characters have a special meaning in database queries, and attempting to insert a string with these special characters in a database could be disastrous. It is possible to suspend the special meaning of a special character by simply adding a backslash in front of the conflicting character. For example, " becomes \" and \ becomes \\. As a rule of thumb, to avoid problems, you want to keep as many backslashes as needed when storing strings in databases. When printing the string, you should remove those slashes. Finally, in many cases you will find yourself with a set of characters that you wish to get rid of, or that you simply want to replace with something else (see the indexer case study). Here are some useful methods for any of these endeavors:

- *chop($str)* or *rtrim($str)*—removes the white spaces at the end of a string and returns the new string.
- *ltrim($str)*—removes the white spaces at the beginning of a string and returns the new string.
- *trim($str)*—removes all white spaces at the beginning and at the end of a string and returns the new string. It is the same as doing *ltrim(chop($str))* or *chop(ltrim($str))*.
- *addslashes($str)* and *stripslashes($str)*—adds or removes backslashes in front of each character that needs to be quoted in database queries, such as a single quote (') or double quotes ("). Always use *addslashes* when inserting a string in a database and *stripslashes* when printing a string retrieved from a database.
- *str_replace($stringtoreplace, $replacement, $str)*—replaces all the iterations of *$stringtoreplace* in *$str* with *$replacement*. In later chapters we will see how to use a regular expression that will make string replacements much more useful. For now simply use a *str_replace* for each replacement you wish to do.

As we shall see in the indexer case study at the end of this chapter, we sometimes need to make sure that all strings have the same casing. This can simply be done by using *strtolower($str)* or *strtoupper($str)*, which respectively turn all letters to lowercase or uppercase. You can also format strings to be used as nicer titles by either making the first letter in the string a capital letter, or even better, capitalizing the first letter of each word (this looks very nice in titles). You do this with either *ucfirst($str)* or *ucwords($str)*, respectively.

If you ever need to reverse a string, this can be easily done with *strrev($str)*—and finally, probably two of the most useful string manipulation functions are *explode* and *implode*. As you can probably imagine with these names, one is the reverse of the other. The goal of an explode is to break a string into an array. This works by providing a string and a separator, and it returns an array containing all the entries that where separated by the separator. For example, *explode("Let us explode this!", " ");* would explode the string using white space as a separator, creating an array containing "Let," "us," "explode," and "this!." Note that the explode function breaks the string only with the separator provided and will consider that, for example, a new line (\n) is a regular character. Because of this behavior, cleaning up the entire string before exploding is highly recommended, as, for example, when replacing new lines (\n) or tabs (\t) with white spaces.

The *implode* method accepts an array and a separator and returns a string containing each element in the array separated by the separator. So, doing *implode($arr, " ")* is similar as running the following code:

```
foreach ($arr as $elem)
  echo $elem." ";
```

There are some alternatives to the explode method when you are trying to extract words from a string that contains many special characters such as double quotes, arithmetic symbols, new lines, tabs, or any such character. The most efficient option would probably be regular expressions, but that section will be covered in a much later chapter. The other alternative is to tokenize the string. To do so, we use the function *strtok($str, $sep)*. This function splits the string *$str* into smaller strings called *tokens*, with each token delimited by any of the characters from *$sep*. The way it works is that each successive call to *strtok* will return the next token. The *$sep* parameter needs to hold a string with all the special characters to be considered separators. When *strtok* cannot find any more tokens, it will return false, which makes this method ideal for use inside a *while* loop. Here is an example taken from www.php.net:

```
<?php
  $string = "This is\tan example\nstring";
/* Use tab and newline as tokenizing characters as well
*/
  $tok = strtok($string, " \n\t");
  while ($tok !== false) {
    echo "Word=$tok<br />";
    $tok = strtok(" \n\t");
  }
?>
```

In this example, the string *$string* is broken down into "this," "is," "an," "example," and "string." Even though there were no white spaces between some of these words, a separator was found, causing *strtok* to recognize that a nonword character was found. Each iteration of the loop will have a single word. Note that only the first call to *strtok* needs to provide the string to use. Any further call to *strtok* will remember what string was being tokenized and the location where the previous called stopped. You may restart the tokenizing or tokenize a different string by providing the string as a parameter again.

This function is obviously different from explode, but it can be used with an array to make an advanced explode that will accept more than one separator. Here is an example:

```php
<?PHP
  /* Function superExplode takes a string to be turned
into an array and a string with all characters to be
considered separators.
  PRE-Conditions: both string are non-empty
  POST-Conditions: An array will be returned containing
each token found */
  function superExplode($str, $sep)
  {
    $i = 0;
    $arr[$i++] = strtok($str, $sep);
    while ($token = strtok($sep))
      $arr[$i++] = $token;
    return $arr;
  }
?>
```

Finding and Comparing

Here are some functions that you can use to compare strings or to find patterns in a string:

- *ord($char)*—returns the ASCII code of a character.
- *strcmp($str1, $str2)*—compares both strings. Returns a negative value if *str1* is less than *str2*, a positive number if *str1* is greater than *str2*, 0 if they are equal. Note that comparisons are case-sensitive, so "*A*" and "*a*" will be two different strings.
- *strcasecmp($str1, $str2)*—case-insensitive comparison. Same as *strcmp* with the difference that two identical letters with different casing (like "*a*" and "*A*") will be considered equal.
- *strnatcmp($str1, $str2)*—natural comparison. Same as *strcmp*, but when a series of digits is found, the value of the entire number is compared rather than comparing digit by digit. For example, *strcmp("a123", "a9")* would say that the second string is greater since 9 > 1, but *strnatcmp* would say the first string is greater since 123 > 9; *strnatcmp* is also case-sensitive.
- *strnatcasecmp($str1, $str2)*—natural, case-insensitive comparison.
- *strpos($str, $tofind, $offset)*—finds the first match of *$tofind* in *$str*, starting the search on the character at position *$offset* ($offset will be

equal to 0 if you omit it). Returns the position of the found match in the string or FALSE if it was not found. If you write this method in a *while* loop, realize that this method might return 0 if the match is found on the first character, but since FALSE == 0, your loop will exit prematurely. You can avoid this by using the identical (===) or not identical (!==) operator, since the 0 returned when a match was found will be an integer, whereas a 0 or FALSE returned when there was no match will be considered a Boolean. For example, if you wish to echo the index of all strings "*match*" in *$str*, you could write

```php
<?PHP
// we assume that $str has a string
$i = 0; // $i will be used to store the index of
        //each match
while (($i = strpos($str, "match", $i)) !== FALSE)
  echo $i++." ";
// We increment $i so that next search starts after
// the last match to avoid an infinite loop
?>
```

- *strrpos($str, $tofind, $offset)*—reverse find. Will find the last location of *$tofind* in *$str* before the index *$offset*. *$offset* can be omitted, in which case it will be considered equal to the length of the string minus one.
- *substr($str, $start, $length)*—returns the substring from *$str* starting at *$start* with *$length* characters. For example, *substr("Hello World", 2, 5);* would return the string "*llo W.*"

Formatting Strings

Here are a set of functions that can be used to print formatted strings:

- *chr($n)*—returns the character that has *$n* as its ASCII code.
- *print($str)*—prints a single string. Similar to echo, and does not need parentheses around its parameter.
- *printf*—works the same way as the function of same name used in C language. It takes a preformatted string that contains a mix of regular characters with special tokens that will be replaced with variables. After the string you must put the variables that will replace the tokens in the same amount and order as you had them in the preformatted string. The tokens can be *%b* for binary integer, *%c* for ASCII character, *%d* for decimal number, *%f* for floating-point number, *%o* for octal number, *%s* for string, *%x* or *%X* for hexadecimal, and *%e* for scientific notation e.g., $1.234E + 4$ instead of 1.234×10^4). For example, if we had a variable *$n* with a number that we wish to print in hexadecimal, and *$str* a string to show up before our number, we could write *printf("My string is %s and my number is %X", $str, $n);*.

• *sprintf*—works the same way as *printf* but instead of printing the string, it returns the final string so that it can be saved in a variable. Technically a *printf(. . .)* is the same as a *print(sprintf(. . .))*.

Manipulating HTML Files

Since PHP was built for the Internet, it contains many useful functions that manipulate Webpages. Some of them assume that you have opened an HTML file and saved its contents in a string, whereas others just accept the URL of the page to process as a parameter. To distinguish those cases, let us use *$str* as a parameter in the first case and *$url* in the second.

The first method is a very useful one that allows retrieval of the META tags information. A META tag is an HTML tag with two parameters called "name" and "content" that describe pretty much anything related to the page. They are usually found in the HEAD section of the page. The *name* attribute informs of the data being stored, and the content attribute holds anything that describes that name. Online searchers such as AltaVista rely strongly on some of the META tags, most specifically the "keywords" META tag. Here is a basic example of what a META tags block could look like:

```
<META name="description" content="This is a silly example, but who cares">
<META name="author" content="Steven A. Gabarró">
<META name="keywords" content="test page, silly, example, PHP, HTML">
<META name="generator" content="Notepad">
```

PHP provides a very useful method to retrieve all the META information as an array called *get_meta_tags($url)*. The returned array is an associative array holding the name of the META tag as a key and the content as the element. If we were to call this function on a file containing the previous example of META tags, our array would be as follows:

```
$arr["description"] == "This is a silly page, but who cares"
$arr["author"] == "Steven A. Gabarró"
$arr["keywords"] == "test page, silly, example, PHP, HTML"
$arr["generator"] == "Notepad"
```

A common problem when mixing HTML and PHP is new lines. When printing a new line (\n) in PHP, we are technically inserting a new line on the resulting HTML code that will be printed by the browser, but as we know, a \n is shown by browsers as a white space. Many times you will be trying to either show information retrieved from a text file or even a database that was not necessarily formatted in HTML, meaning that it contains many new-line characters, but no <BR> tags that would allow the new line to appear on the resulting Webpage. You can solve that by using *nl2br($str)*, which will return a new version of *$str* that will have *
* inserted before all new lines *(\n)*.

Another source of problems are URLs that contain special characters such as white spaces. Many browsers will not accept a link containing white spaces, and will understand those links only if the code of the special character is written. For example, a white space is usually represented as *%20* in a URL. When URL contains those special characters represented as the percentage sign followed by the code of the character, we say that the URL is encoded. If you want to show the same URL with regular characters (e.g., replacing *%20* with a white space), you say that you are getting the decoded version of the URL. You can switch easily between encoded and decoded URLs by using *rawurlencode($url)* and *rawurldecode($url)*, which will return either the encoded or decoded version of the *$url*. As a basic rule, always encode the URLs you are going to insert in an HTML link, and always decode the link names you want to show on the actual page. So, for example, assuming that *$url* is your URL, you could write the following code (code in boldface is PHP code, the rest is regular HTML):

*<A HREF="**<?PHP rawurlencode($url); ?>**"><?PHP rawurldecode($url) ?></A>*

Last but not least, one of my favorite functions that will prove *extremely* useful for our indexer is *strip_tags($str)*. This function takes a string and returns the same string with every single HTML tag removed from it. Here is an example:

```
<?PHP
  $str = "<B>I am</B> a <I>string</I><BR>with loads of
<A HREF=\"http://www.w3c.org\">HTML</A>;
  $str2 = strip_tags($str);
  echo $str2;
?>
```

The variable *$str2* would hold "I am a string with loads of HTML."

PHP INFORMATION FUNCTIONS

PHP has a set of methods used to retrieve information on its actual settings. Here are some of the most important ones:

- *getenv($varname)*—returns the value associated with the environment variable specified in *$varname*. Environment variables include things like *SERVER_NAME*, *SERVER_PROTOCOL*, and *REMOTE_HOST*. Through these variables you can actually retrieve really interesting information like the last page visited, the IP address of the visitor, and many more interesting things ☺. Note that you can also get the same results using *$_SERVER[$varname]*. For example, *$_SERVER["REMOTE_ADDR"]* would give you the IP address of your visitor.

- *get_cfg_var($varname)*—returns the settings for *$varname* as set in the PHP configuration file (*php.ini*).
- *get_current_user()*—returns the name of the owner of the current PHP script. Useful in UNIX/Linux.
- *getmypid()*—returns the process id of the running script.
- *getmyuid()* and *getmygid()*—returns the user id or group id (respectively) of the PHP script's owner.
- *phpinfo()*—As we saw when installing PHP, this function outputs pretty much everything you need to know about your PHP installation. To use www.php.net's words, this method "outputs lots of PHP information."
- *phpversion()*—returns the version of PHP that is running.

CLOSING REMARKS

With all the functions and techniques studied to this point you can write almost any script you wish. The only important thing needed (coming in Chapter 9) is how to send information between different scripts, or how to send information from HTML to PHP using forms (also in Chapter 9). The following chapter will be devoted to PHP5 techniques and object-oriented programming. Now it is the time to test your skills, and the best way is to practice, practice, and practice some more. PHP is a very easy language, but writing scripts will end up taking more time than you expect, so have patience and take your time to make sure that you write the best possible code. The only limit right now is your imagination. To get you started, here is a first PHP assignment.

WRITING A BASIC FILE EXPLORER

In this assignment, we are going to simulate a file explorer. The goal is to use PHP to display the contents of a folder in the same way that a regular file explorer would. Here are some specific items you should make sure to achieve.

Requirements

The following guidelines are recommended:

- To keep it simple, your script should have a variable called *$path* that will hold the path to check.

- You should make sure that the variable *$path* represents a real directory and that you print an error if this is not the case.
- The explorer should now check the contents of the folder
- You should then echo the contents of the folder by first writing all the folders in alphabetical order, followed by all the remaining files also in alphabetical order. For example, if your folder contains the files bla.htm, foo.php, bar.mp3, and the folders Music and Work, you should display in order "Music, Work, bar.mp3, bla.htm, foo.php."
- Try to show what is a folder by either underlining its name using the HTML <U> . . . </U> tag or simply by placing a small icon (using <IMG . . . > tag) in front of it.

Hints

The following tips are also recommended:

- Try not to parse the folder twice. You should be able to open the *$path* after you know that it is a real directory and retrieve all the needed information in one pass.
- The order in which files and folders are read will most likely be the order of creation, so do not assume that folders will always be before files, and do not assume that everything will be sorted alphabetically.
- When sorting data you might want to have two separate arrays holding names (one for directories, one for files) and sort them individually. Another option could be to have a two-dimensional array, where *$arr[$i][0]* is the name and *$arr[$i][1]* is the type. In that case you could use *usort*, using a method that would compare two entries by checking their types first, and then their names if their types are the same.
- Remember to do a *CHDIR before* opening the folder!!

As we learn new techniques, we will refine this explorer to render directories clickable. Our goal will be able to click on a directory to run the same script on that new folder.

CASE STUDY: AN INDEXER/SEARCHER—STEP 1

Overview

If there is a tool that has made the Internet as useful as it is, it would undoubtedly be searchers. Trying to imagine an Internet without Google, Yahoo, AltaVista, and other searchers should bring shivers down your spine. Imaging having to find the lyrics to a song you are looking for by yourself, or find an answer to an aching questions without a tool to do the dirty work for you. Now, since we are learning about Web programming, it is our chance to get behind the wheel and figure out how searchers work, by writing our own.

The Indexer—Step 1

The secret to a great search engine is having great indexing. The process of indexing is the usually long and hard task of gathering as much information on the pages we want to be able to search for and organize our findings. There are tons of different types of indexers, from the basic "keywords" indexers that simply store the information found under the META tag "keywords" to complex full-text indexers with thesaurus that use *n*-dimensional space vectors to store the information of the files (beyond the scope of this book). We are going to settle for something in the middle: a basic full-text indexing with META tag information gathering.

A full-text indexer simply goes through the content of the file being indexed, counting how many times each word appears. This information is then stored in a database, and when a user looks for a word like "Spain," you show all the pages that contained that word, starting with the one that had the word appearing more times. There are several important things to realize when indexing, though.

First, there are useless words that do not need to be indexed. A "useless" word is a word that no one with common sense would try to look for, usually a word that gives no information on the topic of the page. For example, words like "a," "the," "for," "yes," and "no" could be considered "useless." In order to skip useless words, there are several techniques, such as having an array with all the entries to ignore (the safest way). Another faster way is *not* to index a word that has less than a predetermined amount of letters, with the danger of excluding short but important words. For example, a page on databases might contain the abbreviation DB (for database) appearing many times, and should not be ignored. For our indexer, we will simply ignore words of one letter, indexing only words of two or more letters.

Another typical problem when indexing is HTML tags. Obviously when searching for files, you want to be able to know how many times a word appeared, but you seldom care about how many times a specific HTML tag was used. Our function *strip_tags* will be extremely useful! Always remove the HTML tags before proceeding to indexing the words in the file.

Other important thing to keep in mind are letter casing and special characters. Realize that as far as PHP goes, words like "Alicante" (my hometown) and "alicante" are different, but as far as your indexer goes, they should be the same. To solve this, the standard consensus is to lowercase the entire file being indexed. As for special characters, you do not want to record in your database how many times you had a new line, and exclamation point or a double quote. So you need to find a way to get rid of special characters. Regular expressions are usually the best way, but since we will not see them until almost the end of this book, you may use *strtok* or *str_replace*. This way, you can avoid problems like having "hello!" and "hello" appear as two separate words because of the exclamation point. Getting rid of special characters is one of the most important steps in an indexer.

Finally, as stated above, our indexer will also have to gather the META tag information. This step has basically no interference with the full-text indexing, since *get_meta_tags* accepts the URL of the file directly, whereas the full-text indexing will require you to open the file and store its contents in a string so that it can be modified.

In a nutshell, our basic indexer will need to

- Get the META tag information (info) (*get_meta_tags*).
- Open the file, and copy the entire contents in a string variable (set of file functions).
- Strip the tags (*strip_tags*).
- Lowercase everything (*strtolower*).
- Get rid of special characters and count how many times each word appears in the file.
- As far as this first assignment, the indexer should simply output all the gathered info on a page. Of course, the counted words should be sorted alphabetically, and each word should appear only once, followed by the number of times it was found.
- In this assignment we will also simply output the contents of the META tags.

Hints:

- To get rid of special characters, you can do multiple *str_replace* followed by an *explode*, or you can thank me and use the *superExplode* method seen earlier. This way you can use tokenizers and still get an array with all the words.
- If you have an array holding all the words, remember *array_count_values*, which does the counting for you.
- If you have an associative array with words as keys, and numbers as elements (like the one you get after running *array_count_values*), you can sort the array using *ksort*. . . .
- To keep it simple, just have a *$path* variable containing the page to index. In step 2 we will see how to use forms to provide the filename (end of chapter 9).

8

PHP5 and Object-Oriented Programming

OVERVIEW

Even though objects in PHP have existed since version 3, their use has been improved with PHP5, thanks to the use of the script motor Zend 2. In case you have never programmed in any object-oriented programming language (e.g., C++ or Java), I will explain the raw basics so you can follow the explanations. If you wish to look into C++, I recommend that you read *The Design and Evolution of C++* by Bjarne Stroustrup (see alphabetical list in Bibliography at the end of this book).

CLASSES AND OBJECTS

A class is a complex data type that can hold both data and methods. Classes are generally categories of objects; the data it contains are called *data members* or *attributes* and allow definition of a particular instance of that class. The methods inside a class are generally actions that an instance of a class can do, or simply methods that allow access to or modification of data members. For example, you could have a class called *Car* that would hold data members such as *manufacturer, model,* and *year,* and methods like *checkMileage()* or *changeColor().*

Web Application Design and Implementation: Apache 2, PHP5, MySQL, JavaScript, and Linux/UNIX, by Steven A. Gabarró
Copyright © 2007 by John Wiley & Sons, Inc.

An object is an instance of a class, or more basically a specific item that can be part of a class. For example, with the class *Car,* you could have an object *myDodgeViper* (I wish). The object will contain specific data that will define it; for example, in this case *manufacturer* would be equal to *Dodge* and *model* would be equal to *Viper.*

CLASSES IN PHP

To create a class in PHP, you start by writing *class* followed by the name of the class. Once you are in the class, you can create functions as you would outside a class. The difference will be that definitions of functions defined inside a class will be methods of the class. In order to call a method of a class you have two choices: either creating an object of your class and invoking the method (see below) or calling the method statically through the class name:

```php
<?php
class SimpleClass
{
  // member declaration
  public $var = 'a default value';

  // method declaration
  public function displayVar() {
    echo $this->var;
  }
  public static function statMethod(){
    echo "This is a static method";
  }
}
$a = new SimpleClass(); //we create an object of the
                        //class SimpleClass
$a->displayVar(); //we invoke the method displayVar
                  //through the object $a
SimpleClass::statMethod(); // We call the static method
                           //statMethod
?>
```

It is possible to use inheritance in PHP, through the keyword *extends.* Inheritance is the process of *deriving* a class from another one. When you derive from a class (your parent class), you are its child, and inherit any of the parent's data members and methods. This means that you can use any of the parent's public methods without the need to redefine them. To show that a class derives from another one, add *extends ParentClass* at the end of the class definition line. Check the example at the end of the next section.

It is possible for a child class to *override* a parent's method. This basically means changing the behavior of an inherited method, while keeping the same name. If you want to prevent a child class from overriding your methods, write the keyword *final* in front of the parent's method definition, for example

final public function dontChangeMe()

CONSTRUCTORS AND DESTRUCTORS

A constructor is a method that is called whenever an object of a class is created. Its goal is to initialize the data members of the class. In PHP, constructors need to be called *__construct()* and may have any parameters you need. By default a constructor takes no parameters, but you might use parameters to define special initialization data. If, for example, you defined your constructor as *function __construct($a)* (assuming that *$a* will hold a number), you could initialize an object doing *$myObj = new MyClass(12);*.

If your class derives from a parent class, and you wish to call your parent's constructor, you can do *parent::__construct();*.

A destructor does the opposite of a constructor. It is a method called when the script is finishing running and all objects are freed from memory. Its intended use is removal of all data that are no longer needed, and must be named *__destruct()*. Destructors may *not* have parameters.

```php
<?php
  class BaseClass {
    function __construct() {
       print "In BaseClass constructor\n";
    }
    function inheritedFunction() {
      echo "howdy!";
    }
  }
  class SubClass extends BaseClass {
    function __construct() {
      parent::__construct();
      print "In SubClass constructor\n";
    }
  }
$obj = new BaseClass();
$obj2 = new SubClass();
$obj2->inheritedFunction();
?>
```

VISIBILITY

When you are defining a data member or data function, it is possible to set up its visibility. The visibility can be public, private, or protected. *Public* visibility means that the data can be accessed anywhere, *private* means that the data are accessible only within the class itself, and *protected* means that only the class itself, its parents, and its descendants can access it. Data members should always have their visibility written before the data themselves, but it can be omitted in the case of methods that take *public* as default visibility.

```php
<?php
/**
 * Define MyClass
 */
class MyClass
{
  public $public = 'Public';
  protected $protected = 'Protected';
  private $private = 'Private';

  function printHello()
  {
    echo $this->public;
    echo $this->protected;
    echo $this->private;
  }
}
$obj = new MyClass();
echo $obj->public; // Works
echo $obj->protected; // Fatal Error
echo $obj->private; // Fatal Error
$obj->printHello(); // Shows Public, Protected and
                    //Private

class MyClass2 extends MyClass
{
  // We can redeclare the public and protected members,
//but not private
  protected $protected = 'Protected2';

  function printHello()
  {
    echo $this->public;
    echo $this->protected;
    echo $this->private;
  }
}
```

```
$obj2 = new MyClass2();
echo $obj2->public; // Works
echo $obj2->private; // Undefined
echo $obj2->protected; // Fatal Error
$obj2->printHello(); // Shows Public, Protected2, not
                     //Private
?>
```

THE SCOPE RESOLUTION OPERATOR

The scope resolution operator is basically two colons (::). The scope operator was named "Paamayim Nekudotayim" by the Zend team of developers while they were writing Zend engine 0.5 (used in PHP3). It actually means "double colon" in Hebrew. It is a token that allows access to the static, constant, and overridden members and methods of a class, without the need to create an object of that class.

```
<?php
class MyClass {
  const CONST_VALUE = 'A constant value';
}
echo MyClass::CONST_VALUE;
class OtherClass extends MyClass
{
  public static $my_static = 'static var';

  public static function doubleColon() {
    echo parent::CONST_VALUE . "\n";
    echo self::$my_static . "\n";
  }
}
OtherClass::doubleColon();
?>
```

THE STATIC KEYWORD

When you have a method that you would like to access without the need to create an object, you must make the method static (and public). Doing so, you will be allowed to access the method by simply writing the name of the class followed by the scope operator and the method name. Note that since a static method can be called without an instance of the class, you may not use the *$this* object reference inside a static method. A static data member is basically a member that can be accessed without the need of an object. Furthermore, you cannot access a static data member from an object, so it is

accessible only by writing the name of the class, followed by the scope operator and the variable name.

CLASS CONSTANTS

You may define constant values inside classes. Constants are similar to variables, but they cannot be modified. Constants do not use the dollar sign in
their names, and, like static members, they cannot be accessed from an
instance of the class. You may not store a variable, class member, result of a
calculation, or function call inside a constant. Constants are useful when there
is an important data item that you will use throughout your code and that
does not change. You might wonder, why use a constant instead of simply
writing its value? Imagine that you are programming a page that will handle
an array, making sure that you never get more than a specific number of elements, say, 100. You could write the number 100 each time you want to check
the maximum size of the array for comparison, but if in the future you wish
to upgrade your program to accept 1000 numbers, you will have to go through
your code and change every single "100" to "1000." A problem might arise if
you also use "100" for other functions, such as calculating a percentage. By
creating a constant instead of writing the actual data throughout the code,
you allow yourself the flexibility needed to upgrade your code by simply
changing one value: the one written in the constant declaration.

CLASS ABSTRACTION

PHP5 made it possible to create abstract classes. An abstract class is a class
that cannot be instantiated, and is used mainly for inheritance purposes.
Abstract classes will usually have abstract methods, which are basically
methods that are declared but not implemented. If your class contains at least
one abstract method, you must declare the class as abstract, simply adding
the word *abstract* in front of the class name and all abstract methods.

OBJECT INTERFACES

Object interfaces allow you to create code that specifies which methods a class
must implement, without having to define how these methods are handled.
The difference between an abstract class and an interface is that abstract
classes are used for inheritance and can contain both data and methods.
Interfaces can only have methods, which must be implemented by a class.
Interfaces are defined using the *interface* keyword, in the same way as a standard class, but without any of the methods having their contents defined. All
methods declared in an interface must be public.

It is possible to implement more than one interface, by simply writing the names of all implemented interfaces separated by commas. It is not possible to implement two interfaces that share function names, as this would create ambiguity. Also, if your class implements an interface, it must implement all the interface's functions, or be declared as an abstract class, since the non-implemented methods become "abstract."

```php
<?php
// Declare the interface 'iTemplate'
interface iTemplate
{
  public function setVariable($name, $var);
  public function getHtml($template);
}
// Implement the interface
// This will work
  class Template implements iTemplate
  {
    private $vars = array();
    public function setVariable($name, $var)
    {
      $this->vars[$name] = $var;
    }
    public function getHtml($template)
    {
      foreach($this->vars as $name => $value) {
        $template = str_replace('{' . $name . '}', $value, $template);
      }
      return $template;
    }
  }
}
```

COPYING AND CLONING OBJECTS

There is a very important thing to realize about objects, and that is that an object variable is technically a reference to the actual object. Therefore, copying an object by doing *object1 = object2;* simply causes both variables to refer to the same object. In many cases we will not want just a copy of the reference to the object but a copy of the entire contents of the object. To do so, we can use the *clone* operator, for example, *object1 = clone (object2);*

The *clone* operator will create a new object and copy all the attributes from *object2* to *object1*. This may sound like using the equal sign (=), but the main difference is that using *clone* will call any existing __*clone()* method of the class (see below).

It is possible to specify what to do when you are trying to clone an object by creating a method *__clone()*. For example, if you have a class that contains object definitions, you could have a *__clone()* method that will clone the data members rather than doing a shallow copy. Check this example:

```php
<?PHP
  class SubObject
  {
    static $instances = 0;
    public $instance;
    public function __construct() {
      $this->instance = ++self::$instances;
    }
    public function __clone() {
      $this->instance = ++self::$instances;
    }
  }
  class CloneMeWell
  {
    public $object1;
    public $object2;
    function __clone()
    { $this->object1 = clone ($this->object1); }
  }
  $obj1 = new CloneMeWell();
  $obj1->object1 = new SubObject();
  $obj1->object2 = new SubObject();
  $obj2 = clone $obj1;
?>
```

In this example we create an instance of the class CloneMeWell, containing two objects of the class SubObject. The SubObject constructor increases a static data member and saves it in the *$instance* data member. This variable stores how many instances of that class were created. We then make a clone of CloneMeWell, in which we define a *__clone()* method that clones the *$object1* data member, but not the *$object2*. What will happen is that a new instance of CloneMeWell will be created and its *$object1* will be a clone, meaning that a third instance of *SubObject* is created by cloning the *$object1*, but since *$object2* is not cloned but instead simply copied, *$obj1->object2* will refer to the same object than *$obj2->object2*.

COMPARING OBJECTS

There are two ways to compare two objects to determine whether they are the same. You may use the double or triple equal sign. The double equal (==)

will check whether all attributes are the same, and whether the two objects are instances of the same class. For example, an object and its clone would be equal, if compared with ==.

The triple equal (===) will check whether the object variables are identical, meaning that they will refer to the same instance of the same class.

TYPE HINTING

Since PHP5, it has been possible to force function parameters to be either objects or arrays (since PHP 5.1). You may write a method that is meant to work only with a specific class. To do so, either write the name of the class in front of the parameter, or write the word *array* if what you need is an array.

For example, if we wanted to have a function that accepts an object of the class MyClass and an array, you would write

function myFunction(MyClass $classParam, array $theArray);

EXCEPTIONS

Exceptions are a technique used to handle problems found during execution. PHP's exception model is very similar to that of other languages such as Java or C++. The principle is to *try* to run a piece of code, and if there is a problem, you *throw* an exception, which you then have to *catch*. An exception is not really the same as an error, notice, or warning; it is bad behavior that you suspect might occur. Any block of code that you know might cause a problem should be written in a *try* block. If you need to throw an exception, simply use the *throw* keyword, creating a new instance of the class *Exception*. After the *try* block, you should have a *catch* block, which will handle any exception that might occur. If the *try* block had no exceptions, the *catch* block would be ignored. You may read the exception message through a variable declared in a catch block, as an instance of the class Exception. The class Exception contains a method *getMessage()* that returns the message describing the exception.

For example, let us imagine that we want to check for a divide-by-zero exception. Your code would be as follows:

```php
<?PHP
  function divide($a, $b)
  {
    try {
      if ($b == 0)
        throw new Exception("Attempted to divide by zero!");
      return $a / $b;
```

```php
    } catch (Exception $e) {
        echo "Caught exception: ".$e->getMessage()."\n";
    }
  }
?>
```

Here is the structure of the built-in Exception class:

```php
<?php
class Exception
{
  protected $message = 'Unknown exception'; // exception
                                            //message
  protected $code = 0;     // user defined exception code
  protected $file;         // source filename of exception
  protected $line;            // source line of exception
  function __construct($message = null, $code = 0);

  final function getMessage();    // message of exception
  final function getCode();       // code of exception
  final function getFile();       // source filename
  final function getLine();       // source line
  final function getTrace();      // an array of the
                                  backtrace()
  final function getTraceAsString();  // formated string
                                        of trace

  /* Overrideable */
  function __toString();   // formated string for display
}
?>
```

FINAL WORDS

There are many other features and details on object-oriented programming, but with the elements mentioned above, you should have more than enough to get started. At the end of Chapter 13, we will write a class that will help us communicate with a database. The class will contain methods to connect to the database, as well as to gather information in it. You will also see a practical example of exceptions used in the same class.

9

Creating Some Interactivity

OVERVIEW

By now you know all the nuts and bolts of the core set of tools that PHP provides with one major exception: interactivity between pages. The goal of this chapter is to overcome this need and show you the many ways of transmitting information between PHP scripts.

FORMS

Our first technique of communications is *forms*. A form is basically a Webpage that has a set of available input areas for the user to enter information. It also contains a button that allows you to send that information to any page.

Writing a Form in HTML

The first thing to learn is how to create a form in HTML, and how to set it up to send all the data to a PHP script. To do so, use the *<FORM>*... *</FORM>* tags. Inside those tags will be the entire contents of the form, so keep in mind that if you place an input area outside those tags, you will not be able to send the information that the input area contains. The FORM tag takes two main attributes: *action* and *method*. *Action* allows you to specify

Web Application Design and Implementation: Apache 2, PHP5, MySQL, JavaScript, and Linux/UNIX, by Steven A. Gabarró

the script that will run when the form is submitted, and *method* specifies how the information will be sent to the script. The two possible methods are GET and POST. For now, simply write POST, and later on I will explain why that option is better. You may also add a *target* the same way we did with regular links if you want to send the form information to a different window or frame.

Once you have created the working area for your form, it is time to create input areas. Input areas are created with the *<INPUT />* tag, which can be set up with the following attributes:

- *Name*—name given to the input. Probably one of the most important pieces of information, as we will need this name to gather the information in the receiving script.
- *Type*—type of input; see below
- *Value*—default value for the input, if any. If you do not want to set a default value, simply skip this attribute. On radio buttons and check-boxes, this specifies the value associated with the current option. On reset and submit buttons, this specifies the string appearing on the button.
- *Checked*—if your input is a checkbox or a radio button, simply write the word *CHECKED* in the input tag to have the option selected by default.
- *Maxlength*—maximum number of characters that a textbox will accept. When the number is reached, any extra characters that the user tries to write will be ignored.
- *Size*—actual size of the input item. For example, you can use *size* to define the length of a textbox.

Here are the different types of input that exist, and what they are used for:

- *Text*—this is used for regular one-lined textboxes; perfect for login information.
- *Password*—same as *text* with the exception that the characters typed in the box will not show up. Instead, for each character typed you will see a special symbol like an asterisk (*) or black dots, depending on the browser used. You should obviously use this type for password fields, so that no one can eavesdrop on a user who is entering his/her user/pass information.
- *Checkbox*—a checkbox is basically a small square box that can be checked or not checked. Since it is possible to deselect a checkbox by simply click-ing on it, there is no real necessity to group checkboxes together, and they can all work independently. Nevertheless, it is a good idea to group similar checkboxes together. To do this, simply call all the checkboxes

with the same name, followed by brackets. For example, if your group of checkboxes needs to be called "Checks," you should write "Checks[]" for each checkbox under their *name* property. Grouping checkboxes together allows you to gather all the information of the checkboxes as a single array, rather than having one variable per checkbox.

• *Radio*—used to create radio buttons. A radio button is a circle on a screen that can be checked or unchecked. The difference between radio buttons and checkboxes is that radio buttons should always be grouped, as only one option can be selected at any time. You may not click on a selected radio button to unselect it. Instead, you need to click on a different radio button of the same group. This makes the need of grouping radio buttons crucial. If you leave all the radio buttons independent, you will be able to select them all, but unselect none. To group radio buttons, simply give them the same name. In the case of radio buttons there is no need to put the angular brackets that we used with checkboxes, because checkboxes are processed as an array (hence the brackets). You may have several options selected, but since radio buttons can have only one option selected within the same group, there is no need for arrays.

• *Hidden*—probably one of the most useful underused input types. They are useful when transfering information from forms to forms without showing that information to the user. It simply saves the data stored in the "value" attribute and sends it through the form without asking for any input to the user. Note that since this is HTML, the "hidden" field can still be seen and read through the page's code, so *avoid* entering decrypted passwords in "hidden" inputs.

• *Reset*—this will create a button that will reset the form to its initial state, erasing any data that might have been written thus far and replacing them with the default values.

• *Submit*—probably the most important button (at least until we study forms manipulation with JavaScript). This will create a button that will send all the input values to the script specified on the "action" field of your FORM tag.

• *Button*—a simple button like *reset* and *submit* but that has no action. It is useful in JavaScript.

There are actually two more types of input, but they do not use the INPUT tag. These are text areas that are multiline textboxes, and select areas that are menus.

To use a text area, use the *<TEXTAREA>...</TEXTAREA>* with the attributes *name* (same meaning as the name of an INPUT tag), *rows* (number of rows the text area will show on screen), and *cols* (number of columns of character the text area will show on screen). Note that any character between the end of the opening tag and the beginning of the closing tag will be considered the default value, so if you want a totally empty text area of

20 lines and 80 columns, type *<TEXTAREA name="fullText" ROWS=20 COLS=80></TEXTAREA>*. Realize that anything written between the tags will *not* be considered regular HTML; instead it will be considered regular text to be inside the text area. This means that if you have five white spaces between opening and closing tags, it will not translate it all into a single white space on screen as HTML code would; rather, it will actually show five white spaces on the text area.

To use select areas, you first need to use the *<SELECT> . . . </SELECT>* tags with the attributes *name* (same as the other inputs) and *size* (which specifies how many lines to show on screen). Select displays a set of options that are clickable by the user. In this book we will limit ourselves to simple selections (which is the default behavior), but it is actually possible to allow the user to select more than one option at once. Note that if the size of the select is 1, your select becomes a dropdown menu. Once you have defined the SELECT tags, you must add a set of options. Each option is an element that will appear on the list, with an associated value. To add an option, use the *<OPTION />* tag with the attribute *value,* followed by the name you want to show on the menu. Note that using the tag OPTION creates a selectable option with its value, but does not create the text that would show up. The name to show must be written after the tag, and each option should be written on a different line.

Regardless of the input used, realize that the tag that creates the input does only that. To tell the user what to enter in each input, *you* are responsible for writing regular text around your inputs, explaining what they are for, especially for radio buttons and checkboxes (there is nothing more ridiculous on a screen than a bunch of little circles or squares with no name or explanation as to why they are there).

Here is an example of a form with all the different kinds of inputs that will call a script called *forms.php* (which we will see later on) on a blank window:

```
<FORM action="forms.php" method="POST" target="_blank">
  <INPUT type="text" name="text" value="HELLO"
size="20" maxlength="20"><BR>
  <INPUT type="password" name="pass" value="" size="8"
maxlength="8"><BR>
  <INPUT type="radio" name="radio" value="1"/>Radio1<BR>
  <INPUT type="radio" name="radio" value="2"
CHECKED/>Radio2<BR>
  <INPUT type="radio" name="radio"
value="3"/>Radio3<BR>
  <INPUT type="checkbox" name="check[]"
value="4"/>One<BR>
  <INPUT type="checkbox" name="check[]"
value="1"/>Two<BR>
```

```
    <INPUT type="checkbox" name="check[]" value="3"
CHECKED/>Three<BR>
    <INPUT type="hidden" name="hidden" value="boo!"/><BR>
    <TEXTAREA name="textarea" cols="20" rows="5">
    Yipi yipi hey! This text is preceded with new
lines, tabs and white spaces!
    </TEXTAREA><BR>
    <SELECT name="select" size="1">
     <OPTION value="1">Uno
     <OPTION value="2">Dos
     <OPTION value="3">Tres
    </SELECT><BR>
    <INPUT type="submit" name="submit" value="GO!"/><BR>
    <INPUT type="reset"/><BR>
  </FORM>
```

GET versus POST

As mentioned earlier, a form transmits information to your PHP scripts through two possible methods called GET and POST. The GET method will access the script provided in the *action* parameter of your FORM tag by writing the URL of the script followed by all the data that were found in the script. So, for example, if your input contained two textboxes called "name" and "nickname," where I wrote "Steven" and "Bewchy," submitting the form would ask the browser to open the URL yourscript.php?name=Steven&nick name=Bewchy. The syntax is pretty simple; there is a question mark right after the script to run, followed by the series *variable=value*. Different variables are written next to each other by placing an ampersand (&) in between, thus enabling you to see absolutely *all* of the form information sent by simply looking at the address bar on your browser. This is obviously a very poor choice if you are sending important information such as passwords, and the main reason why I never use GET as a form method. The POST method sends all the information directly to the script in a way that is transparent to the user, so the address bar in my previous example would show "yourscript. php."

Retrieving the Form Information on a PHP Script

Once you arrive to a script from a form, you need to first know how the data were sent, and depending on the method you use, one of two arrays: $_GET or $_POST. These arrays are automatically filled when information is received in the page through either method. They are associative arrays where the key is the name of the input, and the element is the value that it was set as. For example, if in "yourscript.php" you received the previous example of "name" and "nickname" through the GET method, you would be able to read the values "Steven" and "Bewchy" by simply writing *$_GET["name"]* and *$_GET["nickname"]*, respectively. It is a good idea to first verify that that data have been sent (with *isset*) before trying to read them in order to avoid unnecessary notices. This can also be used as a security measure to verify that a user has accessed the script through a form and did not attempt to directly write the script's URL. Other fun things you can do is put the $_GET and $_POST arrays in a *foreach* loop to extract all the info sent without even knowing what was sent. Remember that a group of checkboxes sent together will be sent as an array, so keep it in mind and use *foreach* to check which options where selected. When reading the values sent for radio buttons, checkboxes, and select areas, you will receive whatever the *value* parameter was equal to for the selected option. Here is the forms.php file that would process my previous form:

```php
<?PHP
  if (!isset($_POST["text"]))
    echo "You stupid cheater!! You didn't use my form!!!";
  else
  {
    echo strip_tags($_POST["text"])."<BR>";
    $arr = $_POST["check"];
    foreach ($arr as $elem)
      echo $elem." ";
    echo "<BR>";
    echo strip_tags($_POST["textarea"])."<BR>";
// you can access the variables by knowing their name
    foreach ($_POST as $k=>$e)
      echo "Input $k received with value $e<BR>";
// or simply use foreach
  }           ?>
```

Dynamically Creating Forms

Remember that the only real limit to what you can do with PHP is your imagination. If you wish to have a form be automatically generated, just use a PHP script that will echo the tags you need with the dynamic data. For example, imagine that you want to display a dropdown menu where you can select any of the U.S. states, with their zipcode abbreviations as values. It is quite painful to write the entire list with the proper *OPTION* tags each time you need to have that dropdown menu. Instead, you could have an associative array called *$states* in an include file. The array would have the abbreviation as a key and the actual name as a value, so, for example, you would have $states["NJ"] == "New Jersey" and $states["NY"] == "New York." Here is a little script that would create all the options for you:

```
[ . . . ] all the forum definition would be up here [ . . . ]
<SELECT name=State size=1>
<?PHP
  foreach ($states as $k=>$e)
    echo "<OPTION value='".$k."'>".$e."\n";  //don't forget
                                             //the \n

?>
</SELECT>
[ . . . ] rest of html code [ . . . ]
```

TRANSFERRING DATA BETWEEN PHP SCRIPTS

The most basic way to transfer data between PHP scripts is by using the GET method. Because of the way GET data are retrieved in PHP, you do not actually need to receive these data from a form. Simply use the syntax presented before to write variables after the URL of the script to which you wish to send data. So, for example, if I had *$var1* and *$var2* that I wanted to transmit to a new PHP script, I could have a link created by PHP as follows:

```
echo "<A HREF='script2.php?var1=".$var1."&var2=".$var2."'>
Click Me!</A>";
```

Instead of having a link, we can use the *header* function, which, as we will see at the end of this chapter, can automatically redirect the user to the destination page if the proper conditions are met.

Cookies

A better way to share information among different scripts is the use of cookies. But you may ask "What are cookies?" Well, let me quote the *Cambridge Advanced Learner's Dictionary* to answer you:

1. **biscuit** (FLAT CAKE), U.K.
      noun [C] (U.S. cookie)
      a small, flat cake that is dry and usually sweet:
      chocolate/ginger biscuits
      a packet of biscuits
      We had tea and biscuits at 3.30 p.m.
2. **cookie** (BISCUIT), cooky
      noun [C] MAINLY U.S.
      a sweet biscuit:
      chocolate-chip cookies

3. **cookie** (TYPE OF PERSON)
> noun [C] U.S. INFORMAL
> a person of the type mentioned:
> She's a smart/tough cookie.

4. **cookie** (COMPUTING)
> noun [C] SPECIALIZED
> a piece of information stored on your computer that contains information about all the Internet documents that you have looked at

Obviously we are going to concentrate on the fourth definition. A bit more seriously, cookies were created by Netscape and can hold text information of no more than 4 kB. You can have up to 20 cookies per domain and a total of 300 cookies maximum, according to RFC 2109. Cookies are saved on the user's computer and can be returned to the server that created the cookie only in the folder specified on creation. PHP can import the available cookies through the $_COOKIE array.

Cookies are useful when you wish to individualize a Website with different color scheme preferences, as you can use them to remember the login information of your user, or even memorize a shopping cart on a commercial Website.

Cookies can be set in HTML through a Set-Cookie, but we will see only how to create them in PHP. The important thing to remember is the list of parameters cookies need, as you will need that information to create a useful cookie. The first important thing to set up is the name of the cookie, as well as its contents. Other parameters include *expires*, which sets the expiration time of the cookie; the *path*, which specifies where the cookie will be accessible; the *domain*, which states which domain can view the cookie (you can usually leave the option blank to use the current domain); and the *secure* flag, to decide whether you wish to encrypt the cookie.

To create a cookie with PHP, use *setcookie($name, $value, $expires, $path, $domain, $secure);*. Technically you need only the first three parameters; the rest can be left as default. Imagine that you wish to create a cookie called "myCookie" that contains "Hello World!", and you wish the cookie to survive for a full minute. Here is the instruction you would need to run:

setcookie("myCookie", "Hello World!", time()+60);

The function *time()* returns the current UNIX timestamp, which is the number of seconds passed since the Unix Epoch (January 1, 1970 00:00:00 GMT). You may also retrieve the number of milliseconds elapsed since that date with *microtime();*. Since we want our cookie to exist for one minute, we simply need to set the expiration date to the creation time plus 60 seconds.

If later on you wish to access that same cookie, you would read the contents using $_COOKIE["myCookie"], which would hold the string that the cookie contained.

As cookies hold only text data, you might think that they are quite limited, but with our imagination, we can overcome this limitation. Simply use *implode* to create a string with multiple variables concatenated one after the other before writing in the cookie, and use *explode* when reading that same info to split it back the way it was. Here is an example:

```php
<?PHP // COOKIE CREATION
  if (!isset($_COOKIE["helloCookie"])) {
     echo "Cookie not defined<br>";
    $col="#FF0000";
    $size=12;
    $font="Verdana";
    $text="Hello mister cookie!";
    $arr=compact("col","size","font","text");
    $val=implode("|",$arr);
    setcookie("helloCookie",$val,time()+600,"","",0);
    echo "A cookie will be created<br><br>";
  } else {
    echo "<b>Here is the info on the cookie :</b><br><br>";
    $myCookie=$_COOKIE["helloCookie"];
    echo $myCookie;
    $arr=explode("|",$myCookie);
    echo "<b>The following vars where in the cookie
:</b><br><br>";
    foreach ($arr as $k=>$elem) {
      echo "$k=>$elem<br>";
      ${"cookie_$k"} = $elem; //See explanation below
    }
    echo "<br><b>Now let's use the cookie info :</b><br><br>";
    echo "<FONT FACE=\"".$cookie_2."\" COLOR=\"".$cookie_0."\"
  SIZE=\"".$cookie_1."\">".stripslashes($cookie_3)."</FONT>";
    }
?>
```

You probably noticed the line that uses *${"cookie_$k"}* as a variable name. This is a technique that allows you to create several variables with automatically generated names. As you know, the dollar sign $ means that you are writing a variable and the curly braces { } tell PHP that you wish to generate the name of the variable through a combination of strings and other variables. For example, in our code we have $k holding the key of elements in an array, getting the values 0, 1, 2, and 3. This will result in variables called *$cookie_0, $cookie_1, $cookie_2,* and *$cookie_3.*

Sessions

One of the most efficient and easy ways of transferring information between pages without the user's knowledge is to use sessions. Sessions can be imagined as a "magic cloud" that contains all the variables that we need it to hold. The session can be accessed from any PHP script, which can either add more data or read data from the session. The session information is saved in the server computer either on text files (that's the standard behavior) or on the Web server's process memory. This makes session much more flexible than cookies to store data, as the only limit is the size of the server's hard drive.

When a user accesses a page that uses sessions, a unique session identifier is randomly generated and encrypted. This session id is usually stored in the client's computer as a cookie, although you do not need to manually create the cookie, as the session initialization will do this for you. If the browser that the client is using does not accept cookies from your domain, you can still transmit the session identifier between pages with the GET or POST method.

The default session configuration should be good enough for the scope of this book, but here are some settings you can change in your php.ini file (each element will be written as a *setting=default_value,* followed by an explanation of what it does):

- *session.save_handler = files*—this line specifies the way in which the session information will be stored in the server. Other possible values are "mm" for memory, or "user" if you want to manually configure the saving process.
- *session.save_path = C:\PHP\sessiondata*—folder in which the session data will be stored.
- *session.use_cookies = 1*—use cookies? 1 for yes, 0 for no.
- *session.name = PHPSESSID*—name provided to the session.
- *session.auto_start = 0*—I strongly recommend leaving this as 0. You may write 1 if you want a session to start automatically in every single PHP script that you write.

To use session in PHP, you first need to start the session with *session_start()*. If no session was yet created for the user, a session will be created. If a session already existed for this user, starting the session will allow you to access the existing session. Remember that you *must* use *session_start()* if you are planning on using sessions, or the session data will not be accessible. If you want to destroy a session, meaning that you don't want the user to be able to access the session data any longer, use *session_destroy()*. This function is usually one of the last steps of a logout procedure. When a session is started, you may check the name and id of the session with the functions *session_name() and session_id()*, respectively.

In order to use the session, use the array *$_SESSION*. For example, if you want to create a session variable "username" with the value "Bewchy," you simply need to write

$$\$\_SESSION["username"] = "Bewchy";$$

The $_SESSION array works pretty much the same way as $_GET, $_POST, $_SERVER or $_COOKIE. Therefore it is possible to check whether a session variable exists by simply using *isset($_SESSION["varname"])*. You may also delete a session variable using *unset*. Also, since it is an array, you can use *foreach* to retrieve all the data in a session.

The following example is a series of three files. The first one will create a session and store data in it; the second file will check whether the session exists and show any data stored in it; the third file will be a logout procedure that will destroy the session. To navigate between the pages, we will add some basic HTML links:

```
<HTML><HEAD><TITLE>File 1</TITLE></HEAD>
<BODY>
Starting the session . . . <BR>
<?PHP
  session_start();
  $_SESSION["username"] = "Bewchy";
  $_SESSION["realname"] = "Steven";
  $_SESSION["clan"] = "COTW";
?>
Session created<BR>
<A HREF="sessions2.php">Next page!</A>
</BODY>
</HTML>
```

```
<HTML><HEAD><TITLE>File 2</TITLE></HEAD>
<BODY>
  Checking the session . . . <BR>
  <?PHP
  session_start();
  echo session_name()." ".session_id()."<BR>";
  if (!isset($_SESSION["username"]))
  {
  echo "You cheater!!! You tried to sneak in with no
session!<BR>";
  ?>
<A HREF="sessions.php">Go create your session!</A>
  <?PHP
  }
```

```
  else
  {
    echo "Session data is:<BR>";
    foreach($_SESSION as $k=>$e)
      echo $k." ".$e."<BR>";
  ?>
<A HREF="sessions3.php">Next page!</A>
  <?PHP// the previous HTML line is inside the { } of the
       //else, so will
  // only run if the session existed
  }
  ?>
</BODY>
</HTML>
```

```
<HTML><HEAD><TITLE>File 3</TITLE></HEAD>
<BODY>
  Checking the session . . . <BR>
  <?PHP
  session_start();
  if (!isset($_SESSION["username"]))
    echo "Are you trying to destroy a non-existent
session?<BR>";
  else
  {
    echo "Unsetting session variables and destroying
session<BR>";
    unset $_SESSION["username"];
    unset $_SESSION["realname"];
    unset $_SESSION["clan"];
    session_destroy();
  }
  ?>
  Try the <A HREF="sessions2.php">second script</A> now
that there is no session!
  </BODY>
  </HTML>
```

ONE LAST USEFUL FUNCTION AND DESIGN TECHNIQUES

Sometimes you will process information in pages that are not really displaying any data, but that are just PHP scripts that, for example, make sure that the login information is correct before setting up the page for the logged-in user. In those cases we want to be able to redirect the user from the current script to a different one. This can be done with JavaScript, as we will see in Chapter 14, or you can simply use the PHP *header* function.

The function *header* allows you to send a raw HTTP header. For this reason you may use this function only if the headers haven't been sent yet, which means that if a single character has been printed, you will not be able to user *header,* and will get a message saying "headers already sent." I will not get into the details of raw HTTP headers; the only thing you need to know for our situation here is how to utilize this function for redirections. Simply write *header("location:* http://blablabla.com*");* replacing "blablabla.com" with whatever URL you wish to go to. You can, of course, take advantage of this to send GET information by writing, for example, *header("location: myscript.php?var1=1&var2=2&var3=3");*.

Usually when I write a login procedure I start on a standard form. When the user enters the user and password information and clicks on the submit button, I receive all the information in a PHP script that starts by checking the database. If the user and password do not match any record, I use *header* to redirect the user to the login page; if the login information is correct, I set up my session with all the info I might need from the database (email address, name, surname, preferences, etc.) and use *header* to move to the "logged-in" main page.

A *header* can also be used as a basic security tool. If there is a page that should be accessed only if the user is logged in and you are using sessions, you can check one of the session variables right at the beginning of your page and *header* the user back to the login page if that user is not properly logged in. You can also add information on the redirection with the GET method. This is what the top of your "secure" pages could look like this:

```
<?PHP
  if (!isset($_SESSION["user"]))
    header("location: http://mydomain/index.php?reason=nologin");
?>
<HTML>
    <HEAD>
    [ . . . ]
```

ASSIGNMENTS

File Explorer—Step 2

Now that we know how to transmit information between PHP scripts, take the file explorer from Chapter 7 and make it more useful by rendering the folders clickable. The idea is to turn each folder into a link. When you click on a folder name, you should call the same explorer script sending the new path to parse through the GET method. Note that there are always two "directories" that appear in every path: "." and " . . . " The folder "." represents the current working directory, and is not of much use to us, so there is no need to print it. The ".." folder represents the parent directory. Now if you click on "..", you can process the folder the lazy way, meaning that the path will appear with a "/../" at the end. The problem with this technique is that after several clicks your path might look something like "/usr/home/sgabarro/folder/../../sgabarro/folder/," which shows poor design as it actually refers to the folder "/usr/home/sgabarro/folder/." Instead, when you encounter a "..," you should figure out the path of the parent directory by using functions like *strrpos* and *substr*.

CASE STUDY: INDEXER/SEARCHER—STEP 2

In this new step of our indexer, we are going to make our indexer more user-friendly. The last thing a user who wants to index files should need to do is have to open the script source file and modify a $path variable. Instead, use a form.

The other improvement is to make our indexer more flexible, to expedite the indexing of local files. Our indexer will have to accept either regular .htm or .html files (in which case the indexer will do the same as in step 1) or actual folder names. First, if you wish to make your indexer work perfectly well, make sure that you can handle paths written with forward slashes (/), backslashes (\), and in case of folders, paths that either do or do not contain a "closing" slash at the end.

If the input received is a folder, find all the .htm and .html inside that folder and use your indexer on those files. However, if the provided path is a folder, and that folder contains other directories, you should enter those new directories and do the same work. Basically you need to traverse the entire directory structure rooted at the path provided as a parameter, and index every single .htm and .html file. Don't forget to ignore nonhtml files like .php, .mp3, and .zip, as they would probably crash your indexer. To make matters clearer, here is an example of directory structure:

```
┌FolderPassedThroughForm
├file.htm
├──┬aFolder
│  ├┐moreFolders
│  │ ├──morefile.html
│  │ └──script.php
│  └work.pdf
├otherfile.html
├music.mp3
└─┐anotherFolder
  └more.htm
```

In this example, if the form provides *FolderPassedThroughForm* as the initial folder, your indexer should index and display all the information of the files file.htm, morefile.html, otherfile.html, and more.htm; ignoring all the other items. Try to display the full path of each file indexed, as this will help you out on the next step.

10

Making Cleaner Code and Output

CLEANING UP YOUR CODE

One of the drawbacks of embedding HTML and PHP is that it makes code look quite messy. It is also pretty easy to get confused on where HTML ends and PHP starts. If we manage to avoid writing HTML inside PHP code, and if we avoid writing PHP code around regular HTML tags, we can have code that is much easier to read. The problem that this will cause is that it will be more complicated to implement the scripts.

To face this challenge, we will use something called *templates*, and more particularly, a class called FastTemplate. There are many different template options, but I have been using FastTemplate for many years and it is fast and efficient to use. The idea behind templates will be to have pieces of HTML in a small file that will be used as puzzle pieces to finish our Webpages. Each little HTML piece will be called a *template file*, and might contain areas that we will manage to change from our PHP code. Just imagine those dynamic sections as if they were "template variables."

What You Need

The first thing you need is to make sure that you have downloaded the include file. You can see the entire code in Appendix D, and you may download it from the companion Website (the file is called class.FastTemplate.zip).

Web Application Design and Implementation: Apache 2, PHP5, MySQL, JavaScript, and Linux/UNIX, by Steven A. Gabarró
Copyright © 2007 by John Wiley & Sons, Inc.

Note that this version is a debugged version of the standard one you can find online. When I tested the class with the newer versions of PHP, I realized that there were many notices due to outdated writing. I corrected those errors, and the class now works flawlessly with PHP 5.1.2. Extract the zip file in your desired folder (e.g., a folder ./include/ inside your document root), open up the file, and find the variable $WIN32 (it should be around the first few lines of code). If you are running your server on a Windows system, make sure that the variable is set to TRUE. If you are running a UNIX/Linux server, make sure that it's equal to FALSE.

How to Use It?—HTML Side

Your templates should be small sections of HTML code that you want to be able to combine and reuse. For example, you could have a file "tablerow3. html" that would allow you to create a row on a table with three columns. Any area that should be dynamically changed by PHP should contain a "template variable." Template variables should be a word made up of uppercase letters, digits, or the character underscore, and surrounded by curly braces. For example, *{ITEM_1}* is a valid "template variable" name. If we want to have a template to create rows on a table containing three columns, but don't know what each column will contain, we could have the following template file:

```
<TR>
  <TD>{CELL_1}</TD>
  <TD>{CELL_2}</TD>
  <TD>{CELL_3}</TD>
</TR>
```

You could have another file called "mainpage.html" that would contain the table definition in which the rows would be inserted. It could be something like this:

```
<HTML><HEAD></HEAD><BODY>
<TABLE>
{ROWS}
</TABLE>
</BODY></HTML>
```

The most important thing to remember is to place all template files in the same folder. Try to think in terms of reusability and do not be afraid to break your standard page into many different template files. Think that the more template files with "template variables," the more flexibility you will have when building your final output.

How to Use It?—PHP Side

The first thing to do in your PHP is to include the file you just configured with the *include* function. For example, your first line could be *include("./include/class.FastTemplate.php");*

Then you will need to create an object of the class FastTemplate and use some of its methods to set up your final page.

To create a FastTemplate object, decide on its name (e.g., $tpl) and use the FastTemplate constructor, by providing the path to the template files. For example, if your template files are in ./templates/, you would write

$tpl = new FastTemplate("./templates/");

The basic methods needed to use templates are *define*, *assign*, *parse*, and *FastPrint*. *Define* and *FastPrint* will be used only once per page, whereas *assign* and *parse* might occur a variable amount of times, depending on the number of "template variables" used.

The define method takes an associative array in which the elements are the name of the template files to use and their keys are abbreviations of those pages. Choose easy-to-remember names for the keys, as you will refer to the templates through those abbreviations. For example, if we needed to use the files mainpage.html and tablerow3.html, you would write

$tpl->define(array("main"=>"mainpage.html",
"row"=>"tablerow3.html"));

The next step is to use *assign* to set up all the template variables of the template file that we wish to parse. Simply call the *assign* method with the name of the variable you want to set up and the value you want to assign to it. This information will be saved inside the template object and used when you parse a file (see next paragraph). For example, to set up my template variable *{CELL_1}*, I would write

$tpl->assign("CELL_1", $value);

Note that using *assign* on a template variable that was already assigned will overwrite the previous value of that template variable.

Once all the variables of a template file have been set, you may parse the file. Parsing the file means going through the template file, replacing all template variables found with their appropriate values, and storing the final parsed string (file with proper values) in a new template variable to be used later. There are two ways of doing this. The first, and usual way, is to call the *parse* method with the name of a variable that will hold the result of the parsing, and the abbreviation of the file to parse. For example, if we wanted to parse tablerow3.html after we assigned all three cells, you would do

$tpl->parse("ROWS", "row");

The first parameter is usually an existent template variable, particularly, the name of the template variable where you will insert the parsed file. This way of parsing is similar to assign, as it will overwrite the template variable provided as the first parameter on each call.

The other way to parse a file is to use the "append" parsing. The point of the append version is to concatenate successive parsings of the same file (with different data) into a single variable. For example, if our tablerow3.html is supposed to help us build a full table, we will most likely need more than a single row. If we used the regular *parse*, we would be able to have only a single row. In order to use the append method, simply place a period sign (.) immediatly before the name of the file abbreviation. The way you would proceed is to first set up all variables of tablerow3.html, then parse the file doing

$$\$tpl\text{-}>parse("ROWS", ".row");$$

If it is the first time you call this parse, a new template variable *ROWS* would be set up containing the parsing of *row*. Each additional call of the same line will add the result of a new parsing right after the previous content of *ROWS*. Between each call of parse, be sure to reassign the template variables of the parsed file so that each row has the appropriate information, rather than all rows holding the same information. Again, remember that parsing will technically do an assign of a template variable.

Once you have parsed, from the inside out, all the template files needed to create your final output (including the main page), use the method *Fast-Print* by doing

$$\$tpl\text{-}>FastPrint();$$

This method will find the result of the last parsing done and will output the entire string contained in that variable.

Here is an example that would create our dropdown menu with the list of states assuming that we have the variable *$states* containing the associative array explained in Chapter 6. To keep it simple, we will assume that the variable is in an include file *states.php*. I will provide, in order, the code for mainbody.html (main page), option.html (containing a single option line), and templates.php that will do all the work:

```
<HTML>
<HEAD><TITLE>Template example</TITLE>
</HEAD>
<BODY>
  <FORM action=nopage.php method=post>
  <SELECT name=select>
    {OPTIONS}
  </SELECT>
```

```
<INPUT type=submit value=GO>
</FORM>
</BODY>
</HTML>
```

```
<option value="{VALUE}">{NAME}
```

```
<?PHP
  include("./include/states.php");
  include("./include/class.FastTemplate.php");
  $tpl = new FastTemplate("./TEMPLATES");
  $tpl->define(array("page" => "mainbody.html",
      "option" => "option.html"));
    foreach ($states as $k=>$e)
    {
      $tpl->assign("VALUE",$k);
      $tpl->assign("NAME",$e);
      $tpl->parse("OPTIONS",".option"); //We use append
    }
    $tpl->parse("OPTIONS","page");
  /* This parse parses the final page once all options
have been set up. Since the result of this parse will
be printed out and not really used inside any file, and
since the OPTIONS variable will not be needed any
further after the parsing of mainbody.html, I store the
result in the last variable I used (in this case
OPTIONS). I do this to avoid creating an extra entry,
and waste memory space. Technically on the last parsing
the name provided on first parameter is not important.
Realize that we do not need to append either, as we
need only one main body. */
    $tpl->FastPrint();
  ?>
```

CLEANING UP YOUR OUTPUT

To this point, we have been using boring black and white pages, with all settings to default. It is time to bring up some life in our pages, by making a cleaner output.

The first method, which is considered deprecated and poor programming practice, is to use the HTML *<FONT>* ... *</FONT>* tag. This tag allows you to specify the font, size, color, and many other cosmetic settings for a block of text. Since this tag should not be used, I will not waste time discussing it further.

The way you should set up the aspect of your pages should always be through Style Sheets. These style sheets can be defined inside the header of your HTML files, or even better, saved inside style sheet files called Cascading Style Sheets (or *.css* files). We will, of course, concentrate on the latter.

The CSS File

A CSS file is a file that defines categories of input that will have a specific look. It is possible to define properties for any link that HTML accepts, and you may also create independent styles that will be able to attach to any block of data you wish to use. The properties specified in the CSS file define the sizes, fonts, decorations, colors, and many other aspect properties. The list of valid attributes is way too large for me to show in its entirety all here, but it is pretty easy to understand the point of each attribute. You can find an exhaustive list on http://www.pageresource.com/dhtml/cssprops.htm. (Note that CSS files should start with *<!--* and finish with *-->*.)

The way the contents of a CSS file works is quite simple; you only need to write the name of the tag that you wish to change (e.g., the H1 tag) followed by a group of properties between curly braces. Each property is written as *property: value;*.

Some tags, such as links, have several states, and it is possible to have a different aspect for each state. The main states of a link are "link" for regular state, "visited" for a link that has been visited, "hover" for a link that has the cursor placed on top of it, and "active" for a link that refers to a page that is currently opened in a different frame or window. To specify the state you want to set up, write the name of the tag (in our case *A*) followed by a colon and the state (style sheet example will be presented following the next paragraph).

Not only is it possible to create styles for existing tags; you may also define your own classes that can be applied to anything. So, for example, instead of defining a style for H1, one for H2, or one for TD, you can have a class "myclass" and use it on a link, a cell, a paragraph, or pretty much anywhere. To create your class, instead of writing the name of a tag, write the name that you want to give to your class preceded by a period (.). Here is a style sheet example that I actually use systematically in my basic pages:

```
<!--
A:link
  { font-size: 12pt;
    font-weight: bold;
    text-decoration: none;
    color: 000000; }
A:visited
  { font-size: 12pt;
    font-weight: bold;
    text-decoration: none; color: 000000;}
```

```
A:hover
  { font-size: 12pt;
    font-weight: bold;
    text-decoration: none; color: red;}
A:active
  { font-size: 12pt;
    font-weight: bold;
    text-decoration: underline; color: 000000;}
BODY
  { font-size: 12pt;
    font-family: Verdana, Arial, Helvetica, sans-serif }
table
  { font-size: 12pt;
    font-family: Verdana, Arial, Helvetica, sans-serif }
H1
  {color: darkblue;
  font-size: 18pt;
  margin-top: 1pt;
  margin-bottom: 2pt;
  margin-left: 1pt;
  margin-right: 1pt;
  font-family: Verdana, Arial, Helvetica, sans-serif;
}
H2
  { color: black;
    font-size: 16pt;
    font-family: Arial Narrow, Arial, Helvetica, sans-
serif }
H3, H4
  { font-size: 14pt;
    font-weight: bold;
    font-family: Verdana, Arial, Helvetica, sans-serif }
H5
  { font-size: 12pt;
    font-weight: bold;
    font-family: Verdana, Arial, Helvetica, sans-serif }
.myclass {
  font-size: 30pt;
  letter-spacing: 10;
  font-weight: bold;
  font-variant: small-caps;
  color: Yellow;
  background-color: Red;
}
-->
```

Some of the main features of my style sheet, and something that I usually have in all my pages, is nonunderlined links. I personally dislike seeing a link as a typical blue underlined text. Instead, my links simply have the same look as regular text with the only difference that they are in boldface. To let the user know that they are links, I use the hover state of the link and use flashy colors like red; that way, when the user passes the mouse over the link, its appearance will change, capturing the attention of the user. I do have under-lined links, but only when the page referred to by the link is active. Note that colors can be written in hexadecimal, providing a RGB color (red-green-blue), or by simply writing the name of the color.

I also included a .myclass style to show how to create your own class. This class in particular is a silly one that will show up text with the colors of the Spanish flag (red and yellow). I also added humorous attributes such as font_variant, letter_spacing, and background_color.

How to use the style sheet? The first thing to do is to link to the style sheet in your HTML file. Simply insert the following line of HTML inside the *<HEAD>...</HEAD>* section:

<link rel=stylesheet href="styles/mystyle.css" type=text/css>

Of course, don't forget to change the *href* parameter to hold the path to your style sheet file.

The next step is to use the actual styles that are in the CSS file. If you defined a style for a standard tag, simply use the tag, and the style will be applied auto-matically (as long as you are already linked to the style sheet). If you created your own class and you wish to apply it to any tag, simply add the attribute *class* to the tag you wish to change, followed by the name of the class (without the period sign). So, for example, if I want a link to use *myclass*, I would use

```
<A HREF="blabla.html" class="myclass"> . . . </A>
```

If you want to apply your class to a section of your HTML without separating that portion as a link, paragraph, or other "visible" container, you can use the *<DIV>...</DIV>* tag, which will cause your portion of HTML code to be "divided" from the rest of the HTML. This will be very useful when we do some DHTML, as it will allow us to move entire sections around our pages. Of course, you still need to use the *class* attribute, as in this example:

```
Regular text and <DIV class=myclass>funky text!</DIV>.
So easy!
```

Useful Tools

If you are a lucky user of Macromedia's HomeSite software, you have the opportunity to use a program called TopStyle, which ships with HomeSite.

TopStyle is an excellent tool for creating style sheets; it shows all possible attributes on a menu at the right side of the program. It also provides a preview window where you can see what your styles look like while you write them. Please note that I sincerely like the product in question and am not trying to advertise anything.

ASSIGNMENT

Now that you know how to use templates and styles, try applying all that you have learned in this chapter on the file browser that you have been working on in the previous chapters. This means no *<FONT>* tags, no background properties in the *<BODY>* tag, and, of course, not a single HTML tag in your PHP and no PHP inside files containing HTML.

11

Using Databases

OVERVIEW

Now that we are familiar with PHP, it is time to move on to databases, so we can start designing database-driven Websites. This chapter will cover database principles, as well as MySQL basics. The following chapter will be devoted to mixing PHP and MySQL before we move on to JavaScript.

DATABASE BASICS

As the word indicates, a *database* is basically a base of data, or, if you prefer, a set of data with a structure that is similar to real-life situations. It allows you to store any type of information you need, and it can be accessed by any user with the proper rights.

The Entity Relationship Model

An *entity* is a real-life object, such as, for example, "Steven Gabarró," or a receipt for a purchase made on a specific date in a specific store. An *entity type* defines a group of entities with the same characteristics like "workers" or "receipts." Basically, an entity is to an entity type what an object is to a class. An entity is a specific instance of an entity type. Entities can be related

Web Application Design and Implementation: Apache 2, PHP5, MySQL, JavaScript, and Linux/UNIX, by Steven A. Gabarró

FIGURE 11.1 *Entity relationship model.*

through relationships usually named as actions. Each entity type has a set of *attributes* that help define different entities at the same time. For example, name and age would be attributes of the entity type "workers."

When an entity can be identified individually with a single attribute or a small set of attributes, these are considered *index keys*. If there is more than one index key, one of them has to be set as a *primary index key*. If an entity cannot be identified through its own attributes, and if it needs a relation with another entity, it is called a *weak entity*. Any relationship to a weak entity is called a *weak relationship*.

Relationships between entities have a complexity of either 1:1, 1:*n* (or *n*:1), or *n*:*m*. If you have a 1:1 relationship between an *Entity1* and *Entity2*, this means that for each entity of the type *Entity1* there will be a single entity of type *Entity2* related to it and vice versa. A relationship of 1:*n* would mean that an entity of type *Entity1* can have *n* associated entities of type *Entity2*, but a single element of *Entity2* can be associated with only a single item of *Entity1*. The relationship *n*:1 is the reverse of 1:*n*. Finally, a relationship *n*:*m* means that an item of *Entity1* can be related to many items of *Entity2*, and an item of *Entity2* can be related to many items of *Entity1*.

An example of an entity relationship model is shown in Figure 11.1.

More Practical Examples

Let us imagine that you are creating a database to hold the exams you give in a class, as well as the grades of all students. You will need a table *students* that will contain all students with attributes such as *id_student, name, surname,* and *email.* Then you need a table *tests* to hold all tests, although if our tests do not have the same number of questions, it is not a good idea to include the actual questions in the table containing the actual tests. Instead, we will just store *id_test, title,* and *date.* Taking advantage of *id_test,* we will have a table *question_in_test* with the questions used in each test. This could make us think of something interesting: What if a teacher likes to reuse some questions in different tests? Is it a good idea to hold the same full string with the question as two separate entries? Well, I recommend that you *always* avoid redundancies, and storing two full questions with exactly the same data except the *id* of the test seems redundant. Therefore, we will use a separate table *questions* that will contain *id_question, question,* and *answer.* The id of the questions will be used in the table *question_in_test* along with an *id_test* referring to the test it was asked in; *number,* to know in which order it was asked for the test; *value,* indicating the number of points it is worth for that test; and *id_qt,* which will be a primary automatically incremented dull key used to refer to a specific question of a specific test. Finally, we need to hold the grades of each student, which might as well be a grade per question. We will have a table *grade_per_question* with *id_gq* (dull key), *id_student* (the student that took the test), *id_qt* (reference to a question of a test from the *question_in_test* table), and *grade.* Technically we could create an additional table with the grades for a full test per student, but since it is possible to calculate it from data held in other tables, it is not necessary. The final list of tables (and attributes) we have is as follows:

- *students:* id_student, name, surname, email
- *tests:* id_test, title, date
- *questions:* id_question, question, answer
- *question_in_test:* id_qt, id_question, id_test, number, value
- *grade_per_question:* id_gq, id_qt, id_student, grade

Now we need to determine the relationships between the tables. First we have the table *students* that holds a piece of information (id_student) required in the table *grade_per_question*. Each student can have many graded questions, but each entity in grade_per_question can refer to only a single student. Therefore the relationship from *students* to *grade_per_question* is 1:*n*. The table *test* holds id_test, needed in *question_in_test*. Each test can have multiple questions, but an entity in *question_in_test* can refer to only a single test; therefore the relationship from *test* to *question_in_test* is 1:*n*. The table *questions* contains id_question, used in *question_in_test*. Each question can be used in many tests, but each entity inside *question_in_test* can refer to only a single question, so the relationship from *questions* to *question_in_test* is also 1:*n*. The table *question_in_test* contains id_qt, used in *grade_per_question*. A question in a test can have a grade for many students, but an entity inside *grade_per_question* can refer to only a specific question in a specific test; therefore the relationship from *question_in_test* to *grade_per_question* is again 1:*n*. The table *question_in_test* has references to id_question and id_test, but we already took care of the relationships that these references entail. Finally, the table *grade_per_question* has already been assigned all needed relationships. In Figure 11.2 you will see a simplified diagram for this database.

Typical Sources of Error

When working with databases, you should always make sure that all the information is consistent. For example, if we have the database defined in the previous database and you insert an entry in the table *question_in_test,* you should make sure that it refers to the right test with a proper *id_test* and to the right question, with the proper *id_question.* You should systematically check all data inserting when the entity you insert depends on data already in the database.

To avoid problems, and to enhance security, I personally always use a dull key called *id_* followed by the name of the table. I always make that key primary, and autoincremented (automatically incremented), so I do not need to worry about specifying its value when inserting elements. Fields like *email* should always be set as *UNIQUE* to avoid problems. The reason why dull keys help protect your database is that all the information you need to search for a specific entry in any table is simply a number, so if you send that information through pages, anyone trying to hack on your site will see only a number, without knowing what it means. For example, if you are sending a reference to a student through the GET method in PHP, it is much safer to see something like *script.php?id=4* instead of *script.php?student=sgabarro.*

Simplifying the Diagrams

Something I have realized after many years of designing databases is the tediousness of always adding the name of a relationship as well as its type. After you gain some experience understanding relationships, their types become pretty obvious with a simple glance at the tables linked by the relationship. Therefore, I do not write the relationship name or its type. To show the dependences between tables, such as, for example, the dependence of our table *grade_per_question* on the tables *students* and *question_in_test,* I use an arrow pointing from the depending table (let's call this the "primary" table, or table 1) to the dependent table (the "secondary" table, or table 2). This generally means that all my relationships have an arrow on the end of the line that would have corresponded to a "1" in complexity terms. For example, a relationship of 1:1 would be represented with a double-sided (double-barbed) arrow, a relationship of 1:*n* will be expressed by an arrow going from the *n* to the "1," and a relationship of *n:m* will not be expressed by an arrow. A simplified version of our previous database diagram is shown in Figure 11.2.

USING MySQL

MySQL is a database programming language based on the standard ANSI SQL92 but contains several modifications. For example, nested SELECTs were not available in MySQL until version 4.1; MySQL does not support *SELECT . . . INTO TABLE* that the standard SQL accepts; and views became accessible only in version 5.0.1. You probably wonder what all this means.

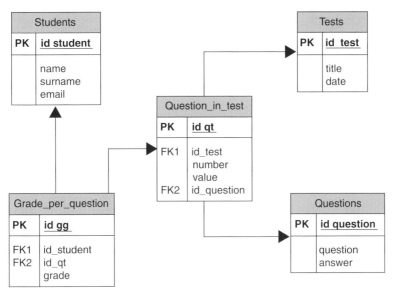

FIGURE 11.2 *Database structure for student grade example.*

Well, no need to know since we do not plan to go that far into MySQL for you to need those features.

MySQL also includes extra features that were not in the standard SQL, such as proper string comparisons, regular expressions, arithmetic on dates, and many other things that again we will not see as we can do all of it with PHP and JavaScript.

MySQL Syntax

Before we go into MySQL syntax, I would like to explain some standard notations that I will use to explain the different commands. Whenever you see a group of text between square brackets in a syntax line (e.g., [UNSIGNED]), this means that the element between brackets is optional and you may use it or not use it depending on what you are trying to achieve.

A group of elements separated by the pipe sign "|" and surrounded by curly braces { } implies a choice. Simply read the pipe as "or"; for example, if you see "{integer | real | string}," this means that the whole block between the opening and closing brace must be replaced by either the word *integer, real,* or *string,* and that exactly one of those blocks must be used, no more, no less. You may also see the pipe sign separating options inside a set of square brackets, meaning a choice between the different options, so that only one option maximum can be used. For example, if you see "[FIRST | AFTER position]," this means that you can write *FIRST, AFTER position* or simply nothing at all.

Words in capital letters (uppercase) will be key syntax words, whereas lowercase words will be used to show what type of information is expected. In the previous example, *position* should be a number representing a position.

Finally, if you see a comma followed by three period signs (, . . .) (ellipses), this means that the element placed before the comma can be repeated as many times as needed.

Data Types

When using MySQL you can use a string by simply surrounding a piece of text with either double or single quotes. Inside a string you may use any of the following special characters: \0 for an ASCII 0 (NULL) character, \' for a single-quote character, \" for a double-quote character, \b for a backspace character, \n for a new-line character, \r for a carriage return character, \t for a tab(ulation) character, \% for the percentage character, and _ for the underscore character. You may also use floating-point numbers (e.g., –12.345), integers (e.g., 678), as well as hexadecimal numbers (e.g., 3FB7A). Finally you may use the *NULL* value to represent the lack of data.

Any name you use to define the structure of your database has a maximum size. For instance, database names, table names, and column (or attribute) names cannot exceed 64 characters. If you wish to use a longer name, you may use aliases, which allow a maximum of 255 characters.

Assuming that you have a database called *classgrades* with the previous example of database structure (see Figure 11.2), you could access a student name by doing *name* if you are inside the table *student, student.name* if you are in the *classgrades* database, but not accessing the table *student,* or simply *classgrades.student.name* if you want to access that field from a different database on the same server. For Web projects you will most likely have only one database with many tables, which will simplify your work.

You may create variables in MySQL using the SET instruction to declare the variable, and *:=* to assign an expression to it. You may declare a variable as *integer, real,* or *string,* and might declare many variables with a single SET instruction. All MySQL variables start with the character @. Here is an example:

> *SET @var1 = integer, @var2 = real, @var3 = string;*
> *@var1 := 4;*

I have never used MySQL variables, as I can accomplish the same functionality with PHP in a much faster and easier way.

MySQL Numeric Data Types

When creating a table in MySQL it is important to know the type you wish to use for each attribute. Here is the list of different usable types, with the explanation of what they mean. You might also see *[U]*, meaning that the type can be set as *UNSIGNED* or *[Z]*, meaning that the type can be set as *ZEROFILL* (indicating that the number will be filled with zeros to the left of the number until all the allowed digits are used). If you see *[(M)]* or *[(M,D)]*, this means that you may specify the maximum number of digits [e.g., *(5)*] or the number of digits for the integer and fractional part of a number in the case of nonintegers [e.g., *(5,2)* would allow five digits before the decimal point and two after]:

- *TINYINT [(M)][U][Z]*—smallest integer number accepted in MySQL: –128 to 127 or 0 to 255 in case of unsigned numbers.
- *BIT*—same as a *TINYINT(1)* for any version of MySQL up to and including 4.1.
- *BOOLEAN or BOOL*—same as *TINYINT(1)*. A value of 0 is considered false; nonzero values are considered true.
- *SMALLINT [(M)][U][Z]*—a small integer between –32,768 and 32,767 in signed numbers and 0 to 65535 for unsigned numbers.
- *MEDIUMINT [(M)][U][Z]*—a medium integer between –8,388,608 and 8,388,607 for signed numbers, and 0 to 16,777,215 for unsigned.
- *INTEGER [(M)][U][Z]*—a regular integer ranging from –2,147,483,648 to 2,147,483,647 and 0 to 4,294,967,295 for unsigned.
- *INT [(M)][U][Z]*—same as *INTEGER*.
- *BIGINT [(M)][U][Z]*—a big integer, ranging from –9,223,372,036,854, 775,808 to 9,223,372,036,854,775,807 and 0 to 18,446,744,073,709,551,615 for unsigned numbers.
- *FLOAT [(M,D)][U][Z]*—a small floating-point number with values ranging from –3.402823466E+38 to –1.175494351E-38, 0, and 1.175494351E-38 to 3.402823466E+38 according to IEEE standard.
- *DOUBLE [(M,D)][U][Z]*—normal-size floating-point number. Allowable values range from –1.7976931348623157E+308 to – 2.2250738585072014E-308, 0, and 20.2250738585072014E-308 to 1.7967931348623157E+308.
- *DECIMAL [(M[,D])][U][Z]*—unpacked fixed-point number. The number is actually stored as a string, using one character for each digit.

Date and Time Data Types

The following types are used to store dates and times:

- *DATE*—used to store any date between "1000-01-01" and "9999-12-31" with the format YYYY-MM-DD (Y for year digit, M for month digit, and D for day digit)

- *DATETIME*—used to store both date and time. The supported range is "1000-01-01 00:00:00" to "9999-12-31 23:59:59." As you can see, the format is YYYY-MM-DD HH:MM:SS.
- *TIMESTAMP [(M)]*—used to store a timestamp, ranging from "1970-01-01 00:00:00" to partway through the year 2037.
- *TIME*—used to store a time ranging from −838:59:59 to 838:59:59.
- *YEAR [(2|4)]*—stores a year in either two- or four-digit format.

String Data Types

Here are the main types that can be used in MySQL to store strings:

- *CHAR(M) [BINARY]*—used to store a string of a specific number of characters (given by M). Note that, for example, a *CHAR(10)* will always use 10 characters in memory, regardless of how many characters you actually need.
- *VARCHAR(M) [BINARY]*—variable-length string. The main difference between a VARCHAR and a CHAR is that in a CHAR the max (maximum) size represents the number of characters used in memory at any time whereas the VARCHAR uses only the exact amount of characters needed, up to the max size. For example, storing "bla" in a *VARCHAR(30)* will not use up 30 characters in memory, but only 3 as needed.
- *TINYBLOB*—a block of data that can hold up to 255 bytes.
- *TINYTEXT*—like a TINYBLOB but holds text data rather than a blob.
- *BLOB* and *TEXT*—bigger blob and text fields than can hold up to 65,535 bytes of binary data (BLOB) or text data (TEXT).
- *MEDIUMBLOB* and *MEDIUMTEXT*—blob and text of up to 16,777,215 bytes or characters.
- *LONGBLOB* and *LONGTEXT*—blob and text of up to 4,294,967,295 bytes [4 GB (gigabytes)] of data.
- *ENUM('value1', 'value2', ...)*—an enumeration. A string object that can have only one value, chosen from the list of values 'value1', 'value2', ..., NULL, or the special ' ' error value. An ENUM can have up to 65,535 distinct values. Data are internally stored as integers.
- *SET('value1', 'value2', ...)*—a set is a string object that can have zero or more values, each of which must be chosen from the list of values 'value1', 'value2', ... A SET can have up to 64 members.

MySQL Operators

In MySQL you will find the traditional arithmetic operators such as +, −, *, and /. You can also use the pipe sign | for a binary or operation, the ampersand

& for binary AND operations, a double "less than" sign << to do a logical shift to the left, and a double "greater than" sign >> to do a logical shift to the right. If you wish to know how many bits there are in a number *n*, simply use *BIT_COUNT(n)*.

Logical operators can be *NOT*, or simply an exclamation point !, for the logical NOT (*!TRUE == FALSE*). You can use *OR*, or the double pipe ||; *AND* or the double ampersand &&.

MySQL Instructions

The following chapters explain the basics of the most important functions as far as Web programming goes. The explanations of some functions will be brief, as their actions will usually be done through PhpMyAdmin, rather than typing the actual SQL query. For the same reasons, I will not go in full depth of all the abilities of each one of the instructions; instead, I will limit discussion of each instruction to its most common use(s).

To create a database, use *CREATE DATABASE name*. To delete the database (along with all its contents), use *DROP DATABASE [IF EXISTS] name*. The option *IF EXISTS* is just an extra flag that you can put to avoid errors in case the name provided does not correspond to an actual database on the server. To force the use of a database, write *USE DATABASE name.*

The code used to create a table in a database is *CREATE [TEMPO-RARY] TABLE [IF NOT EXISTS] table_name [(create_definition1, create_definition2, . . .)]*. When creating a table it is possible to set up its contents through the create definitions. Each one of them can be either one of these:

- *attribute_name type [NOT NULL | NULL][DEFAULT default_value] [AUTO_INCREMENT][PRIMARY KEY][reference_definition]*— used to define a new field in the table
- *PRIMARY KEY (key_column_name, . . .)*—used to specify the fields that will act as primary key
- *UNIQUE (column_name, . . .)*—used to specify which fields are unique

For example, to create the *student* table of the earlier example, assuming that the email address has to be unique, you would write

```
CREATE TABLE 'student' (
  'id_student' SMALLINT UNSIGNED NOT NULL
AUTO_INCREMENT,
  'name' VARCHAR(10) NOT NULL,
  'surname' VARCHAR(20) NOT NULL,
  'email' VARCHAR(30) NOT NULL,
  PRIMARY KEY ('id_student'),
  UNIQUE ('email')
) TYPE = MYISAM COMMENT = 'Super table';
```

The *TYPE* field at the end is not really necessary, but you should include it to force the type of table you are creating. The *COMMENT* field is just an example of how you would insert a comment for a created table.

If you need to alter an already existing table, you may do it by writing *ALTER [IGNORE] TABLE table_name alter_specs [, alter_specs2, . . .]*. The alter_specs can be any of the following:

- *ADD COLUMN create_definition [FIRST | AFTER column_name]*— used to add a new attribute. The create_definition uses the same syntax as with the *CREATE* instruction.
- *ADD PRIMARY KEY (col_name, . . .)*—makes the fields placed between parentheses a primary key of the table.
- *ADD UNIQUE (col_name, . . .)*—sets the fields placed between parentheses as unique.
- *ALTER [COLUMN] col_name {SET DEFAULT default_value | DROP DEFAULT}*—used to set a default value for a field or to remove the current default value.
- *CHANGE [COLUMN] old_name create_definition*—replaces the column *old_name* with the column defined by the *create_definition*.
- *MODIFY [COLUMN] create_definition*—similar to *CHANGE* but will try to figure out the column to be modified through the *create_definition*.
- *DROP [COLUMN] name*—removes an entire column.
- *DROP PRIMARY KEY*—unsets all primary keys.
- *RENAME [AS] new_name*—renames a table.

All these instructions allow you to prepare the database for its use, and even though you will most likely do the same job through PhpMyAdmin without needing to understand the syntax, it is very useful to understand the queries so that you may create an installation script that would set up the database with the proper structure needed for your scripts to work.

The two operations we will do most often through PHP scripts are insertions and searches in the database. In order to insert an element in a table, there are three possible syntaxes:

- *INSERT [LOW_PRIORITY | DELAYED | HIGH_PRIORITY] [INTO] table_name [(col_name, col_name2, . . .)] VALUES (expression1, expression2, . . .) [ON DUPLICATE KEY UPDATE col_name= expression, . . .]*. This is my personal favorite. Simply use the table name followed by the fields for which you wish to specify a value. For example, you could skip values that are autoincremented, and values with a default value if you wish to use that same default value. Finally, after the word *VALUES* you write the expressions that you wish to store in the specified fields in the same order that you wrote the field names.

- *INSERT [LOW_PRIORITY | DELAYED | HIGH_PRIORITY] [INTO] table_name [(col_name, col_name, . . .)] SELECT . . . [ON DUPLICATE KEY UPDATE col_name=expression, . . .].* This is used whenever the insertion depends on a selection (see next section).
- *INSERT [LOW_PRIORITY | DELAYED | HIGH_PRIORITY] [INTO] table_name SET col_name=expression, col_name2=expression2, . . . [ON DUPLICATE KEY UPDATE col_name=expression, . . .].* This is similar to the first case but with a slightly different syntax.

For example, to insert a new user in our previous example, we could write

> *INSERT INTO students (name, surname, email) VALUES ('Steven', 'Gabarró', 'sgabarro@stevens.edu');*

The *ON DUPLICATE KEY UPDATE . . .* section allows you to update the fields of existing entries if you attempt to input an entry with a conflicting key or unique field. For example, in our case, the field *email* is UNIQUE, so if I attempt to insert a new entry with the same email address (sgabarro@ stevens.edu), the MySQL server will find the field that contained that unique field and update the entry by looking at the series of assignments placed after the *ON DUPLICATE . . .*

If you are trying to update an entire field but, for example, preserving the primary key, you can use *REPLACE*, which works exactly the same way as *INSERT*, except that it does not accept the *ON DUPLICATE KEY UPDATE* field. Instead, in case of a duplicate field, the conflicting entry is removed and replaced with the new entry. For example, if the *id_student* for the entry containing my name were 5 and I wanted to update my email address, I could do

> *REPLACE INTO students (id_student, email) VALUES (5, 'sgabarro@cs.stevens.edu');*

Another final way to update a series of entries is to use *UPDATE* with the following syntax:

UPDATE [LOW_PRIORITY] table_name SET col_name=expression1 [, col2=expr2, . . .] [WHERE where_condition] [ORDER BY col_name] [LIMIT row_count]

The way *UPDATE* works is simple; you provide a condition as part of the *where_condition* that will match all the elements you want to update, and it will change the specified columns for all the matches found. If you provide an *ORDER BY* statement, the updates will be done in the order of the sorted elements. Finally, the *row_count* is used as a limit and represents the maximum number of rows to update. If you do not provide a limit, all matches will be updated. Also, if you do not provide a *WHERE* statement, all entries in the table will be matched and updated (based on the limit). For example, assuming that we had an extra field *age* in my table *students*, we could decide to look at every student alphabetically ordered by their last names (surnames), and make the 10 first 20-year-old students in the list one year older by writing

> *UPDATE students SET age = age + 1 WHERE age*
> *= 20 ORDER BY surname LIMIT 10*

In order to delete an entry from a table, we use *DELETE [LOW_PRIORITY] FROM table_name [WHERE where_definition][ORDER BY column] [LIMIT rows]*. Skipping the *WHERE* section will match all the elements in the table and delete all the entries that the *LIMIT* allows you. For example, to delete the first 20 students using alphabetical order based on the surname, you would write

> *DELETE FROM students ORDER BY surname LIMIT 20*

Assuming that you already inserted data in your database, the operation you will use more often is called *SELECT*. A *SELECT* is used to look for information in one or more tables that matches specific criteria. The following displayed routine in bold, is the full syntax accepted for a *SELECT;* it may seem overwhelming, but as you will see in a later example, it is quite simple once you skip some of the optional sections. I will explain the important options that you might need and skip the rest, which is usually needed only in advanced database manipulation.

SELECT
  [ALL | DISTINCT | DISTINCTROW]
  [HIGH_PRIORITY]
  [STRAIGHT_JOIN]
  [SQL_SMALL_RESULT] [SQL_BIG_RESULT]
[SQL_BUFFER_RESULT]
  [SQL_CACHE | SQL NO_CACHE] [SQL_CALC_FOUND_ROWS]
select_expression, . . .
[FROM table_references
  [WHERE condition]
  [GROUP BY {col_name | expression | position}
    [ASC | DESC], . . . [WITH ROLLUP]]
  [HAVING where_condition]
  [ORDER BY {col_name | expr | position}
    [ASC | DESC], . . .]
  [LIMIT {[offset,] row_count | row_count OFFSET offset}]
  [PROCEDURE procedure name (argument list)]
  [INTO OUFILE 'file name' export_options | INTO DUMPFILE 'file name']
  [FOR UPDATE | LOCK IN SHARE MODE]]

Pretty scary, isn't it? ☺

To simplify this a bit, let me show you the options that I have personally used in the past; I will explain each of them. If you wish to learn what the others do, refer to http://dev.mysql.com/doc/refman/5.0/en/select.html:

SELECT select_expression [, select_expression2, . . .] FROM table_ reference1 [, table_reference2, . . .] [WHERE condition][GROUP BY col_name [ASC ⏐ DESC]] [HAVING where_condition] [ORDER BY col_name [ASC ⏐ DEC]] [LIMIT [offset,]count][INTO DUMPFILE 'exportfile']]

The *select_expressions* represent which data are being searched. Usually it is a series of attributes from the tables in which we are searching. If you wish to gather the information for all the fields in the tables searched, you can use the * (asterisk) symbol. Another useful tool when looking for data gathered from separate tables is to use aliases to the tables searched. For example, if you define an alias *t1* for the first table containing the data you are searching, and *t2* for the second table that you need (see next paragraph for table alias definition), you could write for example *SELECT t1.column1, t2.column2, . . .*

The table references are the list of tables in which to look for the information needed. When looking inside a single table, simply write its name, but if you are searching in different tables, it is preferable to provide them with an alias using the keyword *AS* so that the aliases can be used in the *select_ expression*. For example, you could have *SELECT t1.name, t2.salary FROM employee AS t1, info AS t2. . . .* This would create an alias *t1* to the table *employee*, and an alias *t2* to the table *info.*

The *where_condition* is the same type of expression as seen before. It is used to select the right matches that you need. For example, you could group an employee's name with that person's salary, extracted from tables *employee* and *info,* assuming that the name of the employee is the main identifier needed in the *info* table by doing *SELECT t1.name, t2.salary FROM employee AS t1, info AS t2 WHERE t1.name = t2.name.* Of course, we assume that both tables have a field *name.* This query will find all pairs of entries with the same name and return the value of the name field from the *employee* table and the *salary* field from the *info* field for each of those matches.

The *GROUP BY* section allows you to group results by a specific field. It is quite similar to *ORDER BY.* The options *ASC* and *DESC* mean "ascending order" and "descending order," respectively.

The option *HAVING* is quite similar to *WHERE* but runs at the end of the query, right on the set of values that were found owing to the *WHERE* definition. The *HAVING* field allows you to use functions, whereas *WHERE* does not.

ORDER BY is the regular sorting, as used in other instructions. Note that an *ORDER BY* statement can accept several table names that allow you to create several levels of ordering. For example, *ORDER BY surname, name ASC* would do a sorting of the data by surname, and if there were several entries with the same surname, those entries would be sorted by name.

The option *LIMIT* is a bit more flexible when using a *SELECT,* allowing you to not only specify how many elements to match but also know which is the first element to be considered. This is a really useful tool when you want to limit the number of results shown on a page, and facilitates the creation of multiple pages to show data. For example, in a commercial Website where you would sell several hundred products, you should avoid showing them all on the same page. Instead, you should split them into smaller groups, for example, 10 items per page. The standard in these cases is to have small numbers that represent the pages—for example, with page 1 showing elements 0–9, page 2 showing elements 10–19, and so on. This method could be implemented by calculating the *LIMIT* value by checking the current page. We come up with the formula *first_item = (page − 1) * 10.* Just to verify, the first item of page 4 would be the 31st entry (index 30) in the list of matches, and $(4 − 1) * 10 == 30$, so it is all good! This value represents the offset that should be followed by the amount of elements that we want to gather. For example, to view the 10 items on page 5, we would calculate the offset doing $(5 − 1) *$ $10 == 40$, and use a *LIMIT 40,10.*

Finally, *INTO DUMPFILE* allows dumping the results of the query in a file for its further processing. As a last example, let us imagine that we want to gather all the info on users with an *id* greater than 50 and save it in the file "results.txt." You could do

> *SELECT * FROM users WHERE id_user > 50 INTO DUMPFILE 'results.txt';*

Using Functions in MySQL

There are many useful functions in MySQL that allow advanced database programming directly through the SQL command prompt. Nevertheless, we have learned how to use PHP, and we will always access MySQL through PHP scripts. This means that it is *much* simpler for us to do the work directly in PHP and use the results of the PHP functions as input for our SQL queries.

12

Using PhpMyAdmin

OVERVIEW

PhpMyAdmin is probably the most useful and simple database management tool I have used. It allows the manipulation of a MySQL database, using PHP, through a very user-friendly interface. This short chapter will guide you through the steps of creating and setting up your database.

CREATING A DATABASE

The first thing you need to do when creating a database is to have its layout prepared. It is important to know exactly what the database will hold, what tables it will include, and what fields will define the tables. The next step is to create the actual database.

In PhpMyAdmin main page, you will see a text area such as that shown in Figure 12.1

In that field you should enter the name of the database you wish to create and then click on "create." If the database already exists, select it from the dropdown menu on the left frame. Once you have selected the database you wish to access (or created a new one), you will see its name appear on the left frame, along with the name of every table it contains.

Web Application Design and Implementation: Apache 2, PHP5, MySQL, JavaScript, and Linux/UNIX, by Steven A. Gabarró
Copyright © 2007 by John Wiley & Sons, Inc.

FIGURE 12.1 *PhpMyAdmin homepage.*

CREATING TABLES

Once you select a database and you see the list of tables on the left, you may click on a table name on the left menu to check the structure of that table. Clicking the icon to the left of the table name will show its contents. If there are no tables, you will see a screen like that shown in Figure 12.2.

The top menu gives access to *Structure* (to view the structure of the database), *SQL* (where you can type in your own SQL queries, or import a SQL file), *Export* (which allows you to export the structure and data of the database), *Query* (used to create queries through dropdown menus, when you are uncertain of SQL syntax), *Operations* (to copy the database, rename it, change its character set, etc.), and *Drop,* which deletes the database along with all the data it contains.

To create a new table, enter its name in the *Name* field, and the amount of attributes it will contain in the *Fields* attribute. You can always modify this later, but it is preferable to know the details beforehand. Each time you are in the database structure page, you have the possibility of creating a new table.

Once you select the number of fields for the new table, you will see a screen similar to the screenshot in Figure 12.3, with as many lines as number you provided for the *Fields* value. For each line you must insert (in this order) the name of the field (how you will refer to it in your scripts), its type (through the dropdown menu), its length (see chapter 11), its collation (just leave as default), any attributes (like UNSIGNED or UNSIGNED_ZEROFILL),

FIGURE 12.2 *Table creation page.*

FIGURE 12.3 *Filling in the details of a new table.*

FIGURE 12.4   *Database structure view.*

whether you wish to allow the field to accept being null or not, a default value (if any), whether it is an AUTO_INCREMENT field (ideal for ids) and, through the radio buttons, whether the field is a primary key, index key, or a unique or regular field. The last checkbox allows creation of a *full-text,* which is a way to group several fields together as one massive text field.

After you fill in all the details of your new table, you can insert some comments, and then submit it so that the table is created. You should see its name on the left frame menu, as in Figure 12.4.

ACCESSING AN EXISTING TABLE

Click on the name of the table you wish to view in the left menu. This will take you to the table menu (see Figure 12.5), where you can view the table structure, *Browse* the data in the table, send a *SQL* query, *Insert* new entries, *Export* the table and its contents, do several *Operations* on the table, *Empty* its contents, or *Drop* the entire table along with its data.

EXPORTING/IMPORTING A DATABASE STRUCTURE AND CONTENT

Usually phpMyAdmin is used to create the general database structure, leaving the elements' insertion to your own PHP scripts. Sometimes it is useful to create installation scripts that will use PHP to create the needed database

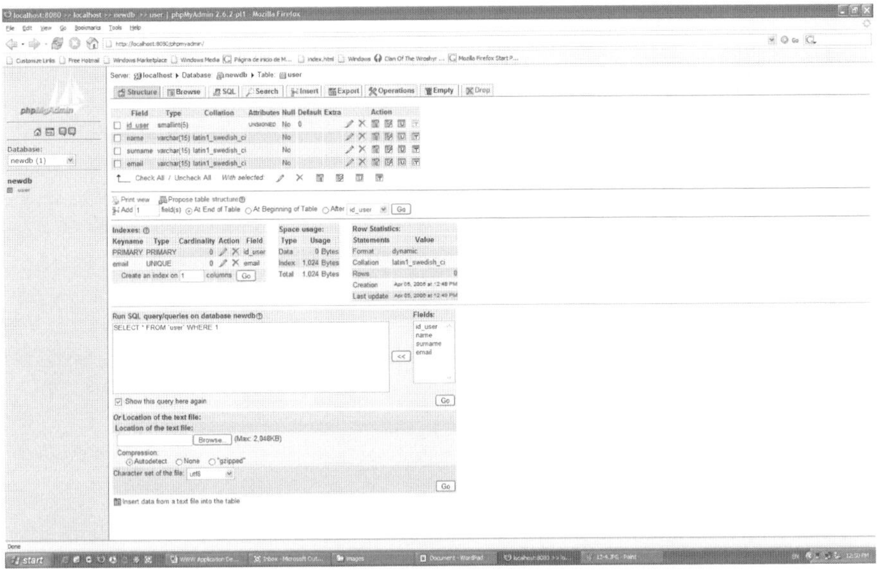

FIGURE 12.5 *Table structure view.*

and table structure in the database server. To do so, follow the directions in the next chapter to write a PHP script that will run all the needed SQL queries, such as "CREATE DB" or "CREATE TABLE."

Another way of setting up your database on another computer is to use the export/import feature. Select the database you wish to export from the drop-down menu on the left and select the *Export* tab (see Figure 12.6).

Once you are there, select the format to export to (SQL is usually the best choice, as it will create a simple text file with all the SQL queries that will create and populate your database). You may choose whether you wish to export the database structure, the data, or both, as well as setting up other options on the way the import will work. Finally, select the "Save as file" option so that you can save the export. If you don't select "Save as file," the actual export file will simply show up in your browser, rather than allowing you to download it. You may also choose to compress the file as a zip or gzip (I personally use gzip when exporting), to make the export file smaller. Note that exporting a database exports its contents, but not the database name, so you will need to create the database before you can import the structure.

Once the file is created and saved in your computer, transfer it to the server in which you wish to install your database. We will assume that you have installed phpMyAdmin in the destination computer. Create a database with the same name as your source database, and select the *SQL* option (third icon from left in the toolbar shown in Figure 12.7).

From there, click on the *Browse* button, select the export file you saved, and click on the lower *Go* button. The other *Go* button is used when you

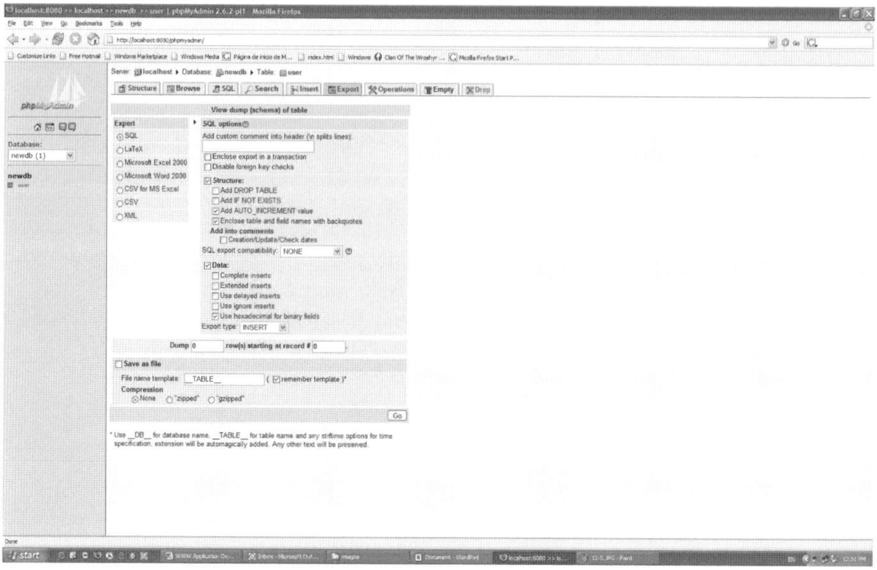

FIGURE 12.6 Export interface.

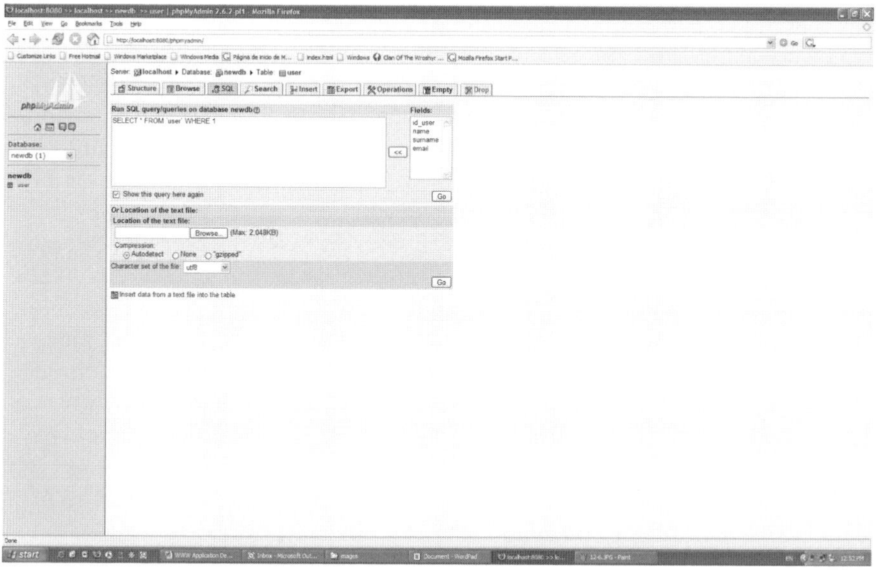

FIGURE 12.7 SQL queries interface, import page.

manually write your SQL queries. Make sure that the file is smaller than the size specified (2048 KB in my screenshot), or the operation might time out. If your file is larger, you can break it down into several small files and import them one by one.

ASSIGNMENT—FINAL PROJECT

When I teach this course, this is the point where I ask students to specify their idea for a final project. The reason I wait until I finish the basics of databases is because all database-driven Websites should be designed around the database, so it is important to have enough knowledge of database structures to come up with a proper database layout for the project. The main rules I enforce are:

- Create a team (minimum one person, maximum three or four, depending on the project). The harder the project, the more people I allow to work on it. Ideally I like to have projects of at least two students as it forces them to learn how to work together in teams.
- Start thinking of a final project idea; the project *must* be a database-driven Website written in PHP. I allow free choice of database (excluding MS Access) as the principles remain the same regardless of whether they decide to use MySQL, PostgreSQL, or other similar database. Typical projects include bulletin boards similar to phpBB, eBusiness Websites, image galleries, and online journals.
- Write a page describing the project, and who will be the team members. I require students to write the description in a single page to learn how to transmit important information in a small amount of text, going straight to the point.
- When students have no project ideas, I usually choose one for them, but I tend to suggest fairly complex projects such as email or FTP clients coded in PHP. This usually motivates students to use their imaginations and create Websites that they might use in the future.
- Finally, some JavaScript features must be added before the final presentation of the project.

Once the project proposal is submitted, it is the professor's decision to accept the project as is or to add features that seem are necessary. Once the project is approved, the student must take the project through three main phases:

1. First they need to come up with the database layout, which needs to be reviewed by the professor and approved.
2. About a week or two before the final presentation day, the students should go through what I call a "CEO" (chief executive officer) presentation.

This teaches some basic principles of real-world communication, based on the principle that CEOs will give you a maximum of 5 minutes to impress them. This is usually a fun role-playing chance, where the professor pretends to know nothing about Web technologies. The students must show the progress on their projects in exactly 5 minutes and convince the CEO that their project will be beneficial for the "fictitious" company that the CEO is representing. Of course, they must make sure that they can explain their projects in very simple words, avoiding sentences like "We will handle user authentication through sessions, storing the session ID in a cookie for further use." Instead, the presentation should emphasize the main functionalities of the project, as well as the appearance (CEOs will want it to look nice) rather than the "how it works."

3. The final presentation usually runs for about 15 minutes and should be what I call the "CIO" (chief information officer) presentation. A CIO knows about technology, and therefore the presentation should have a much higher technical level than for the CEO presentation. In this presentation the students should efficiently show every aspect of their Website, which needs to be flawless (I take great pleasure in attempting basic security breaches to students' projects). They should, of course, explain how the scripts work and show important portions of code.

In the last chapter of the book you will find a long step-by-step development cycle that I use on my Websites and that I recommend. It also includes some examples of security breaches that can happen in a PHP project.

13

Creating Database- Driven Websites with PHP/MySQL

OVERVIEW

Once you have designed and created the database you want to use, it is possible to access its contents with PHP. The easiest way to proceed is to create the database and its tables with a tool like phpMyAdmin, and then use PHP scripts to manipulate the data in the database.

CONNECTING TO YOUR MySQL SERVER WITH PHP

When you wish to check the contents of your database with PHP, the first thing to do is to connect to it, using the method *mysql_connect*. This function requires three extremely important parameters: the host (or server where the DB is installed and running), the user (should be the same one you set up for phpMyAdmin), and the password for that user. Generally the host will always be *localhost* unless your Web server and database server are installed in two separate machines.

Instead of directly using the *mysql_connect*, I would recommend creating an include file in which you will write wrapper functions for all the standard methods. A wrapper function will run the standard one, making sure everything works fine, or quit the script if there is a problem. The include file should

Web Application Design and Implementation: Apache 2, PHP5, MySQL, JavaScript, and Linux/UNIX, by Steven A. Gabarró
Copyright © 2007 by John Wiley & Sons, Inc.

also include the user, password, and server information so that the information is centralized in a single file. The file should be kept in a *safe folder*!!! Here is what the beginning of the include file should look like:

```php
<?PHP
  $MySQL_Host="localhost";
  $MySQL_User="user";
  $MySQL_Pass="pass";
  function connect()
  {
    global $MySQL_Host, $MySQL_User, $MySQL_Pass;
    if (! $linkid=mysql_connect("$MySQL_Host", "$MySQL_
User",   "$MySQL_Pass"))
    {
      echo "Impossible to connect to ", $MySQL_Host,
"<BR>";
      exit;
    }
    return $linkid;
  }
?>
```

Note that our new function connect will return the same value that *mysql_connect* returns. This $linkid will be the resource needed for us to send any query to our database server. To actually connect using our function, we need to first include our include file and then simply call our function connect, like this:

```php
<?PHP
  include("/usr/home/sgabarro/includes/myinclude.inc.php");
  $lkid = connect();
?>
```

SUBMITTING SQL QUERIES

So far our code simply connects to the database and does nothing else. To add extra functionality, there are many methods, as we shall see; but once you know MySQL syntax, you only need the method to send a query and the methods to read the results from those queries. Whenever you wish to access a database, create a string holding a SQL query, and use either *mysql_db_query* or *mysql_query*. The first one takes a database name and the query; the second takes the SQL query and the link id provided by connect. If you use the second method, you must first select the database to use on your MySQL server using *mysql_select_db*. I personally prefer the second option, but I also have a wrapper method for this task:

```
function send_sql($sql, $link, $db) {
  if (! ($succ = mysql_select_db($db))) {
    echo mysql_error();
    exit;
  }
  if (! ($res = mysql_query($sql, $link))) {
    echo mysql_error();
    exit;
  }
  return $res;
}
```

Note the use of *mysql_error()*, which prints the last error returned by the MySQL server. Usually my scripts will use only a single database, so I write *send_sql* with just two parameters, and I hard-code the database to access on the *my_select_db* line. This function should be in the same file as *connect*. Here is an example of how you would retrieve all the info for a user "Bewchy" assuming that our DB name is "Examples" and our table name is "Users":

```
<?PHP
  include("include.inc.php");
  $link = connect();
  $db = "Examples";
  $sql = "SELECT * FROM Users WHERE username='Bewchy'";
  if ($res = send_sql($sql, $link, $db))
    echo "The query worked, now let us learn how to
use the returned var";
  ?>
```

PROCESSING THE RESULTS OF A QUERY

As you probably noticed, when sending a SQL query, the *send_sql* function returns a variable that we called $res. This variable is a resource handler, and contains all the information related to the query sent. For example, if you tried to find a series of users, $res would hold the details of all the matches found. These data can be read with several methods; my favorite is the function *mysql_fetch_row*. This function receives a resource handler as an input and returns the next row. Each row is an entity that was returned after the query. What is nice about this method is that it will return an array with all the details in the order they were requested. Also, this function returns FALSE if there are no more rows, so you can easily use it in a loop to process all the results. You can also use the function *mysql_num_rows($res)*, which will return the number of rows the resource handler contained. If, for example, your query was "SELECT user, password FROM Users WHERE age=26," doing send_sql should return a resource handler with all the usernames and passwords of all the 26-year-old users. Assuming that we called $res = send_sql($sql, $link, $db), here is some code you could use to check all the entries:

```php
<?PHP
  // we assume that the query was already done
  if (mysql_num_rows($res) == 0)
    echo "No match found!";
  else
    while ($row = mysql_fetch_row($res))
      echo "User: ".$row[0]."<BR>Password: ".$row[1]."<BR>";
?>
```

EXAMPLE OF LOGIN PROCEDURE

When you have a page that requires users to log in using a username and password, I usually have a login.php script that checks user validity. If it is, I gather all the needed info for that user and store it in a session, right before I redirect the page to the "logged-in" area, which, of course, will ensure that the session is properly set up. Something I like to do is store all passwords with MD5 encryption, to increase security. This means that to verify username/password information, I need to encrypt the password received through the login page also with MD5, and see if it matches the one stored in the database. A basic way to check for proper username/password is to attempt to find all users with same username and encrypted password. If you set up your database properly, fields like "username" will be unique, so you know that you can receive only a single match or none at all. Here is a basic login. php procedure, assuming that our "users" database contains (in order) the fields *id_user*, *username*, *pass*, *name*, *surname*, and *email*:

```php
<?PHP
  include ("include.inc.php");
  session_start();
  $link = connect();
  $sql = "SELECT * FROM users WHERE user='".$_
SESSION["user"]."' AND pass=MD5('".$_SESSION["pass"]."')";
  if (! $res = send_sql($sql, $link, "examples"))
  {
    echo "Database problem!!!"
    exit;
  }
  if (mysql_num_rows($res) == 0)
    header("Location: index.php");
```

```
// no need to put an else, since if any of the previous
//"if" was true, we would have left the page by now.
$arr = mysql_fetch_row($res);
$_SESSION["id"] = $arr[0];
$_SESSION["user"] = $arr[1];
$_SESSION["name"] = $arr[2];
$_SESSION["surname"] = $arr[3];
$_SESSION["email"] = $arr[4];
header("Location: index_logged.php");
?>
```

OTHER USEFUL FUNCTIONS

Here is a list of functions you might find more or less useful:

- *int mysql_affected_rows($linkid)*—returns the number of affected rows in the previous MySQL operation.
- *bool mysql_close($link)*—closes the MySQL connection.
- *bool mysql_data_seek($res, $row)*—moves the internal pointer of a resource handler to the row $row. The next call of *mysql_fetch_row()* would return that row.
- *resource mysql_list_dbs($lid)*—lists all the databases available in the MySQL server through a result pointer. To retrieve a specific name of database, use *mysql_db_name($res, $row)*.
- *mysql_drop_db($dbname, $link)*—deletes a MySQL database along with all its tables and data.
- *int mysql_errno($link)*—returns the error number from the previous MySQL operation. To get the string of that error message, use *mysql_error($link)* instead.
- *object mysql_fetch_field($res)*—returns an object containing the field information. This can be used to obtain information about fields in the provided query result. The main fields you might find useful in the returned object are *name* for the field name, *table* for the name of the table the column belongs to, and *def* for the default value of that column. Other properties include *max_length, not_null, primary_key, unique_key, multiple_key, numeric, blob, type, unsigned*, and *zerofill*.
- *array mysql_fetch_lengths($res)*—returns an array that corresponds to the lengths of each field in the last row fetched by MySQL.
- *bool mysql_free_result($res)*—frees the result memory.
- *int mysql_insert_id($link)*—returns the ID generated from the previous INSERT operation. Very useful to know the value of an AUTO_INCREMENT field right after inserting an element.

- *int mysql_num_fields($res)*—get the number of fields in a result.
- *string mysql_result($res, $row)*—get the contents of a specific result as a string.

GROUPING OUR METHODS IN A CLASS

As I was trying to find an example of object-oriented programming in PHP, I realized how useful a *database* class would be. Inside we would have all the methods we need to help out with any database operation we might want to do. It will also hold all the data that we might need, like resource, handlers, username, password, host, and link id.

The class will contain a method *setup* that will accept the host, username, password, and default database to use for our remaining queries. This function will also connect to the database. This function should be the first one to call, although it can be omitted as long as you change the class code to include your default host, username, and password instead of "localhost," "root," and "." The function *pick_db* will allow you to pick a new database, or choose one if you never used *setup*. This can also be skipped if you give the member $db a default value with the database name you will always use. Then we have a destructor that frees up memory and disconnects for the server, a function *disconnect* to disconnect, a function *connect* to connect to the server, a function *send_sql* (pretty much the same that we mentioned earlier in this chapter), with the added feature that it will connect to the database in case this had not yet been done. The function *printout* will show the contents of a resource handler as a table; *next_row*, which returns the next row in the resource handler; *insert_id*, which will return the last AUTO_INCREMENT value set by an INSERT; and *new_db*, which creates a new database and sets it up as the default database to use.

Feel free to add your own methods; there are many other things that you might find useful to use; this is meant to serve only as an example. Note that I used exceptions in some functions to illustrate how to use them.

Here is the code:

```
<?PHP
  /*********************************************************
  **                                                     **
  **    Class database written by Steven A. Gabarró    **
  **                                                     **
  *********************************************************/

  class database
```

```
{
  private $link;
  private $res;
  private $host = "localhost"; // change to your own
                               //default value
  private $user = "root"; // change to your own
                          //default value
  private $pass = ""; // change to your own default
                      //value
  private $db;

  // sets user, pass and host and connects
  public function setup($u, $p, $h, $db)
  {
    $this->user = $u;
    $this->pass = $p;
    $this->host = $h;
    $this->db = $db;
    if (isset($this->link))
      $this->disconnect();
    $this->connect();
  }
  // Changes the database in which all queries will
  //be performed
  public function pick_db($db)
  {
    $this->db = $db;
  }

  // destructor disconnects
  public function __destruct()
  {
    $this->disconnect();
  }

  //Closes the connection to the DB
  //public function disconnect()
  {
    if (isset($this->link))
      mysql_close($this->link);
    unset($this->link);
  }

  // connects to the DB or disconnects/reconnects if
  //a connection already existed
  public function connect()
```

```php
    {
      if (!isset($this->link))
      {
        try {
          if (!$this->link=mysql_connect($this->host,
$this->user, $this->pass))
            throw new Exception("Cannot Connect to
".$this->host);
        } catch (Exception $e)
        {
          echo $e->getMessage();
          exit;
        }
      }
      else
      {
        $this->disconnect();
        $this->connect();
      }
    }

    // sends a SQL query
    public function send_sql($sql) {
      if (!isset($this->link))
        $this->connect();
      try {
        if (! $succ = mysql_select_db($this->db))
          throw new Exception("Could not select the
database ".$this->db);
        if (! $this->res = mysql_query($sql, $this->link))
          throw new Exception("Could not send query");
      } catch (Exception $e)
      {
        echo $e->getMessage()."<BR>";
        echo mysql_error();
        exit;
      }
      return $this->res;
    }

    // Shows the contents of the $res as a table
    public function printout() {
      if (isset($this->res) && (mysql_num_rows($this-
>res) > 0))
      {
        mysql_data_seek($this->res, 0);
```

```
    $num=mysql_num_fields($this->res);
    echo "<table border=1>";
    echo "<tr>";
    for ($i=0;$i<$num;$i++){
      echo "<th>";
      echo mysql_field_name($this->res,$i);
      echo "</th>";
    }
    echo "</tr>";
    while ($row = mysql_fetch_row($this->res)) {
      echo "<tr>";
      foreach ($row as $elem) {
        echo "<td>$elem</td>";
      }
      echo "</tr>";
    }
    echo "</table>";
  }
  else
    echo "There is nothing to print!<BR>";
}
// returns an array with the next row
public function next_row()
{
  if (isset($this->res))
    return mysql_fetch_row($this->res);
  echo "You need to make a query first!!!";
  return false;
}
// returns the last AUTO_INCREMENT data created
public function insert_id()
{
  if (isset($this->link))
  {
    $id = mysql_insert_id($this->link);
    if ($id == 0)
      echo "You did not insert an element that cause
an auto-increment ID to be created!<BR>";
    return $id;
  }
  echo "You are not connected to the database!";
  return false;
}
// Creates a new DB and selects it
public function new_db($name)
```

```php
  {
    if (!isset($this->link))
      $this->connect();
    $query = "CREATE DATABASE IF NOT EXISTS".$name;
    try {
      if (mysql_query($query, $this->link))
        throw new Exception("Cannot create database
".$name);
      $this->db = $name;
    } catch (Exception $e)
    {
      echo $e->getMessage()."<BR>";
      echo mysql_error();
      exit;
    }
  }
}
?>
```

Here is a small function that illustrates how the previous class would be used:

```php
<?PHP
  include ("./databaseClass.php");

  $db = new database();
  $db->setup("dbuser", "dbpass", "dbhost", "dbname");
  $query = "SELECT * FROM user";
  $res = $db->send_sql($query);
  echo "Found ".mysql_num_rows($res). " rows<BR>";
  $row = $db->next_row();
  echo $row[0]."<BR>";
  $row = $db->next_row();
  echo $row[1]."<BR>";
  $db->printout();
  $db->insert_id();
  $db->new_db("testing");
  $db->disconnect();
  $db->insert_id();
?>
```

INDEXER/SEARCHER—STEPS 3 AND 4

The next phase for our indexer/searcher is to start using our database to hold the results from our indexing as well as reading the information in the database to perform a search.

Step 3 will consist in taking our previous version (step 2) and modifying the code so that instead of outputting the results on a page, everything will be stored in a database. It is entirely up to you to decide on your database structure, but remember that you want to be able to search all that information effectively. The important data we will need to hold are

- Filename
- File URL
- Metatags for each file
- Full-text count of the words of each file

To avoid redundancy with the words, I would recommend using a *words* table with simply a word and an id. Then you would refer to the word found through its id. An example of what your database might look like is shown in Figure 13.1. Every attribute in **boldface** is a "unique" field, underlined fields are primary keys (PK is for primary key, FK for foreign key).

Step 4 consists in writing the search module of our indexer/searcher. It should consist of a textbox, and either a select box, radio buttons, or checkboxes. The textbox is where users would enter the words they are looking for, and the other element will allow users to specify whether to perform a full-text search, a metatags search, or both. This step is actually the easiest one as long as you have a good database layout.

Once the user enters the word to search for, you should output the names of all the files containing the word. Each name should have a link to the file, and should display the number of iterations of the word you were searching for. The pages should be displayed in order of importance, putting the page with the most iterations of the searched word right on top. You can also add

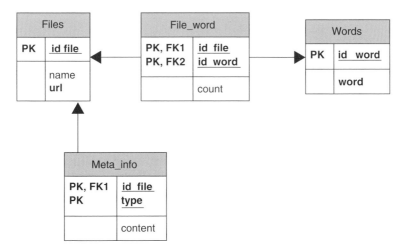

FIGURE 13.1 *Sample database structure for the indexer/searcher.*

extra features such as wildcard searching. For example, you could allow a user who is looking for any words containing the string "abc" to write things like **abc**. This is easily done by replacing the asterisks by a percentage sign, as the % is the "wildcard" character in MySQL. To look for a nonfull match, do not use *attribute = value;* instead use the *LIKE* operator. For example, if you wanted to search for any user whose name includes the letter "z," your SQL query would be

SELECT * FROM 'users' WHERE name LIKE '%z%'

Another fun feature is to add a "highlight" link that would load a prepro-cessed version of the page. The preprocessing would basically be a PHP script that would open the page, replace the word you were looking for by the same word with a "highlight style" (such as all-capital letters, yellow background with red lettering) throughout the original text and then display the updated version of the page.

14

JavaScript—A Client-Side Scripting Language

INTRODUCTION

Remember that JavaScript is a Web programming language that runs client-side. It runs on almost any browser, although different browsers will run slightly different versions on JavaScript. This is important to realize, as some instructions that work on MS Internet Explorer might not work on Mozilla Firefox or Netscape Navigator and vice versa. The reason for this is the lack of real standard, and the fact that there is no single organization deciding on what JavaScript should handle or not (as opposed to HTML's W3C). My recommendation, when writing in JavaScript, is to check the browser version and to always test your script on the most popular browsers out there. If you do not wish to make your scripts compatible with different browsers (which usually takes a longer time to write), you should at least test the version of the browser and give users a warning, letting them know that the scripts might not work.

Other than a browser to test your scripts, you need only a basic text editor to write the scripts. You do not even need a Web server, since double-clicking on your HTML files containing JavaScript will be good enough to see if they work.

JavaScript code is usually embedded in the middle of HTML pages. To start a block of JavaScript, write *<SCRIPT LANGUAGE = "JavaScript">* and finish the block with *</SCRIPT>*. The *SCRIPT* tags in this case act like

Web Application Design and Implementation: Apache 2, PHP5, MySQL, JavaScript, and Linux/UNIX, by Steven A. Gabarró
Copyright © 2007 by John Wiley & Sons, Inc.

the *<?PHP* and *?>* for PHP. Once you are in between opening and closing *SCRIPT* tags, make sure you respect all JavaScript syntax rules!

As we saw on Chapter 2, JavaScript is an object-based language, so most of our time will be spent using preexisting objects to do our job. One thing to remember is that the language is case-sensitive, so make sure to use the proper mix of upper- and lowercasing when calling an object's method or attribute!

When we studied PHP, we saw that it works by executing the code on the server, and sending the final result of the script directly to the client's browser. JavaScript runs client-side, having all its code downloaded along with the HTML. For this reason, all the JavaScript is run line by line as the page is being read and displayed. For example, if you have some JavaScript between two HTML paragraphs, the first paragraph will be displayed, then the JavaScript will run, and the second paragraph will appear on the page only after the entire script is finished running. Here is an example of a page containing a script that will change the background color of the page. You do not need to understand how it works; we are just trying to see the basic structure of a page containing JavaScript and how the script is executed step by step:

```
<HTML>
<HEAD><TITLE>JavaScript example 1</TITLE></HEAD>
<BODY>
  First block!<BR>
  <SCRIPT LANGUAGE="JavaScript">
    alert("First block");
  </SCRIPT>
  Second block!<BR>
  <SCRIPT LANGUAGE="JavaScript">
    alert("Second block");
  </SCRIPT>
  And now we change the background color to flashy
yellow<BR>
    <SCRIPT LANGUAGE="JavaScript">
    alert("Change Background!");
    document.bgColor = "Yellow";
    </SCRIPT>
  </BODY>
</HTML>
```

The function *alert* used creates an alert window, which blocks the script until the user clicks on "OK." As you can see, when an alert is waiting to be clicked on, it blocks the interpretation of the HTML file and nothing else is displayed until we unblock the script.

Comments work in JavaScript the same way as they did in PHP, meaning that you can use either the double slashes or the /* . . . */.

JavaScript SYNTAX

Types of Data and Variables

In JavaScript, as in PHP, any data help has a type associated with it, which can be numerical, text, or, of course, more complex data such as arrays or objects. When writing a string, make sure to surround it by either double or single quotes. You may also use any of the typical special characters such as \b for backspace, \n for new line, \r for return carrier, \t for a tab, \' to show a single quote, \" for double quotes, \\ for backslash, or \xNN (where NN is a hexadecimal number) to write the character with ASCII code "NN." You can also use *true* and *false*.

As in PHP, JavaScript does not need to specify the type that a variable will hold, and you can therefore switch the contents of a variable from a number to a string, to an object, or to anything you need. Variables in JavaScript do not need special characters such as the dollar sign used in PHP. For this reason, for the browser to understand that a word refers to a variable, you need to declare that variable, by putting the keyword *var* in front of the variable name the first time you use it. Variable names must start with a letter, and can be composed of any letters, numbers, and the underscore symbol (_). Here is a small example of how you would declare a variable, we will assign a number to it, and then switch to a string (this code should, of course, be surrounded by the *SCRIPT* tags!):

```
var myVar;
myVar = 23456;
alert(myVar);
myVar = "Hello World!";
alert(myVar);
```

Remember to put a semicolon at the end of each line of code. As you can see, *alert* is very flexible, and can show any data of primitive types.

Operations and Calculations

To assign a value to a variable, simply use the equal sign. You may use numerical calculations between variables with the typical arithmetic symbols +, −, *, /. The plus sign can also be used to concatenate strings, so you could output a mix of strings and variables by writing, for example, *alert ("Variable 1 is " + var1 + "and variable 2 is " + var2);*.

You can use the same postincrement (var++), preincrement (++var), postdecrement (var−−) and predecrement (−−var) used in PHP. You can also precede the equal sign with an operator to do things like *myVar *= 5;*. Remember that something of the type *variable operator = expression* is equivalent to *variable = variable operator expression*. You may therefore use it not only with numbers but also with, for example, strings *myString += "this will be concatenated to myString";*. JavaScript handles the basic operator precedence, so expressions like $1 + 2 * 3$ will return 7 $(1 + (2 * 3))$ and not 9 $((1 + 2) * 3)$.

Two very useful methods will allow you to find a number inside of a string. You can use *parseInt(string)*, which returns the first integer found in the string or *NaN* if no string was found; or *parseFloat(string)*, which returns the first floating-point number found in the string or *NaN* if there were no numbers. NaN stands for "not a number" and means that a string contains no numerical data. These two functions work only if the number you are looking for is right at the beginning of the string (white spaces may precede the number). If you try to parse a string of the type "string 123," these methods will return NaN. You can actually test a string to see if it is a number using *isNaN ()*. Realize that this method tells you if the parameter provided is not a number, so it will return false if the parameter was a number: it would mean that it is *not* NaN; therefore it is a number (you must love double negations ☺). For example, *isNaN(234)* will return false and *isNaN("Hello")* would return true.

Here is an example of a miles-to-kilometers converter script. Since JavaScript is client-side, we can directly ask the user for input data without the need of forms. To do so we will use the *prompt* method, which takes two parameters: the string to display (what you want the user to input), and the default value. The function *prompt* will pop up an entry box for the user to enter some information, and will return whatever the user wrote. Also, instead of doing an *alert* as in the previous examples, we will use *document.write()*, which is basically the JavaScript equivalent of PHP's *echo*. This way we will show the results on the Webpage rather than on an alert window.

```
<HTML>
  <HEAD><TITLE>Conversions!</TITLE></HEAD>
  <BODY>
  I don't understand miles, so give me kilometers
please!<BR>
    <SCRIPT LANGUAGE="JavaScript">
      var inputVar = prompt("Enter the number of miles
to convert", 60);
      if (isNaN(parseFloat(inputVar)))
        alert("You didn't enter a number!! This is
      unacceptable!");
      else
      {
        var result = parseFloat(inputVar) * 1.609344;
        // conversion data provided by Google
        document.write(parseFloat(inputVar) + " miles is
the same as " + result + " km");
      }
    </SCRIPT>
  <BR>Thanks for using the converter!
  </BODY>
</HTML>
```

Arrays

If you wish to use arrays, you need to specify that the variable you will use is an array. This is done by creating an object of the class Array by writing

var myArray = new Array();

The Array constructor can actually accept the series of elements to insert in the array. Since JavaScript's variables can be of any type, you can hold a mix of different data types in the same array. To access or modify data in an array, you can use the angle brackets with the index of the element to modify. Note that as in PHP, the elements inserted in an array do not need to have successive indices, and it is possible to have an array with only three elements located at indices 2, 23, and 325, for example. Here is a basic array manipulation example:

```
var myArray;
myArray = new Array("Uno", 2, "3.0");
myArray[3] = "Four";
```

As with PHP, array indices start at 0 by default. You can create multidimensional arrays by simply making an array element become a *new Array()*; thus each new level of arrays would use a new set of angled brackets with an index. Here is how you would create the same "friends" array that we saw in the PHP version of multidimensional arrays. Remember, our goal was to have a set of names and list of relatives for each entry in our friends array. So technically we need a three-dimensional array. The first dimension tells us which friend we are dealing with, the second dimension allows us to read either the friend's name or the array of relatives, and the third dimension holds the names of the relatives:

```
var friendsArray = new Array();
friendsArray[0] = new Array();
  friendsArray[0][0] = "Steven";
  friendsArray[0][1] = new Array();
    friendsArray[0][1][0] = "Peter";
    friendsArray[0][1][1] = "Jackie";
    friendsArray[0][1][2] = "Romina";
friendsArray[1] = new Array();
  friendArray[1][0] = "Christian";
  friendArray[1][1] = new Array();
    friendArray[1][1][0] = "Jose";
    friendArray[1][1][1] = "Liliane";
    friendArray[1][1][2] = "Daniel";
// and so on
```

Decisions

As in PHP, JavaScript can check different conditions and branch to different sections of the code depending on the value found. To do so we can use the common comparison operators "==" for equals, "<" for less than, ">" for greater than, "<=" for less than or equal to, ">=" for greater than or equal to, and "!=" for different. You can combine different boolean expressions with "&&" for AND, "||" for OR, and "!" for NOT.

When using the *if* statement in JavaScript, there is one basic difference, residing in the *elseif.* In PHP *elseif* has to be written as a single word, but in JavaScript it is two separate words. The general syntax would therefore be:

if (condition)
{ }
else if (anotherCondition)
{ }
else
{ }

You may also use the *switch . . . case* the exact same way as in PHP (don't forget to use *break*). Here is an example of using both switch and if statements. We will prompt the user for a number; if the user inputs something that is NaN, we will say there's a problem; if it is a number, we will say "hello" if it is 0 or 1, "goodbye" if it is 2, and "hooah!" otherwise:

```
var input = prompt("Enter a number", 0);
if (isNaN(input))
  document.write("Not a number!");
else
{
  switch (input)
  {
    case 0:
    case 1:
      document.write("Hello");
      break;
    case 2:
      document.write("Goodbye");
      break;
    default:
      document.write("Hooah!");
  }
}
```

Loops

In JavaScript, you may use the exact same basic loops used in PHP (except for the *foreach* loop). Just as a reminder, here are three quick loop examples.

Remember that if you are creating a new variable in the first section of a *for* loop, you will still need to write the keyword *var*:

```
var n = 5; var j = 10; var k = 15;
for(var i = 0; i < n; i++)
  document.write(i + " ");
while (i < j)
  document.write((i++) + " ");
do
{ document.write(i + " ");
} while ((i++) < k);
```

In case you feel deprived for not having the great *foreach* to process all the elements in an array, feel that way no more, since JavaScript has the equivalent *for . . . in*. The basic syntax is *for (index in array)* and allows you to get all the valid indices in an array, skipping the indices of empty cells. For example, you could print all the contents of an array doing

```
var index;
for (index in myArray)
{
  document.write(myArray[index]);
}
```

Finally, you can use *break* and *continue* as we did in PHP. The first will quit a loop, and the latter will force the next iteration of a loop.

Using Functions

To create a function, simply write *function functionName(parameter1, parameter2, . . .)*. As in PHP, the type of parameters or return value can be anything, so it does not need to be defined. For example, if we wanted to create a function to convert miles into kilometers, we would write the following code:

```
function milesToKm(miles)
{
  if (isNaN(miles))
    alert ("Error in function milesToKm: Parameter
provided is NaN!!");
  else
    return (miles * 1.609344);
}
```

To use the function later on, you would simply write, for example, *var myKm = milesToKm(60);*.

USING OBJECTS

Recall that an object is an instance of a class, which means an element that holds both data members that define it, as well as methods. For example, an object "car" can have the properties "color," "brand," or "mileage." The methods inside the object are actions that can be done with the particular object. For an object car you could have *fillTank()*, *changeColor()*, and so on.

To create an object you need to use the keyword *new*, like this:

var myVar = new ObjectName(constructor parameters);

Remember that JavaScript is an object-based language, not an object-oriented language. Therefore you may not create new classes, but you may use any of the preexisting ones. We already have used Arrays, and as you might have noticed, we used the keyword *new* to create arrays. This is due to the fact that arrays are actually objects! We will now see some of the most important available classes that can be used in JavaScript to create objects.

The String Objects

Yes! Strings are objects too!! They are special objects that do not necessarily need the keyword *new* to be created. You can create strings either by simply writing a string between single or double quotes, or by using *new String()*, in which case the constructor can receive a string or a number. For example, *var string1 = new String(123.345);* will create the string "123.345." As you can see, converting from numbers to strings is really simple. Here is a list of major data members and methods that can be used with strings (you do not need a variable to use these methods and you may use them right after a string between double quotes, e.g., *"hello".length* would return 5):

- *length*—for example, *myString.length* is a data member holding the number of characters in the string.
- *charAt(position)*—for example, *myString.charAt(4)* returns the character at the position provided as a parameter. Note that indices start at 0, so our example would return the fifth character.
- *charCodeAt(position)*—same as *charAt* but returns the ASCII code of the character rather than the character itself.
- *fromCharCode(list of numbers)*—this method is actually used to create strings from a set of ASCII codes. Instead of writing a name of object in front of the method, use the class name *String*. You could write, for example, *var myString = String.fromCharCode(61, 62, 63);*, which would create the string "*abc*."
- indexOf(string, position)—for example, *myString.indexOf("tofind", 0)* will find the index of the first match of the provided string (*"tofind"*)

starting at the index provided (0). The second parameter is optional, but very useful if trying to find a series of matches.

- *lastIndexOf(string, position)*—same as *indexOf* but searches backward. If the position is omitted, the search is done from the very end of the string.
- *substring(beginning, end)*—returns the substring from the calling string starting at position beginning and finishing before index end. It is very important to realize that the last character returned will always be at index *end-1*. For example, if *myString* holds "*Hello*," doing *myString.substring(1, 3)* would return the string "*el*."
- substr(beginning, length)—similar to *substring*. Returns the *substring* starting at beginning and having length characters. For example, *"Hello".substr(3, 2)* would return "*lo*."
- *toLowerCase()*—for example, *myString.toLowerCase()*. Turns *myString* to all lowercase.
- *toUpperCase()*—for example, *myString.toUpperCase()*. Turns *myString* to all uppercase.

The Math Class

The Math class contains many static methods, meaning that there is no need to create an object of the class Math in order to use them. Simply write *Math.* followed by the name of the data member or method to use. Here is the list of the most important methods and static data members:

- Math.PI—returns the value of Π
- Math.abs(number)—returns the absolute value of *number*
- Math.ceil(number)—returns *number* rounded up
- Math.floor(number)—returns *number* rounded down
- Math.round(number)—rounds the *number*
- Math.pow(x, y)—calculates *x* to the power of *y* (x^y)

One last and fun function of the Math class is *random()*. Unlike PHP, random will always return a number between 0 included and 1 excluded. From there it is up to you to figure out how to achieve the range of numbers you want to have. Here is an interesting application. Imagine that you are writing a script for role players, and you are trying to get a dice-rolling script that will calculate a series of dice rolls. A very popular role playing rule set called the "d20 system," used in games such as "Star Wars RPG" or "Dungeon & Dragons," is based on rolling a die with 20 sides, numbered 1 to 20. Now, we know that our random-number generator will return a value (let us call it *x*) between 0 and 1. We have

$$0 <= x < 1$$

Since we want to get values of up to 20, we can multiply x by 20, getting

$$0 \leqslant 20\, x < 20$$

One problem is that, we may get 0 and yet we will never reach 20. Since our smaller number will always need to be 1, we can add one:

$$1 \leqslant 20\, x + 1 < 21$$

Now we have to realize that the number we will get will be a floating-point number. In order to turn it into an integer, we will need to round it. If we round up, our range will be 1–21, which is not good. If we use the regular *round,* we might still get number 21 which is out of bounds. Instead, we can use *floor* since the largest number we will get is 20.9999999999[...], which, rounded down, is still 20. Our final formula gives us

$$1 \leqslant \text{floor}(20\, x + 1) \leqslant 20$$

Here is the script that would calculate our dice rolls:

```
<HTML>
<HEAD><Title>d20 System dice roller v1</Title>
</HEAD>
<BODY>
  <SCRIPT LANGUAGE="JavaScript">
    var numberOfThrows;
    var diceRoll;
    do
    {
      numberOfThrows = parseInt(prompt("How many times
should I roll the dice? Enter a number please.", 1));
    } while (isNaN(numberOfThrows));
    // we bug the user until he enters an actual
    //number.
    document.write("Let's roll!!<BR>");
    for (var i = 0; i < numberOfThrows; i++)
    {
      diceRoll = Math.floor(Math.random() * 20 + 1);
      document.write(diceRoll + "<BR>");
    }
  </SCRIPT>
  If you want to reroll, press F5 or click on the
browser's refresh button.
</BODY>
</HTML>
```

The Array Objects

As we saw earlier, arrays are technically objects created doing *new Array()*. Here is a list of important methods and data members; we will assume that *myArray* is already holding an array with the numbers 12, 2, 69, 51, and 666:

- *myArray.length*—returns the number of elements in the array.
- *myArray.concat(myArray2)*—returns the concatenation of *myArray* and *myArray2*.
- *myArray.slice(b,e)*—same as substring for *Strings*. Will return the subarray starting at index *b* and finishing at index *e – 1*. For example, *myArray. slice(1,4)* would return an array holding the values 2, 69, and 51.
- *myArray.join(mySeparator)*—same as PHP's implode. Creates a string with all the elements in *myArray* concatenated with *mySeparator*. For example, *myArray.join("+–+");* would create the string *"12+–+2+–+69+–+51+–+666."*
- *myArray.sort()*—sorts *myArray*.
- *myArray.reverse()*—reverses *myArray*. If you wish to do a reverse sort of an array, you could do *myArray.sort()* followed by *myArray.reverse()* and *"voilà!."*

THE DATE OBJECTS

A quite useful class in JavaScript is the *Date* class, which allows you to store any date. To create an object with the current date and time, simply write *var date = new Date();*. You may also use three other constructors if you are trying to create a date object for a date different from the current one.

The first alternative is to provide a number, particularly the number of milliseconds elapsed since January 1, 1970 at 00:00:00 GMT. For example, if you do *var date = new Date (303178567890);* you are creating a Date object based on August 10, 1979 around (20:15 hours) (8:15 p.m.).

Obviously, creating a date like this is useful only if you want to create an object using a saved UNIX timestamp that you might have received through a PHP script. To create a *Date* object for an older date, write the date as a string with *Day Month Year*, for example, *var date = new Date("10 August 1979");*.

The final alternative if you want a specific time but do not know the number of milliseconds elapsed is to use a *Date* constructor that accepts seven parameters in the following order: year, month, day, hour, minute, second, and millisecond. Note that in JavaScript, the list of months actually starts at index 0. This means that January is 0 and December is 11. Therefore, to create a date based on August 10, 1979 at 5:30 hours (5:30 a.m.), 20 seconds and 14 milliseconds, you would write *var date = new Date(1979, 7, 10, 5, 30, 20, 14);*

One last thing to remember when writing times with this format is that all times use the military 24-hour system, so if you wish to say that it is 3:00 p.m., you must write 15:00 hours. Basically, just add 12 to p.m. times to get the military time.

Once a Date object has been created, it is possible to extract individual items from it, or modify settings individually. Here are the available methods, assuming that our object is called *myDate*:

- *myDate.getDate()*—gets the month date. In my previous examples it would be "10."
- *myDate.getDay()*—gets the day of the week, where 0 is Sunday, 1 is Monday and so on until Saturday, which is 6.
- *myDate.getMonth()*—gets the month number. Remember that January is 0, and December is 11 (yes, Christmas is on 11/25 when you are using JavaScript ☺).
- *myDate.getYear()* and *myDate.getFullYear()*—returns the year, in either "short" version or full version. For example, for the year 1979, *getYear()* would return 79, and *getFullYear()* would return 1979. For this reason, *getYear()* on a year like 2006 will return 106 because *getYear()* returns the number of years passed since 1900.
- *myDate.getHours()*, *myDate.getMinutes()*, *myDate.getSeconds()*, and *myDate.getMilliseconds()*—returns the hour, minute, second, and millisecond, respectively.
- *myDate.setDate(n)*—sets the date to *n*. Note that there will be no *setDay()* since the weekday is calculated automatically, and you cannot change the course of time and decide that a date that was a Monday will become a Wednesday!!
- *myDate.setMont(n)*—sets the month to *n*. Remember, January is month 0!
- *myDat.setYear(n)*—sets the year to *n*.
- *myDate.setHours(n)*, *myDate.setMinutes(n)*, *myDate.setSeconds(n)*, *myDate.setMilliseconds(n)*—sets the hours, minutes, seconds, and milliseconds to *n*. If you set a value greater than the regular maximum for the quantity being set, the date will be modified accordingly. For example, setting the hours to 36 would move the date forward one day (24 hours) and set the hour to noon.

There is something *extremely* important to realize when using dates in JavaScript. Since the language is client-side, any date gathered will be the date of the *client*! This also means that if users change the clock settings on their computers, your script will think it is a totally different date! Obviously this is unacceptable. You might think that no one is silly enough not to realize that, but let me tell you a little (true) story. As the Spaniard I am, I love soccer, and my favorite team happens to be a team from a major city in Spain that is not the capital. I will not say the actual name of the team because I do not wish to get into trouble with them. Any soccer fans probably guessed the team I root for. Anyway, in order to please their fans, they had a page with live text description of their games. To build up anticipation waiting for the next game, they had a counter saying how long you had to wait for it. The script worked by checking the current time and comparing it to the game time—except that they programmed it in a client-side programming language, and did not account for the time difference. So, there was I in the United States wanting to know how my team was doing at the exact time the game was being played, but the page said I had to wait 6 hours for the game to start, simply because there is a 6-hour difference between that major coastal Spanish city and U.S. west coast. The moral of this story is "Remember which side you are gathering the time from!" The client side will give you the user's time; the server side will give you the server's time, which won't be affected by the time zone of visitors.

Luckily, JavaScript has a way to solve this issue: using UTC times. UTC is the Coordinated Universal Time (UTC sounded better than CUT) implemented in 1964, and more commonly known as GMT (Greenwich Mean Time). Basically it sets the center of all time zones in Greenwich (southeast of London, U.K.). Eastern Standard Time (EST) is GMT − 5, Central European Time (CET) is GMT + 1, and so on. Once you have a *Date* object, you can create a nice formatted string of the full date using the methods *myDate.toLocaleString()* if you want to get the local time, or *myDate.toUTCString()*, which will represent the same date as UTC. For example if the current time is 13:15 (1:15 p.m.) in local time and I am in the U.S. east coast, the time shown by *toUTCString()* will be 18:15 (6:15 p.m.). You may also retrieve the time zone offset (number of minutes offset between UTC and local time) using *myDate.getTimezoneOffset()*.

You may also set or get individual sections of the date directly in UTC format, by directly using any of the previous methods adding the word UTC next to *get* or *set*. For example, *myDate.getUTCDate()* will get the UTC date, and *myDate.setUTCHours(n)* will set the hours of the UTC time (which obviously changes the local time accordingly).

15

Programming the Browser

OVERVIEW

In this chapter, we will see how you can use JavaScript to access any section of HTML files, as well as the actual browser window. To access all these features, we need to use the Window object and its components.

THE WINDOW OBJECT

The window object holds data members and methods that will allow you to interact with the actual browser window. It is a global object, which means that you do not need to actually write its name when calling its methods. We already saw a method from the window object: the function *alert*. Technically you should type *window.alert("Hello")* to use this method, but we can omit the *window.* section. The window object also allows you to change things like the message appearing on the status bar of your browser (the area that shows the progress when downloading a page, and displays "Done" when the page is loaded). You may do this by modifying the data member *defaultStatus*. For example, writing *window.defaultStatus = "Hello and Welcome!"*; will write the welcome message in the status bar. Later on, when we start using timers, we will see how to create scrolling text on the status bar. As with *alert*, you

Web Application Design and Implementation: Apache 2, PHP5, MySQL, JavaScript, and Linux/UNIX, by Steven A. Gabarró
Copyright © 2007 by John Wiley & Sons, Inc.

do not need to write *window.* and may simply use *defaultStatus = "This is cool!"*.

The most interesting thing about the window object is the objects it contains. These are the *location, history, navigator, screen*, and *document* objects. Since all these objects are part of *window*, you may write, for example, either *window.document*, or simply *document*.

The Location Object

The location object allows to change the location of the window, forcing a redirect if set to a page different from the one currently running. You can use two different redirections:

- *location.replace("newpage.html")*—changes the current page with "*newpage.html*" in the history stack. This means that the page that called this method will disappear from the browser's history, and only the new one will appear.
- *location.href("newpage.html")*—also redirects the browser to the new page, but simply adds the new page on the history stack. Once you are in the *newpage.html*, you can go back to the page that used the method by simply clicking "back."

The History Object

The history object allows you to move through the browser's history. It has three main methods:

- *history.back()*—same effect as clicking on the "back" button of the browser.
- *history.forward()*—same effect as clicking on the "forward" button of the browser.
- *history.go(n)*—allows one to move forward or backward *n* times. If *n* is negative, it is the same as clicking "back" *n* times; if it is positive, it is the same as clicking "forward" *n* times.

The Navigator Object

The navigator object gives information about the browser, including the software used, its version, or the operating system it is using. Here is an example of how you could extract information on the browser. From here you could use the *indexOf* method to find strings like *MSIE* or *Firefox* to check the browser version (note that *mimeTypes* and *plugins* refer to an array):

```
<HTML>
  <HEAD>
    <TITLE>Navigator Example</TITLE>
  </HEAD>
  <BODY>
  <SCRIPT LANGUAGE="JavaScript">
    var navData = navigator.appCodeName + "<BR>";
    navData += navigator.appName + "<BR>";
    navData += navigator.appVersion + "<BR>";
    navData += navigator.cookieEnabled + "<BR>";
    navData += navigator.mimeTypes + "<BR>";
    navData += navigator.platform + "<BR>";
    navData += navigator.plugins + "<BR>";
    navData += navigator.userAgent + "<BR>";
    document.write(navData);
  </SCRIPT>
  </BODY>
</HTML>
```

The Screen Object

The screen object provides information on the screen such as *screen.height* for the client's screen height in pixels, *screen.width* for the screen width, or *screen.colorDepth* for the number of color bits used:

```
<HTML>
  <HEAD>
    <TITLE>Screen Object</TITLE>
  </HEAD>
  <BODY>
  <SCRIPT LANGUAGE="JavaScript">
    var screenData = "You are running with a resolution
of ";
    screenData += screen.width + " by " + screen.height;
    screenData += " with a color depth of " + screen.
colorDepth;
    document.write(screenData);
  </SCRIPT>
  </BODY>
</HTML>
```

The Document Object

The document object is probably the most important object inside *window*. It refers to the actual page being displayed. We already saw a method from this object: *write*, which adds text to a page. The document object also includes arrays such as *forms*, *images*, and *links*, which allow you to access and set up all the data inside forms, images, and links in the page.

The main problem of the *document* object is that browsers might have different properties inside it, making it harder for the developer to write multibrowser code. For example, Netscape Navigator contains an array *tags* in the *document* object that Microsoft Internet Explorer does not support. Let us concentrate on the basic arrays inside the *document* object.

First, we have the *images* array. Each time you use an image with the *<IMG>* tag, there is a reference to that image that is added to the *images* array. The very first image will be at *document.images[0]*, the second image in *document.images[1]*, and so on. You may also add a *name* attribute to the *IMG* tag, allowing you to refer to the image through the link's name. For example an image defined as *<IMG SRC="bewchy.gif" NAME="myImage">* can be accessed by doing *document.images["myImage"]*. When you have a reference to an image, you may change any attribute inside the tag by simply writing a period (.) followed by the name of the attribute to change. The following example prompts the user for an image URL and replaces the image on the page with the one provided in the prompt:

```
<HTML>
  <HEAD>
    <TITLE>Image Loader</TITLE>
  </HEAD>
  <BODY>
    <IMG SRC="" NAME="image1">
    <SCRIPT LANGUAGE="JavaScript">
      var url = prompt("Enter an image URL",
  "http://wroshyr.free.fr/images/bewchy.gif");
      document.images["image1"].src = url;
    </SCRIPT>
  </BODY>
</HTML>
```

The next array is the *links* array. It does the same as the image array, but instead of storing all links created with the *<IMG>* tag, it stores references to all links created with the *<A>* tag. As with the images, you may also provide a name to the links so that they are easier to refer to. Since it is also possible to change any of the links' tag attributes, you can drive a user crazy by switching the destinations of your links by doing, for example, *document. links[0].href = "differentpage.html"*.

Last but not least, we have the *forms* array, which holds references to all the forms in the page. You might think that its usefulness is limited since pages usually contain at most a single form, and you probably wouldn't want to change its properties such as *action* or *method*, or your receiving script wouldn't work properly. Well, when you have access to a *form* element, you can actually have access to every tag inside that form, which means that you can edit the properties of every single input, and even *add and remove options in a select input*!

Since there is usually only one form, the simplest thing to do is to give a name to the form inside the *FORM* tag, allowing you to refer to it through its name. For example, if you define a

<FORM ACTION="script.php" METHOD=POST NAME="myForm">

you will be able to access the actual form doing *document.forms["myForm"]*, *document.forms[0]*, or even *document.myForm*. My favorite is the third option. To access an input tag located inside a form *myForm*, use the period sign followed by the name of the input. Here is an example of a script that would change the appearance of a "submit" button; to make the code shorter, our form will not have any *action* or *input*:

```
<HTML>
  <HEAD>
    <TITLE>Changing  Button</TITLE>
  </HEAD>
  <BODY>
    <FORM  NAME="myForm">
      <INPUT  TYPE="Button"  VALUE="Name  that  WILL  change"
NAME="myButton">
    </FORM>
    <SCRIPT  LANGUAGE="JavaScript">
      alert("Let  us  change  the  button  name!!!");
      document.myForm.myButton.value  =  "I  changed!!
Woohoo!";
    </SCRIPT>
  </BODY>
</HTML>
```

If you do not know the names of the inputs (or are too lazy too scroll up/down your code to read it), or if you wish to make a set of operations with every single one of them, you can use a single *form* reference as an array. You can therefore check the number of inputs in the form (including *selects*, and *textareas*) by doing *document.yourFormName.length*. If you wish to access the third input in the form, you can do *document.yourFormName[2]* (remember that arrays start their indices at 0).

Some form inputs have special behaviors, such as checkboxes and radio buttons. Recall that you can group a set of checkboxes or a set of radio buttons by giving the same name to each different option. Thus, the objects referring to each one of those blocks can be used in JavaScript as an array, in which the index identifies which option you are accessing. You can also determine whether an option is checked by comparing the *checked* attribute to true. For example, if you want to determine whether the third radio button on a series of radio buttons called *myRadio* is checked, you can do

> *if(document.myForm.myRadio[2].checked == true)*
>   *doSomething();*

You can also select and deselect options by accessing the one you wish to modify and updating the value of the attribute *checked* to FALSE if you are deselecting or TRUE if you are selecting it.

In the case of a *SELECT* input, you can access each option individually, and even add or remove options. To access a specific option we use the *options* array, which is automatically made part of each *select* object. The value of each option can be value modified (with *.value*) or even the text next to the option (with *.text*). To remove an option from a select menu, simply set the option to be equal to *null.* To add a new option, we create an object of the type *Option*, providing its constructor with the text to appear next to it, and the value associated with that option. Note that all created options are placed at the end of the menu, but since all options are in an *options* array, you can use array operations to switch the elements around. You can also check which option is selected by accessing the data member *selectedIndex* of a select area anytime. For example, to change the text in a menu option when you select it, you could do

> *document.myForm.mySelect.options[document.myForm.mySelect.*
> *selectedIndex].text = "This was the selected option";*

One last useful thing that you can do in JavaScript is force the submission of a form (even if there is no "submit" button!). Simply use the method *submit()* from a form object. For example

> *document.myForm.submit();*

Here is an example that allows you to add and remove options in a drop-down menu:

```
<HTML>
  <HEAD>
  <SCRIPT LANGUAGE=JavaScript>
  function butRemove_onclick()
  {
    var sel = document.form1.selectArea;
    sel.options[sel.selectedIndex] = null;
  }
```

```
  function butAdd_onclick()
  {
    var sel = document.form1.selectArea;
    var newoption = new Option();
    var pos = sel.options.length;
    sel.options[pos] = newoption;
    sel.options[pos].text = document.form1.option.value;
    sel.options[pos].value = document.form1.optionValue.
value;
  }
  </SCRIPT>
  </HEAD>
<BODY>
  <FORM NAME=form1>
  <SELECT NAME=selectArea SIZE=1>
      <OPTION VALUE=0 SELECTED>Example Option
  </SELECT>
  <BR>
  Option:<INPUT TYPE="text" NAME="option">...VALUE:<INPUT
TYPE="text" NAME="optionValue"><BR>
  <INPUT TYPE="button" VALUE="Remove Selected Option"
NAME=butRemove onclick="butRemove_onclick()">
  <INPUT TYPE="button" VALUE="Add Option" NAME=butAdd
onclick="butAdd_onclick()">
  <BR>
  </FORM>
</BODY>
</HTML>
```

USING EVENTS

Probably one of the most interesting things about JavaScript is the opportunity to use events. An event is an action that is triggered by an action by the client. For example, you can have an event happening when a page finishes loading, when the client clicks on a button or link, or when the mouse cursor is placed over certain areas. Events are assigned directly as a parameter of the tag that will handle the event. For example, if you want to start an action when the page finishes loading, the event is set in the *BODY* tag; if you want a link to behave in a specific way, you would put the handler in the *A* tag; and so on. Events start with *on* followed by the actual event to handle, these are the main events:

- *onClick*—triggered when the element is clicked on
- *onMouseOver*—triggered when the mouse is place over the element

- *onMouseOut*—triggered when the mouse leaves the element
- *onMouseDown*—triggered when the mouse button is pressed (a click is a combination of *mousedown* and *mouseup*)
- *onMouseUp*—triggered when the mouse button is released over the element
- *onKeyDown*—as *onMouseDown* but with the keyboard
- *onKeyUp*—same as *onMouseUp* but with the keyboard
- *onKeyPress*—same as on *mouseclick* but with the keyboard (same as *onKeyDown* followed by *onKeyUp*)
- *onLoad*—triggered when the element finishes loading (usually put in the *BODY* tag)
- *onUnload*—triggered when you leave a page
- *onChange*—triggered when the element changes (useful mostly in text fields)
- *onSelect*—triggered when a menu option is selected
- *onResize*—triggered when the window is resized (would be placed inside the *BODY* tag)
- *onReset*—triggered when a form is reset
- *onMove*—triggered when the window is moved (would be placed inside the *BODY* tag)
- *onFocus*—triggered when an element gains the focus (cursor entering a text area, for example)
- *onError*—triggered when there is a JavaScript error
- *onDragDrop*—triggered when an element is dragged and dropped in the browser window
- *onBlur*—triggered when an element looses focus
- *onAbort*—triggered when the loading of a page is interrupted

Once you know which event you want to use, you must decide what action to take. The general procedure is to create a function in JavaScript that will be called by your event handler. Then simply write the name of the method between double quotes next to the event, inside the tag that will handle the event. For example, *<BODY onload = "loadfunction()">* would call the JavaScript function *loadfunction()* whenever the body of the page finishes loading. Note that you may also call the methods with any parameter you wish to use, so you can use the same function for different elements. I personally like putting all my event functions inside the *HEAD* tags, which helps keep the body as clean as possible, concentrating all functions outside it. This also allows the functions to load before the body does, so that as soon as you need to use them, the browser already knows about them.

Here is a fun little example. We will have a link with an *onClick* attribute that will popup an alert message, a button input with an *onMouseOver* that will change its face value, and an *onClick* that will change the page to www.google.com. Note that the event names are not case-sensitive, so you may write *onClick* or *onclick*:

```
<HTML>
<HEAD>
  <TITLE>Link that goes nowhere and onLoad</TITLE>
  <SCRIPT LANGUAGE="JavaScript">
    function link_onclick()
    {
      alert("You clicked on the link! But I refuse to go
anywhere!!");
      return false;
    }
    function button_onmouseover()
    {
      document.form1.mybutton.value = "You placed the
cursor on me!!! I will take you to Google.";
    }
    function button_onclick()
    {
      location.href = "http://www.google.com";
    }
  </SCRIPT>
</HEAD>
<BODY>
  Take me to <A HREF="http://www.google.com/"
onclick="return link_onclick()">Google</A>!
  <FORM name="form1">
    <input type="button" name="mybutton"
     onmouseover="button_onmouseover()"
     onclick="button_onclick()"
     value="Place the mouse over me!">
  </form>
</BODY>
</HTML>
```

As you probably noticed, when using the event *onClick* I actually wrote *return* in front of the function name, and my function returns a value. This is a very useful feature that is used mostly on links and forms (through the "submit" button, actually). Writing *return* basically means that your function will return a value that should not be ignored, and that should be *true* or *false*. Now, here comes the fun part! If the value is true, the element works normally, as if the return were not there, but if your return value is *false*, the element will not perform its standard task, leaving the user in the page. This is *extremely* useful on forms as you can verify the contents of the form before submitting it and let the users know about any errors so that they can correct them before sending the data through the form. To do this, you would simply have an *onClick* property on your "submit" button that would call the method that will verify all data, returning false if a problem was encountered.

Two methods are very useful on forms containing text areas. Ideally, when you are writing a form, you should always include some JavaScript to test the form before sending any data to your PHP scripts. This allows a first layer of data verification done on the client, which is much faster than transmitting the data to a PHP script; have the PHP script verify the data; and redirect the client to the first page if an error is found. Verifications done in JavaScript allow you to avoid the burden of constant back and forth with the server. A typical problem that can be found in forms is bad type of data input in a textbox; for example, you may be expecting an email address and the user leaves the field empty, or inputs a text that is not an email address. In those cases you want to inform the user of the error and to change the data. In those cases you can call the methods *focus()* and *select()*, to place the user in the field that needs changing. These methods should be called from a form element object; an example would be *document.myForm.myInput.focus()*. The method *focus()* will give the focus to the entry, and the method *select()* allows you to select the entire text that was entered. When a field needs to be changed, there is nothing better than to do a *focus()* of the problematic field, followed by *select()*. This way the user simply needs to enter the new data, automatically overwriting the previous text.

One last useful point is to realize that any of the objects accessed through the document object can be stored in variables to ease up the typing. For example, you could do

var myButton = document.myForm1.button;

From then on, you would be able to access your button simply typing *myButton*.

TIMERS

JavaScript has the ability to create two main types of timers: one-shot timers and regular timers, called "intervals." One-shot timers allow you to decide on a specific amount of milliseconds to wait before a function is called. Using the function *setTimeout*, for example, you could do

var timerID = setTimeout("myFunction()", 5000);

This would create a timer that would wait 5 seconds before calling *myFunction()*. The returned ID is very important as it will be needed if you want to stop the timer. Simply use *clearTimeout(timerID)* to stop the timeout.

Regular timers are like timeouts, except that they restart the timer after each timeout. The function used in that case is *setInterval("functionName()", time)*; for example

var timerID = setInterval("alert('Hello')", 5000);

This would run the *alert('Hello')* every 5 seconds. As with timeouts, you can clear the interval by doing *clearInterval(timerID)*.

TIME TO PRACTICE!

Now that you know the basics of event programming, try writing a script containing a button that keeps track of how many times it has been clicked. Realize that variables defined outside a function are considered global. They are accessible inside any function, so you can use that fact to your advantage. Also remember that the text on a button is set by its attribute *value*.

Another fun thing to do is an event log. Create a form with different types of inputs, such as radio buttons, regular buttons, text and password fields, and text areas. Now make sure that you have at least one large text area that you will use to keep track of all events that occur. Set up each input you created with all the events you might want to test out, and have each event function display the latest event at the end of the large text area. Remember that you can access the contents of a text area through the *value* field of the tag, and also that you can concatenate text using the plus (+) sign. Also, if you wish to include a "clear" button, you can either simply include a "reset" button or create a regular button with an event that will write an empty string ("") in the value field of your text area by doing

document.myForm.textArea1.value = "";

Finally, use intervals or timeouts to create a banner changer. Have a set of images with their URLs stored in an array, and set a timer that will change the image every few seconds.

16

Windows and Frames

In the previous chapter we studied the window object and its contents, concentrating on the document object. The goal of this chapter is see how JavaScript can communicate between windows and frames, which effectively means communicating between separate Webpages.

FRAMES AND JavaScript

When you create a frame in a Webpage, each frame will have its own *window* object; it is therefore possible to access any of the object *window* contains on each separate frame. You can always check the name of any created frame by accessing the *name* field of your frame, which is accessed by writing *window.name.* To make matters even nicer for us developers, you may also access the parent of any frame you have, as well as any child. Imagine that you have created a frameset page containing two frames called *frameLeft* and *frameRight*. When you are in either frame, you can access the page that created those frames (the one with the frameset definition) by simply typing *window.parent.* This will refer to the window object of the parent; from there you can access anything defined in the parent as if you were in the parent's page, including functions, variables, and form references. Whenever you wish to access a function or variable defined in your parent's page, you can do so

Web Application Design and Implementation: Apache 2, PHP5, MySQL, JavaScript, and Linux/UNIX, by Steven A. Gabarró
Copyright © 2007 by John Wiley & Sons, Inc.

by writing the name of the method or variable after *window.parent*. Here is an example of a frameset page containing a method that will pop up an alert box saying "Hello." The frameset will define two children, *frameLeft* and *frameRight*, with one button each. Whenever the user clicks on either button, we will call the method written in the parent frameset. To make things more interesting, our method will accept the name of the calling frame as a parameter. Obviously our left and right frames do the same, except that they will send a different value to the parent's method. We can use *window.name* in the frame's code to directly send the right name.

Frameset definition:

```
<HTML>
  <HEAD>
    <TITLE>Basic Frames Example</TITLE>
    <SCRIPT LANGUAGE="JavaScript">
      function sayHi(name)
      {
        alert ("Hello " + name);
      }
    </SCRIPT>
  </HEAD>
  <FRAMESET cols="50%,*">
    <FRAME name="frameLeft" SRC="page.html">
    <FRAME name="frameRight" SRC="page.html">
  </FRAMESET>
</HTML>
```

Frame's page:

```
<HTML>
  <HEAD>
  </HEAD>
  <BODY>
    <INPUT type="button" value="Click me!"
onclick="window.parent.sayHi(window.name)">
  </BODY>
</HTML>
```

Since we know that we access a frame's parent, you might be wondering if it is possible to access frames in a more complex layout, in which a frameset may contain a frameset inside it. Well. . . . Of course, you can! Not only can you move up in the frames, you can also check a frameset child either using the *frames* array, or simply using the name of the array inside the *window* object of the frameset page. Also if the parent of a frame has a parent, this "grandparent" can be accessed by adding a new *.parent* for each level you wish to climb in the frame's hierarchy. If you wish to access the parent of all frameset (usually called the "root" or the "top"), you can do *window.top*. The most important step when you are attempting to work with more complex frames is to really know your frame's hierarchy well.

Let us suppose that our page is cut into three frames, with frameTitle on top, and frameMenu and frameBody underneath. Our menu frame will have a dropdown menu with several city names; when a city is selected, we will keep track of all selected cities on the frameBody inside a text area. The frameTitle will have a page showing how many times you changed cities, writing the message using a button, since we haven't seen how to modify regular text yet.

Frameset definition:

```
<HTML>
  <HEAD>
    <TITLE>Frames Example</TITLE>
  </HEAD>
  <FRAMESET ROWS="200, *">
    <FRAME name="frameTitle" SRC="title.html">
    <FRAMESET cols="200, *">
      <FRAME name="frameMenu" SRC="menu.html">
      <FRAME name="frameBody" SRC="body.html">
    </FRAMESET>
  </FRAMESET>
</HTML>
```

frameTitle:

```
<HTML>
  <HEAD>
  <SCRIPT LANGUAGE="JavaScript">
    var count = 0;
    function change_button()
    {
      count++;
      document.myForm.myButton.value = count +
"selected cities so far";
    }
  </SCRIPT>
  </HEAD>
  <BODY>
    <FORM name="myForm">
      <INPUT type="Button" name="myButton" value="0
selected cities so far">
    </FORM>
  </BODY>
</HTML>
```

frameMenu

```
<HTML>
  <HEAD>
  <SCRIPT LANGUAGE="JavaScript">
    function select_onchange()
    {
      window.top.frameTitle.change_button();
      window.parent.frameBody.change_text();
    }
    var test = 0;
  </SCRIPT>
  </HEAD>
  <BODY>
    <FORM name="myForm">
      <SELECT name="mySelect"
onchange="select_onchange()">
        <OPTION value=0>Alicante
        <OPTION value=1>Hoboken
        <OPTION value=2>New York City
        <OPTION value=3>Barcelona
      </SELECT>
    </FORM>
  </BODY>
</HTML>
```

frameBody:

```
<HTML>
  <HEAD>
    <SCRIPT LANGUAGE="JavaScript">
      function change_text()
      {
        var myTextArea = document.myForm.myText;
        var menuSelect = window.parent.frameMenu.
document.myForm.mySelect;
        myTextArea.value = myTextArea.value + menuSelect.
options[menuSelect.selectedIndex].text + "\n"
      }
    </SCRIPT>
  </HEAD>
  <BODY>
    <FORM name="myForm">
      <TEXTAREA name="myText" COLS=50
ROWS=25></TEXTAREA>
    </FORM>
  </BODY>
</HTML>
```

WINDOWS AND JavaScript

Probably one of the most annoying things on the Internet are the popup windows that 90% of pages abuse. Well, now it is your chance to create popup windows! JavaScript allows the creation of windows and the communication between different windows. Of course, we will not concentrate on how to annoy users, but rather how to make intelligent popups that close themselves when they are no longer needed.

We already saw a basic technique for creating popup windows. The idea was to provide a name in the *target* field of a link, making sure that the name had not been used yet (creating the new window with that name), or by using *_blank*, which would always create a new window with no name. JavaScript will allow us to go a step further and create new windows with the set of properties we need.

The basic syntax of window creation is calling the *open* method from the *window* object. The function takes three parameters: the page to open, the title to give to the window, and a list of window features. For example, if you wanted to create a popup that opens a file called *popup.html*, you could have the following script. In order to make our popup intelligent, we are adding an *onUnload* in the *BODY*. This event will be triggered when you leave the page that opened the popup, and it will close the popup window that was created. To close a window, simply use the method *close()*:

```
<HTML>
  <HEAD>
    <TITLE>Popup example</TITLE>
    <SCRIPT LANGUAGE="JavaScript">
      var newWindow = window.open("http://www.google.com",
"myWindow", "width=500,height=500");
      function closeIt()
      {
        alert ("Goodbye!");
        newWindow.close();
        return true;
      }
    </SCRIPT>

  </HEAD>
  <BODY onunload="return closeIt()">
    Go <A HREF="http://www.stevens.edu">elsewhere</A>.
  </BODY>
</HTML>
```

A good thing about the *open* method is that if you attempt to open a new popup with the same name under the same variable, the previous popup is updated, instead of creating a new popup. The object returned by *open* is extremely important as it is a reference to the new window's *window* object. Thus, you can access anything in the new window by using the previously seen objects such as *document* and *location*.

The third parameter in the *open* method is probably the most interesting one, as it allows you to fully customize the look of the new window. It should be a string with no white spaces so that it works in all browsers (Netscape does not like white spaces in this parameter). You may use any of these attributes:

- *copyHistory*—can be *yes* or *no;* allows you to specify whether you want to copy the history stack of the opening window.
- *directories*—can be *yes* or *no;* allows you to either show or hide the directory buttons.
- *height*—height of the window in pixels.
- *left*—left starting position; basically, the amount of pixels between the window's left border and the screen's left border.
- *location*—can be *yes* or *no;* allows you to show or to hide the location field.
- *menubar*—*yes* or *no;* allows you to show or hide the menu bar.
- *resizable*—*yes* or *no;* allows the user to resize or not to resize the window.
- *scrollbars*—*yes* or *no;* allows scrollbars to appear when needed or not. If you make a window that is not resizable and has no scrollbars, make sure that it is big enough to display all that you want to show.
- *status*—*yes* or *no;* show or do not show the status bar.
- *toolbar*—*yes* or *no;* show or do not show the toolbar.
- *top*—top starting position; basically, the number of pixels between the top of the window and the top of the screen.
- *width*—width of the window in pixels.

Imagine that you want to create a window that will be opened right in the middle of the screen, meaning that its center should be the same as the screen's center. Then you want the window to be a third the size of the screen. The first thing to do is to calculate the size. This is done using *screen.height* and *screen.width*. We just need to divide the numbers there by 2 to get our "half-size." The position is a bit harder. If you used half of the screen's height and width, you would be basically choosing the center of the screen as a coordinate, but using those values on our *top* and *left* field would make our window's top left corner to be at the center of the screen, and we do not want that. Since our window is meant to be centered and we already know its size, we know that the number of pixels from (for example) the top of the window and its center will be the window's height divided by 2. Since we know the distance from the top of the screen to the center of the screen, we can simply subtract that value by half the size of the window, letting us know the coordinate to use for our top. Use the same principle to calculate the left coordinate. The code would be something like this:

```
Var newWindow;
function open_centered_window(urlToOpen)
{ var height = screen.height / 3;
  var width = screen.width / 3;
  var top = (screen.height / 2)- (height / 2);
  var left = (screen.width / 2) - (width / 2);
  var features = "width=" + width + ", height=" +
height + ", top=" + top + ", left=" + left;
  newWindow = window.open(urlToOpen, "myWindow",
features);
  }
```

When we create a new window, since we get an object reference to the new window, the popup creator can always access the contents of the popup. Now, if you wish to do the opposite (accessing the creator window from the popup), use the *opener* object of your window. If you have a window *main* that opens a pop-up *child* that opens a window *grandchild*, you can access child from grandchild doing *window.opener* and even main from grandchild doing *window.opener.opener*. Each opener object will refer to the *window* object of you opener; from there you may access any form element, image, and so on.

One last fun thing you can do with windows is moving and resizing them. This can be done through the window object, so it can be done to any opener window, popup, or the window itself. There are two ways to resize and move: changing the coordinates/size through an offset, or giving the final value the fields it should have. Moving is done with *theWindow.moveTo(left, top)* or *theWindow.moveBy(leftoffset, topOffset)*. Resizing is done through *theWindow.resizeTo(width, height)* or *theWindow.resizeBy(widthOffset, heightOffset)*. To show this, we are going to create two windows. The main one will simply contain a button to open or close the second window. We will actually use the same button to open and close the window. Our popup window will contain two text fields and two buttons. The text fields will allow us to enter a number of pixels for height and width, and will contain an *onChange* event that will apply the changes whenever they are made. The two buttons will be used to either center the window, or have it move to a random location. If the user manually changes the size of the main window, we will update the remote controller with the new size of the window. The randomizing of the location and size of the main window will be done in such a way that the resulting window will always be inside the limits of the screen, and with a size small enough so that the bottom right corner will not protrude out of the desktop.

Main window:

```
<HTML>
  <HEAD>
    <TITLE>Popup example</TITLE>
    <SCRIPT LANGUAGE="JavaScript">
      var newWindow;
      var status = 0;
  function popupopenclose()
  {
    if (status == 0)
    {
      openWindow();
      document.form1.myButton.value = "Close Window";
      status = 1;
    }
    else
    {
      closeWindow();
      document.form1.myButton.value = "Open Window";
      status = 0;
    }
  }

  function openWindow()
  {
    newWindow = window.open("remote.html","Remote",
"width=250,height=250");
  }
  function closeWindow()
  {
    if (typeof(newWindow) != "undefined")
    {
      if (newWindow.closed == false)
      {
        newWindow.close();
      }
    }
  }
  function changeSize()
  {
    if (window.outerHeight > 0)
    {
      newWindow.document.myForm.height.value = window.
outerHeight;
```

```
      newWindow.document.myForm.width.value = window.
outerWidth;
      }
   }
    </SCRIPT>
  </HEAD>
  <BODY onunload="closeWindow()"
onResize="changeSize()">
    <FORM NAME=form1>
    <INPUT TYPE="button" VALUE="Open Remote"
NAME=myButton  onclick="popupopenclose()">
    </FORM>
  </BODY>
  </HTML>
```

Remote Controller Window:

```
<HTML>
  <HEAD><TITLE>Remote controller!</TITLE>
  <SCRIPT LANGUAGE="JavaScript">
    var height = 500;
    var width = 500;
    var left = 200;
    var top = 200;
    function applyChanges()
    {
      window.opener.moveTo(left, top);
      window.opener.resizeTo(width, height);
    }
    function updateWindow()
    {
      height = document.myForm.height.value;
      width = document.myForm.width.value;
      applyChanges();
    }
    function centerWindow()
    {
      top = (screen.height / 2) - (height / 2);
      left = (screen.width / 2) - (width / 2);
      applyChanges();
    }
    function randomWindow()
    {
      top = Math.round(Math.random() * screen.height);
      left = Math.round(Math.random() * screen.width);
```

```
        height = Math.round(Math.random() * (screen.
height - top));
        width = Math.round(Math.random() * (screen.width
- left));
      applyChanges();
    }
  </SCRIPT>
  </HEAD>
  <BODY>
    <FORM name=myForm>
  Height: <INPUT onChange="updateWindow()"
name="height" value="500" type="text"><BR>
    Width: <INPUT onChange="updateWindow()" name="width"
value="500" type="text"><BR>
    <INPUT name="center" type="button"
onclick="centerWindow()" value="Center Window"><BR>
    <INPUT name="random" type="button"
onclick="randomWindow()" value="Random Window"><BR>
  </FORM>
  </BODY>
  </HTML>
```

There is only one thing in the code that you might not know yet: *outerHeight* and *outerWidth*. These are basically properties of any window object that tell you the size of the outside of the browser window. If you want to know the size of the actual document, ignoring its borders, use *innerHeight* and *innerWidth*. Unfortunately, these properties depend on the platform. They work great on Firefox but not on Internet Explorer (IE) version 6+, for example. That is the reason why there is a condition checking *window.outerHeight* in the main window. If you try to access that value on IE, you will get "undefined."

ASSIGNMENTS

At this point you can do most of the fun features of JavaScript, so open up your mind, use your imagination, and try writing scripts that allow you to communicate between different frames in different windows. Try playing around with forms, updating data remotely, and have fun! The more fun you have practicing, the better you will learn.

ONE LAST FUNNY EXAMPLE

Here is a really cool example of an annoying window. It is a perfect example of how annoying popup windows can become. Before you write it down and try it out, be advised that I am not responsible for any problems that may arise. Nothing major should happen, but if you don't watch out, you might end up with several hundred browser windows moving around your desktop. When you are tired of seeing the effects, you should kill all the windows either through your task bar or task manager. That being said, let me explain how this little devilish window works, and why you need to be careful with it (unless you have a popup blocker). The idea of this popup window is to show several things. First we have an example of interval timers, which we use to call a method that will calculate the new coordinates and size of the window. Then we see how to move and resize an existing window. We also see how to use events to detect when a key is being pressed or the mouse is clicked inside the window. Finally, we see an example on how to create a popup window. What the script will do is constantly move and resize a window around your desktop (on a very basic pattern). This should be annoying enough, but to make matters worse, the moment a key is being pressed, we will create a new window that loads the same page, so that we have two annoying windows. Clicking anywhere on the page will have the same effect. Note that the event used for the key detection is *onKeyDown*, which means that the event is not happening as a combination of key down and key up (full key press), but just when the key goes down. Now, since most operating systems will repeat the key if it stays pressed, holding the key down will be considered as a lot of separate events. I tried pressing it for about a full second and ended up with around 20 windows. Of course, having *onKeyDown* as the event also means that if the users tries using ALT + F4 (default combination of keys to close a window), they will open a new window (because of the button being pressed) and close it (because of the "closing" combination of keys), but if they hold the key down too long, the windows might be created faster than they are deleted. Well, here is the code, I hope you enjoy it ☺:

```
<HTML>
<HEAD>
  <TITLE>OMG THIS SUCKS!</TITLE>
<SCRIPT language="JavaScript">
  var size = 800;
  var direction = 1;
  var myTimerID = setInterval("startannoying()", 1);
  function newwindow()
  {
    window.open("annoyingwindow.html", "", "");
  }
  function startannoying()
  {
    if (direction == 0)
    {
      size += 10;
```

```
    if (size == 800)
      direction = 1;
  }
  else
  {
    size -= 10;
    if (size == 100)
    {
      direction = 0;
    }
  }
  window.resizeTo(size,size);
  window.moveTo(size, size);
}
</SCRIPT>
</HEAD>
<BODY onkeydown="newwindow()" onmousedown="newwindow()">
  I wouldn't touch the keyboard or click on the window
if I was you!!
</BODY>
</HTML>
```

You could actually make this worse by, for example, adding an *onUnload*, in case the user tries (and manages) to hit the "back" button. Any "improvements" to make the page more annoying are entirely up to your imagination.

17

String Manipulations Revisited

OVERVIEW

We have seen the basics of string manipulations, with methods such as *charAt(), charCodeAt(), indexOf(), lastIndexOf(), substr(), substring(), toUpperCase(), toLowerCase(),* or even the attribute *length* to determine the size of a string. It is now time to take string manipulations a step further, see more useful methods, and study regular expressions. We will finish this chapter talking about the use of regular expressions in PHP, but for now let us talk about JavaScript.

NEW BASIC STRING METHODS

Back in Chapter 14, we saw that arrays had a method called *join* that allowed the creation of a string from a set of array elements. This was the same as a PHP implode. You might be wondering whether there is an equivalent to PHP's explode in JavaScript, and the answer obviously is "Yes." The function is called ***split()*** and takes a delimiter as parameter. For example, assuming that you have a string called *myString*, you could write *myString.split(',')* if you wanted to use the comma as a separator. There is something very important to realize when you use split. If your string finishes with the separator, you will have an entry that is an empty string. So if you do

Web Application Design and Implementation: Apache 2, PHP5, MySQL, JavaScript, and Linux/UNIX, by Steven A. Gabarró
Copyright © 2007 by John Wiley & Sons, Inc.

> var myString = "a,b,c,d,";
> var myArray = myString.split(',');

your array would actually hold "*a*," "*b*," "*c*," "*d*," and "".

Another interesting function, which will acquire an entirely new dimension in a few paragraphs after we do regular expressions, is *replace(match, replacement)*. For example, you could do *myString.replace("winter", "summer")* to have a sunnier day. As we will see later on, the match can actually be a regular expression, which will allow you to change as many matches as needed.

Next we have *search;* for example, *myString.search("Bewchy")* would return the string's position or -1 if the string were not found. You might wonder what the difference is between this and *indexOf.* Simply put, *search* accepts regular expressions; *indexOf* does not.

The final basic method is *match,* for example, *myString.match("1234").* This creates an array with all the matches found on the string. In our example it would create an array with as many entries as times you found *1234* on *myString.* Each entry will have the exact same *1234* data. You might wonder why you would use this method! Well, it will become *much* more useful when we combine it with regular expressions, as it will give us all matches on our expression.

REGULAR EXPRESSIONS IN JavaScript

A regular expression is basically a string that has a specific syntax, which allows you to find groups of similar strings. For example, they can be used to see if a string is an email address by checking the string for the key elements that all email addresses should contain.

To use regular expressions in JavaScript, we use the *RegExp* objects. You can create a new object by writing the regular expression either directly between slashes or as a string. The following example creates two variables with the same regular expression that will attempt to find three digits (I personally always use the first type):

> var myRegExp = /\d{3}/;
> var myRegExp2 = new RegExp("\d{3}");

A regular expression tries to ascertain, character by character, what your expression holds inside a string. Check this example:

> var myString = "bar, barman, barmaid, Bar, barcode";
> var myRegExp = /bar/;
> myString = myString.replace(myRegExp, "Club");

The idea is to change all "*bar*" iterations with "*Club,*" but if you try the example, the result will be "*Club, barman, barmaid, Bar, barcode.*" Only the first one would be replaced. If you wish to match all iterations, you need to add the "*global match*" modifier, which will try to match the expression in the entire string. Simply add a "*g*" after the closing slash. This would still raise an issue, as we have a string *Bar* with capital B. Since *B* is different from *b*, it would still not match the second word *Bar*. You can solve this with the "case-insensitive" modifier, by putting a letter "i" at the end of the regular expression. Our regular expression becomes

var myRegExp = /bar/gi;

With this regular expression, the result would be "Club, Clubman, Clubmaid, Club, Clubcode".

To make expressions more useful, you can use any of the following special characters:

- \d—represents any digit (0–9)
- \D—any nondigit character
- \w—any word character [A–Z, a–z, 0–9, or underscore (_)]
- \W—any nonword character
- \s—any non-white-space character
- .—any single character
- [. . .]—put characters instead of the periods, and it will match any of the characters between brackets. For example, *[abc]* will match *a* or *b* or *c*. You can represent a range of values with the – sign; for example, *[a–s]* would be any letter from *a* to *s*.
- [^ . . .]—any one character except those inside the brackets. For example, *[^abc]* will match any character EXCEPT for *a, b,* or *c.*

When there is a character (including any of the previous special characters), you can use any of the following suffixes, to be placed right after the actual character that is repeated. If you want a group of characters to be repeated, surround the group with parenthesis. Here is the set of repetition characters:

- *{n}*—match *n* of the previous items. For example, */a{4}/* would match *aaaa.*
- *{n,}*—matches *n* or more of the previous item. For example, */a{2,}/* would match *aa, aaa, aaaa,* and so on with *a*s as many a symbols as needed.
- *{n,m}*—matches at least *n* and at most *m* of the previous item. For example, */a{2,4}/* would match *aa, aaa,* and *aaaa.*
- ?—match the previous item 0 or 1 times. For example, */a?/* will match *a* and lack of *a.* It's the same as using *{0,1}.*

- +—match the previous item 1 or more times. Same as doing *{1,}*.
- *—match the previous item 0 or more times. Same as doing *{0,}*.

For example, to find a number like 1-800-555-5555, we can use either one of these two:

> *var myRegExp = /\d-\d{3}-\d{3}-\d{4}/;*
> *var myAltRegExp = /\d-(\d{3}-){2}\d{4}/;*

It is also possible to use a series of characters that allow forcing the position of a regular expression. Here is the list:

- ^—placed in front of a pattern, it will ensure that the match is found at the beginning of the string. For example, */^Hello/* would check whether *Hello* is right at the beginning of the string.
- *$*—placed at the end of a pattern, it will ensure that the match is found at the end of the string. For example, */Goodbye$/* would check whether the string finishes with *Goodbye*.
- \b—matches a word boundary. A word boundary is basically a limiter that does not count as a character, which means that a word was just written or is about to start.
- \B—matches a nonword boundary.

Check this example to understand word boundaries:

> *var myString = "Hello World!!! This isn't really cool is it?";*
> *var myRegExp = /\b/g;*
> *myString = myString.replace(myRegExp, "|");*

In this little piece of code we are replacing word boundaries all across the string (due to the global match modifier) with a pipe (|). The resulting string would be "*|Hello| |World|!!! |this| |isn|'|t| |really| |cool| |is| |it|?*." Therefore, if we wanted to improve our previous *bar* example, to have only the full word *bar* matched, you would use the regular expression */\bbar\b/gi* .

Remember that you can group regular expression in parentheses; so, for example */\b((ab){2,3}c)+\b/gi* would match globally (and case-insensitively) any full word (surrounded by word boundaries) that will have two or three groups of *ab* followed by a *c*, 1 or more times. For example, "*ababc*" is a match, and so is "*abababcababc*," but not "*ababab c*," since there is a word boundary before *c* is found.

Another useful feature of regular expressions is the reuse of previous matches. For example, you could have a string with comma-separated strings, and you could try to see if the same word appears twice in a row anywhere in the string. To do this, we must first group in parentheses the pattern that will be repeated, and then refer to it with a backslash followed by the position of the pattern (only the parenthesized patterns count). Our regular expression to match successive identical words separated by a comma and a white space would be */(\w+), \1/*. Basically, we try to find any word character one or more times, followed by a comma, a white space, and the exact same group of word characters found before the comma.

Sometimes you might have two possible choices of matches, and you might want to match only one of two choices. You can use a pipe (|), which is the "OR" character. For example, writing */a(b|c)d/* would match either *abd* or *acd*, but never *abcd*, *abc* or *ad*.

REGULAR EXPRESSIONS IN PHP

Using regular expressions in PHP is the same as using regular expressions in JavaScript, so I grouped both languages in this chapter. When using regular expressions in PHP, our regular expressions will be written as a string rather than using the slashes. For example, instead of writing */abc/* to match the string *abc,* we would use *"abc"*, with the double quotes. Other than that, the basics are the same; you can use any of the grouping, and position characters. You can also use *[[:alnum:]]* to match an alphanumerical data (digit or letter), *[[:digit:]]* to match a digit, and *[[:alpha:]]* to match a alphabetical character.

Once you have created your regular expression, you must use any of the regular expression functions that PHP has. First, we have *ereg*, which accepts a regular expression, a string where the regular expression needs to be found, and an optional array that will hold the series of matches. The function returns the length of the match for the pattern or *FALSE* if there were no matches. Imagine that you want to see if a date is formatted the regular American way of month-day-year and print its European equivalent in the format day/month/year. First we would write a regular expression that would help us see if there were a match, making sure to group in parentheses every group that we want to move around. Each parenthesized group will be accessible individually through the array sent as parameter. The entry at index 1 will hold the submatch for the first set of parentheses, the entry at index 2 will hold the second pattern, and so on. Index 0 will have the full match. Here is the code that would check the expression and print the new version:

```
if (ereg("([0-9]{1,2})-([0-9]{1,2})-([0-9]{4})", $dateString, $matches))
    echo $matches[2]."/".$matches[1]."/".$matches[3];
else
    echo "Invalid date format: ".$dateString;
```

You may also use *eregi*, which does the same, but ignoring the character case. It is like adding the *i* modifier at the end of a regular expression in JavaScript.

To replace patterns with other strings, use *ereg_replace($pattern, $replacement, $string)* or *eregi_replace($pattern, $replacement, $string)* for the same as a case-insensitive match find.

If you wish to gather information on all the different matches, use the function *split(pattern, string, limit)*. This function returns an array with all the matched elements. The *limit* is an optional parameter if you wish to store a maximum number of matches. You can also use *spliti* to do the same but case-insensitively. For example, if you wanted to find all words of two or more characters in a string (e.g., as in an indexer), you could do

$$\$arr = spliti(\text{``[[:alpha:]]\{2,\}''}, \$str);$$

The Set of PCRE

It is commonly known that the language Perl is one of the best languages for string manipulation, mainly because of its powerful regular expressions methods. Since there is nothing wrong in admitting that a different programming language is more powerful in a small set of operations, PHP decided to bring what made Perl so special into PHP, by creating the set of PCRE (Perl-compatible regular expressions).

The PCRE allows use of the same regular expressions as in JavaScript, meaning that you *must* put the slashes before and after your patterns. You will still need the double quotes around the entire expression. For example, to match the string *php* in a PCRE function, your regular expression should be "*/php/*." The good thing about this is that you can use the same modifiers used in JavaScript, such as *i* for case-insensitive. It also allows you to use the *x* modifier, which helps in creating commented multiline regular expressions. The *x* modifier basically indicates that all the white spaces in the patterns should be ignored, as well as any character between a pound sign (#) and the end of a line. This would allow you to turn a regular expression like */\bphp\b/i* into

> / #begin pattern
>   \b   #find word boundary
>   php #followed by "php"
>   \b   #then another word boundary
> /xi

Another modifier that can be added after the closing slash is the letter *e*. When used, it allows the use of subpattern matches similar to *\1* in JavaScript. This feature will be usable with the function *preg_replace()*, with the difference that it needs a double backslash (as shown below).

Finally, you may use any of the following special characters with any PCRE: \d for digit, \D for nondigit, \s for white space character, \S for non-white-space character, \w for word character, \W for nonword character, \b for word boundary, \B for nonword boundary, \A for start of subject, \z for end of subject, and \Z for end of subject or new line. For more information you may go to www.pcre.org.

Here is an example of how to use the *e* attribute to replace all tag names in a string to uppercase. To match all tag names, and not its attributes, find a character "less than," maybe followed by a slash (in case of a closing tag) and a series of word characters, followed by another set of characters different from "greater than," followed by "greater than." Since the character slash is a special character, to use it we need to "escape" it by preceding it with a backslash, so if you see "\/," it is not a strange capital V (or inverted uppercase Greek letter lambda); it is a backslash followed by a forward slash. Our regular expression would be "/(< \/?)(\w+)([^>]* >)/e". The three groups in parentheses are as follows: opening "less than," tag name, parameters, if any, with closing "greater than." To change the string to enable it to hold all-uppercase tags, you would do

> *$newString = preg_replace("/(<\/?)(\w+)([^>]*>)/e", "'\\1'.*
> strtoupper('\\2').'\\3'", $str);*

The other main PCRE functions used in PHP are

- *preg_match($pattern, $string, $array)*—the array is optional; this attempts to match the pattern on the string. If the array is provided, *$array[0]* would hold the text that matched the full pattern, *$array[1]* would hold the text that matched the first parenthesized subpattern, *$array[2]* would hold the text that matched the second parenthesized subpattern, and so on. This function looks for only one match.
- *preg_match_all($pattern, $str, $matches, $order)*—this will find all matches of *$pattern* in *$str* and store them in the array *$matches*. The *$order* can be *PREG_PATTERN_ORDER or PREG_SET_ORDER*. The first choice will organize the matches so that *$matches[0]* is an array of all the full-pattern matches, *$matches[1]* the array with all the matches on the first parenthesized subpattern, and so on. The second option will have *$matches[0]* holding an array of the first set of matches (meaning that *$matches[0][0]* would be the first full match, *$matches[0][1]* would be the contents of the first subpattern for the same match, and so on); *matches[1]* would be the second set of matches, and so on. I personally prefer using *PREG_PATTERN_ORDER*, as it helps out when you want to show information per type of match (full or partial).
- *preg_replace($pattern, $replacement, $str, $limit)*—if *$limit* is omitted or set to -1, all occurrences of *$pattern* in *$str* are replaced with *$replacement*. You can use (as we saw earlier) \\0, \\1 for substring matches. Note that you can *only* use single digits, meaning that only the full match and the first nine subpatterns can be referred to.

- *preg_split($pattern, $str, $limit, $flag)*—same as *split* but using PCRE. *$limit* is optional, and *$flag* can be *PREG_SPLIT_NO_EMPTY*, which will gather only nonempty matches.

- *preg_quote($s, $delimiter)*—puts a backslash in front of every character that is part of the regular expression syntax. The *$delimiter* is optional, but will also be escaped if included. The characters affected are \ + * ? *[ ] ^ $ ( ) { } = ! < > | :*

18

JavaScript and DHTML

OVERVIEW

You might be wondering what DHTML is, and, as do many people, you probably think it is a new language. Well, you would be wrong. DHTML stands for Dynamic HTML, which is a "high-tech" word used to define the possibility of changing an already loaded page. When we changed images, and moved windows, we were doing DHTML. In this chapter we will take this one step further, seeing how to change text, positioning of elements, and almost anything.

One very important thing to realize is that DHTML is technically done through JavaScript; therefore the scripts we will write might not work in every single browser. It is important to test your scripts and try to force yourself to use cross-platform objects and properties.

POSITIONING ELEMENTS

One of the main aspects of DHTML is elements positioning; it is possible to pinpoint the exact location of any element. Each location is given in pixels as a top left coordinate of the beginning of the element. Positioning can be either absolute or relative. When the positioning is set as absolute, the number of pixels specified indicates the location of the block from the top left corner of the inside of the browser. If the location is set as relative, the coordinate

Web Application Design and Implementation: Apache 2, PHP5, MySQL, JavaScript, and Linux/UNIX, by Steven A. Gabarró
Copyright © 2007 by John Wiley & Sons, Inc.

provided is calculated from the top left of the container. Note that the actual coordinates can be set as part of the item's style by using the *top* and *left* properties. To illustrate positioning, we will create a colored box, using the *height* and *width* style attributes. Imagine that you have the following classes in your style sheet:

```
<!--
  .Box { top: 100px;
    left: 100px;
    height: 300px;
    width: 300px;
    background-color: red;
    position: absolute; }
  .ParagraphStyle { top: 100px;
      left: 100px;
      color: yellow;
      position: relative; }
-->
```

This example yields a red box of 300 × 300 pixels, with its top left at 100 × 100 pixels from the top left of the browser:

```
<HTML>
  <HEAD>
    <TITLE>Positioning Example</TITLE>
    <LINK rel=stylesheet href=mystyle.css type=text/css>
  <BODY>
    <DIV CLASS="Box">
      <P CLASS="ParagraphStyle">
        This is cool!!!
      </P>
    </P>
  </BODY>
</HTML>
```

Besides the possibility of positioning any element anywhere, it is also possible to access *any* tag in a page, and modify its contents. We already saw how to do this with basic tags like links, images, and forms (with its elements), but it can also be done with paragraphs, *DIV* sections, or almost anything. To do so, provide the attribute *ID* to the tag you want to access. For example, you can set a paragraph to be accessible by doing

<P ID="myParagraph">...</P>

Once you have a set of opening/closing tags with an ID set to it, you may access the text inside it using the attribute *innerText*. For example, if we have the previous paragraph, you could change its contents by changing *myParagraph.innerText*. Note that *innerText does not* work on Firefox; instead, you should use *textContent*. As with any of the basic tags we saw earlier, you can update any property of the elements. Properties include any of the attributes in the style sheet. To change a style simply use the word *style,* followed by the style attribute to change. For example, you can change the *left* position of a paragraph to "200" by doing

myParagraph.style.left = "200px";

You can also add any event handler to paragraphs or other items, to enable you to change text when the mouse gets over it or out, even when you click it. This way you can create sections of your page that will behave like links without being links! Simply add an *onclick* property that will change the *location.href,* and you have made a link for yourself.

Be creative, but do not abuse the flourishes as they might become annoying to users. A nice use of paragraph positioning is scrolling news headers. You could have a section on top of your page with a paragraph that will scroll text thanks to an interval timer.

You can actually use coordinates that are negative when positioning an element. This means that they are placed outside the actual body of the page, making them hidden. From there you can use events to bring those sections in or out of the page, which is great for dynamic menus. Later on we will see how we can create this sort of menus.

As you probably realized using *innerText,* it only captures text skipping any HTML in the block. If you wish to set the contents of a paragraph or other element to contain HTML tags, you can use the properties *innerHTML* and *outerHTML*. The first will allow setting or reading all the contents between the opening and closing tags. The latter actually allows you to change the contents as well as the containing tags. This can be used to create an HTML code preview viewer as in the following example. This example works *only* with Microsoft Internet Explorer (IE). After it you will see a similar example that works on Firefox:

```
<HTML>
  <HEAD>
  <SCRIPT LANGUAGE=JavaScript>
  function setHTML()
  {
    if (radInnerOuter[0].checked == true)
    {
      div1.innerHTML = textarea1.value
    }
    else
```

```
    {
      div1.outerHTML = textarea1.value;
    }
  }
  function getHTML()
  {
    if (radInnerOuter[0].checked == true)
    {
      textarea1.value = div1.innerHTML;
    }
    else
    {
      textarea1.value = div1.outerHTML;
    }
  }
  </SCRIPT>
  </HEAD>
  <BODY>
  <DIV ID="div1">
    Write your HTML code in the box below!</H1>
  </DIV>
  <BR><TEXTAREA COLS=50 ROWS=20 ID=textarea1
NAME=textarea1></TEXTAREA>
  InnerHTML <INPUT TYPE="radio" NAME="radInnerOuter"
CHECKED>
  outerHTML <INPUT TYPE="radio" NAME="radInnerOuter">
  <INPUT TYPE="button" VALUE="Get HTML" NAME="bttnGet"
onclick="getHTML()">
  <INPUT TYPE="button" VALUE="Set HTML" NAME="bttnSet"
onclick="setHTML()">
  </BODY>
</HTML>
```

Here is a similar example that works on Firefox. Since *outerHTML* does not work on Firefox, we will illustrate the difference between *innerHTML* and *innerText,* or Firefox's equivalent *textContent.* As you will note, *textContent* will not parse any HTML contained in the text, whereas *innerHTML* will check the HTML code and process it.

```
<HTML>
  <HEAD>
    <SCRIPT LANGUAGE=JavaScript>
  function set()
  {
    if (document.form1.radTextHTML[0].checked == true)
```

```
    {
        div1.innerHTML = document.form1.textarea1.value
    }
    else
    {
        div1.textContent = document.form1.textarea1.value;
    }
}
function get()
{
    if (document.form1.radTextHTML[0].checked == true)
    {
        document.form1.textarea1.value = div1.innerHTML;
    }
    else
    {
        document.form1.textarea1.value = div1.textContent;
    }
}
</SCRIPT>
</HEAD>
<BODY>
<DIV ID="div1">
    <H1>Write your HTML code in the box below!</H1>
</DIV>
<FORM NAME="form1">
<BR><TEXTAREA COLS=60 ROWS=10 ID=textarea1
NAME=textarea1></TEXTAREA>
<BR>
<BR>
InnerHTML <INPUT TYPE="radio" NAME="radTextHTML"
CHECKED>
ContentText <INPUT TYPE="radio" NAME="radTextHTML"><P>
<INPUT TYPE="button" VALUE="Get" NAME="bttnGet"
onclick="get()">
<INPUT TYPE="button" VALUE="Set" NAME="bttnSet"
onclick="set()">
</BODY>
</HTML>
```

If you wish to update the inner or outer text or HTML of a block without changing the entire contents, you can use *insertAdjacentText* or *insertAdjacentHTML*. These are two methods that accept the location of the insertion, followed by the block to insert. The value of the first parameter can be *beforeBegin* to insert before the opening tag of a block, *afterBegin* to insert after the opening tag, and before the current text/HTML, *beforeEnd* to insert right before the closing tag, and *afterEnd* to insert after the closing tag. For example, *myDiv.insertAdjacentText("beforeEnd", "<BR>");* would insert a break of line at the end of *myDiv* but before its closing tag.

Another fun feature of DHTML is the ability to detect the source of an event. In IE, for example, you can use the *event* object, which holds information on the location of the mouse cursor, or what caused each event. Here are the contents of the *event* object:

- *event.screenX*—gives the *X* coordinate of the cursor.
- *event.screenY*—gives the *Y* coordinate of the cursor.
- *event.button*—returns a number representing the mouse button that causes the last event: 0 for no button pressed, 1 for left button, 2 for right button, 3 for left + right, 4 for middle button, 5 for left + middle, 6 for right + middle, and 7 for all three buttons (which is fun if you want to compel users to have a three-button mouse ☺).
- *event.fromElement*—returns the element in which the mouse was before the event occurred. For example, if you had a *onMouseOut* event on a button called *myButton* in your form *myForm*, when the mouse leaves the button the *even.fromElement* would be the same as *document. myForm.myButton*.
- *event.srcElement*—returns the element that caused the event.
- *event.toElement*—returns the element to which your mouse is moving when the event occurred.

WRITING DYNAMIC MENUS IN DHTML

Imagine that you are trying to imitate the typical window menus that every application has (with *File, Edit, View,* etc.) but inside a Webpage. The idea is that you want to show a table with a set of options; if you click on any of them, you "activate" the menus, which would show a table with all the submenus for each of those options, right under the main title. In order to do so, we could have a set of tables with the submenus, each table would be a submenu and would be in a separate *DIV* section. The idea is to keep the submenus "hidden" and make them appear in the page when the right option is selected.

To "hide" a submenu, we will place its *DIV* at a set of negative coordinates, placing it in a higher and further left position than the top left corner of the browser, effectively making it invisible. Once the option is selected, we will place the submenu right under the main option. We will combine this technique with several *onmouseover, onmouseout,* and *onclick* maneuvers.

The *onclick* will be used to know whether you are in "menus" mode or not, just like when you click on *File*. After the first click, you want to show all the submenus by simply placing the mouse over its title. Whenever we move out of at menu title, we will hide its submenu, unless we place the cursor on that same submenu. Finally after a click is made, we will switch back to "no-menu" mode, hiding all submenus. Below you will see the code to achieve this on Internet Explorer (this is just a basic example; most links will not even work). Be sure to check the companion Website for the Firefox-compatible version, as well as many other examples:

```
<HTML>
  <HEAD>
    <TITLE>DHTML Menus Example - MSIE Version</TITLE>
    <SCRIPT LANGUAGE="JavaScript">
    var showMenus = 0;
      function hideMenu(num)
      {
        var toHideId = (num.id).substring(3);
        var destinationId = (event.srcElement.id).
substring(3);
        if (toHideId != destinationId||(showMenus == 0))
        {
          num.style.top = -500;
          num.style.left = -500;
        }
      }
      function pickMenu(num)
      {
        hideMenu(div0);
        hideMenu(div1);
        hideMenu(div2);
        var src = event.srcElement;
        if (showMenus == 1)
        {
          num.style.top = parseInt(src.style.top) + src.
height;
          num.style.left = parseInt(src.style.left);
        }

      }
      function toggle(num)
      {
        if (showMenus == 1)
        {
          hideMenu(div0);
          hideMenu(div1);
          hideMenu(div2);
```

```
        showMenus = 0;
      }
      else
      {
        showMenus = 1;
        pickMenu(num);
      }
    }
  </SCRIPT>
</HEAD>
<BODY>
  <IMG SRC="file.gif" ID="img0" onmouseover="pickMenu
(div0)" onmouseout="hideMenu(div0)" onclick="toggle(div0)"
style="position:absolute;left:10px;top:10px;">
  <IMG SRC="links.gif" ID="img1" onmouseover="pickMenu
(div1)" onmouseout="hideMenu(div1)" onclick="toggle(div1)"
style="position:absolute;left:115px;top:10px;">
  <IMG SRC="help.gif" ID="img2" onmouseover="pickMenu
(div2)" onmouseout="hideMenu(div2)" onclick="toggle(div2)"
style="position:absolute;left:220px;top:10px;">
  <DIV ID="div0" STYLE="position:
absolute;top:-500;left:-500;width:100px;">
    <TABLE border=1>
    <TR>
      <TD><A HREF="">Option 1</A></TD>
    </TR>
    <TR>
      <TD><A HREF="">Option 2</A></TD>
    </TR>
    <TR>
      <TD><A HREF="">Option 3</A></TD>
    </TR>
    <TR>
      <TD><A HREF="">Option 4</A></TD>
    </TR>
    </TABLE>
  </DIV>
  <DIV ID="div1" STYLE="position:absolute;top:-500;
left:-500;">
    <TABLE border=1>
    <TR>
      <TD><A HREF="http://www.google.com">Google</A></TD>
    </TR>
    <TR>
      <TD><A HREF="http://www.stevens.edu">Stevens</A></TD>
```

```
    </TR>
    <TR>
      <TD><A HREF="http://www.wiley.com">Wiley</A></TD>
    </TR>
    </TABLE>
  </DIV>
  <DIV ID="div2" STYLE="position:absolute;top:-500;
left:-500;">
    <TABLE border=1>
    <TR>
      <TD><A HREF="">About</A></TD>
    </TR>
    <TR>
      <TD><A HREF="">Help Me</A></TD>
    </TR>
    </TABLE>
  </DIV>
  </BODY>
</HTML>
```

YOUR TURN!!

Now that you know about DHTML, try to write a script that will show moving paragraphs on the screen. Remember, you can set the position of a paragraph *myParagraph* by doing

myParagraph.style.top and *myPararaph.style.left*;

19

Putting It All Together!

OVERVIEW

With so many techniques and approaches, you might feel a bit lost trying to know how to organize your development phases, what you should start with, and what language should be used for what. This chapter provides the guidelines for applying the design techniques I have used in the past and that have always proved to work. As an example, we will imagine that we are writing a Web-based commerce site. These guidelines are general to any language; at the end of this chapter I will get more specific on the strong points of each language and what languages should be used and when.

PROCEDURE

Step 1—Understanding the Problem and Finding the Solution

This is probably one of the most important steps in Web development, and actually any type of programming. Designing your scripts properly depend on this. You *must* understand what is that you are trying to achieve and then figure out how to solve that problem. Usually the solution is found through several meetings between the developer's group and their managers. It is a good idea to have project sponsors at the first meetings so that they can state clearly what they are paying for and what they would like to accomplish.

Web Application Design and Implementation: Apache 2, PHP5, MySQL, JavaScript, and Linux/UNIX, by Steven A. Gabarró
Copyright © 2007 by John Wiley & Sons, Inc.

Once the first meeting has taken place with the decided scope of the project, you need to visualize how the final product will behave and what modules will be required. For example, if we are writing an e-business site, we know that we will need a payment module for costumers to pay for their purchases, a shopping cart system to keep track of purchases, a username/password system to remember regular users, an administrator panel to add items to our store, and scripts that will show the products to the clients by extracting the details from the database, allowing items to be searched by name, price range, or even category. To keep the example simple, and since I know what most computer science students like to do in their spare time, we will assume that we are coding a Website that will sell videogames.

Step 2—Designing the Database

The reason why we call these Websites "database-driven" programs is simple—the entire page revolves around a central database. This means that creating the database should *always* be the first part of your development cycle, after knowing how you plan to solve the problem. Always try to create a database with the least possible redundancies, and my advice is to try to have tables that hold only the crucial information for that table. If there is a set of data that complements a table but is not essential for the table itself (e.g., a list of user preferences would complement a user's table), you should create a separate table linked to the main one, rather than including the all the properties in a single table. The reason for this is that if you do a query on a large table, more information will have to be fetched, taking longer times to run the queries.

We have established that we want a Website to sell videogames, so we will need a table called *videogames* with attributes like *id_game, name, esrb_rating, description,* and *image_url*. Then we know that we will need to remember client's details, so we will use a *user* table with *id_user, name, surname, email, username, password,* and *level*. I am adding the level field to handle clients versus administrators. It just needs to be a little flag that will have a set value for regular shoppers, and a different value for Website administrators, granting them the right to modify the contents of the site, such as adding and removing games, reviewing orders, deleting users, adding more administrators, and so on.

As we said, we want to be able to search games by categories, yet you probably noticed that I did not add a category field. There is nothing wrong with writing a string with all the categories that a game is part of; for consistency with category names, I will create a *categories* table with *id_category* and *category*. This will store the names of the categories and associate each one with a simple number. This is the way I always write my databases so that I never need to transmit a string to extract information from one table to another. Instead, I always use dull keys, making it harder for a hacker to know what information I transmit between scripts.

Obviously this table still does not tell us which categories a game belongs in, so we need to create a *game_category* table with *id_game_category* (not strictly needed, but I want to keep it simple and avoid the need to combine two attributes as my primary key), *id_game*, and *id_category.* This will allow me to store all the categories of all the games. If a game has more than one category, it will have two entries in that table. This is a good example of a *n,m* relationship, where each game can have many categories, and each category can be applied to many games.

Following the same type of logic, even though the number of possible game platforms is limited, there are always new platforms appearing every few years. In order to keep our database as robust and flexible as possible, we will have a *platforms* table with *id_platform* and *platform*, similar to the *categories* table. As you probably noticed earlier, the *videogames* table had no reference to platform or price, because the same game may be available in different platforms, and its price will likely depend on its platform. For example, a handheld version of a game will always be less expensive than the same game on the newest generation of consoles. We will therefore use a *game_platform* with *id_game_platform* (this is the id used), *id_game, id_platform,* and *price.*

We then need to keep track of shopping carts. Most basic commercial Websites simply store the shopping cart in a session or a set of cookies, loosing all its contents if the user leaves the current computer and logs in on a different one later on. Instead of this behavior, we instruct the computer to memorize all shopping carts of registered users, so that the next time they log in, the items they tried to purchase will still be available. Each user is supposed to have only a single cart, so to keep things simple, we will use *id_user* as the primary key for the carts. If the user is not logged in, we will not store the cart in the database, using sessions instead. Basically, shoppers would get in the page, start shopping, and if they log in, their shopping carts will be stored in the database. If they were already logged in, updating the carts would update the database as well. Our table *cart* will hold *id_user, date,* and *total_price.* To store the items in the cart and its quantities, we can use a table *game_in_cart* with *id_game_in_cart* (dull id), *id_user* (reference to a specific shopping cart), *id_game_platform* (reference to a game in a specific platform), and *quantity.* The price can be calculated through the *game_platform* table.

Once the user decides to check out the shopping cart (i.e., finishes shopping), you need to ask for information such as shipping address, billing address, and payment information. Each user may have several credit cards, each associated with its own billing address information, and can also have a group of possible shipping addresses (in case the order is to be sent home, to the office or to a friend). To make our database as flexible as possible, we will have a table *addresses* with *id_address, id_user, line1, line2, city, zip,* and *phone;* and a table *payment* with *id_payment, id_address, type* (Visa, MasterCard, American Express, or other payment method), *number, expiration*

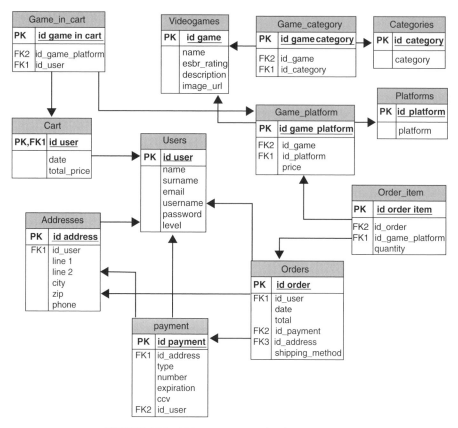

FIGURE 19.1 *Videogame store database structure.*

date, ccv (security code), and *id_user* (we could do without it, since we can extract the user information through the *id_address*, but it would simplify the task of searching for payment methods for a specific user).

After the user confirms the payment method as well as the shipping and billing address, the shopping cart is upgraded to an "order," and will be stored in a table *orders* with *id_order, id_user, date, total, id_payment* (for payment method and billing address), *id_address* (for shipping address), *shipping_method*. The specific items of each order will be in a table *order_item* with *id_order_item, id_order, id_game_platform, quantity*.

The final layout of our database is shown in Figure 19.1.

Step 3—Main Functionalities

Once you have created the database, you should create the main functionalities of your Website. Start concentrating on making sure the Website works, as clients would much rather see an ugly Website that can do what it is supposed to do, rather than a pretty page that has errors all over the place and does nothing at all.

Try to start with the important tasks first, as they will be the key parts of the project, but keep in mind what will need to be done in further steps. It is a good idea to set some data inside the database so that you can tell whether the scripts work well.

In our game-selling Website I would probably start writing the code to show all the games in the database, with 10 titles per page, taking advantage of the *LIMIT* property used in MySQL when performing a *SELECT*. The next step would be to extract the categories and platforms for which we have games from the database and write a script that would show the games for a specific platform and/or category by simply clicking on a link.

Once you can display all items correctly, work on the user login procedure. This should not take too long. At the same time create the forms to attract new users and add information like addresses and payment information. Make sure that the login script creates a session and that the session is kept alive until the user logs out. Of course, write the logout procedure that will destroy the session.

Next, start working on the add-to-cart function that should be attached to each displayed game on the page. Then work on the scripts that would help you update the cart, such as removing items, adding items, or changing the quantities of items already in there. Finally, work on the checkout procedure, turning a cart into an order.

If you write all the previously mentioned functionalities, the core of the project is done, and you can start pitching the progress to your team mates to try and find usability problems and bugs.

Step 4—Backside

You should always create an administrator panel to help you handle the data in your Website. For example, to add a new user or other entry in the database, it is much more recommendable to do so via your own scripts, rather than going straight to the database manager and adding the data manually.

Since you already wrote a login page, and in your database you have a flag *level,* add a check during login that will test whether the user is an administrator, and, if so, direct the user to an Admin panel.

The Admin panel should have scripts allowing the removal of items, as well as adding new categories, platforms, games, removing users, making a user an Admin, and pretty much anything that would update the contents of the database. To test out the functionalities, simply try adding a few items through the newly built Admin panel, then switch to a regular user and see if the products appear as they should.

Step 5—Improvements on Functionality

Once you have finished with the basic functionality of both the user and administrative portions of the site, you may start having fun with advanced functionality. This could include a searching tool to look for items by name, platform, esbr, price, or anything you might want to provide. You can do a "news" page that would show the most recent releases, based on the release date on the database, as well as the current date. You could also have an "upcoming" section with the games that are about to appear. The whole point of this is to improve the functionality of your Webpage, based on recommendations from tester users, project managers, and other team mates. Do not get too far away from your initial agreement; if you ask any project manager, you will learn that "Scope creep will kill you!"—meaning that if you keep changing the specifications of the project after you already agreed on them, your project will be delayed, potentially making you loose your window of opportunity as well as many development hours (and time is money). The "updates" should concentrate on bug fixes, and increased robustness on the project.

A typical thing that should be done in this step is to add forms verification for every single form on the Website. You should check all the data transmitted from page to page and make sure that it contains what it should.

At the end of this step your entire Website should be functional, but might not look the best. So let us advance to step 6.

Step 6—Improvements on Looks

Once you know that your pages work, you might start playing around with different style sheets. The best thing to do as you are developing the pages is to think about what different styles you will need and start providing class names to all the elements that will need a style. Then create an empty style sheet and link to it. In this step we edit the style sheet in question and experiment with colors, fonts, sizes, and even layouts.

Step 7—Thorough Testing, Hacking Attempts

So, you finally have a Website with all the required functionalities, you have an administrator control panel, the page uses a nice style sheet that you think your supervisor will like, and you probably think that you are finished with the project . . . unfortunately it is *not yet* the case. This step is probably one of the most overlooked steps in Web development, and it is the fundamental difference between a good Website and an excellent one.

In this phase you should group yourself with some friends or coworkers and attempt to break your Website (make sure that you have backups of the pages and database before you start). By "breaking" the Website I mean trying to insert corrupt data, hacking into the administrator panel without proper authorization, and things like that. It is actually quite funny to do and forces you to use your imagination to try and figure out the most obscure way to make the pages not work as intended.

A typical thing I do when testing my students' Websites is attempt to insert HTML code in any form containing data that will be displayed. For example, you could write things like *<FONT COLOR="WHITE">* if the background color is white when asked for a name; that way you force all following text to appear in white, virtually "erasing" all data that should appear on the page. The data would still be there, but would show up as white over white. Sometimes I decide to insert JavaScript like *<SCRIPT LANGUAGE= "JavaScript">alert("i pwn u n00b!")</SCRIPT>*, which will produce an alert message every time the field in question is read. This is usually an easy way to illustrate a serious problem, as it could allow a user to enter a JavaScript code that would generate popup windows opening malicious Websites. Those Websites could have the same appearance as your legitimate Website, and could be asking users to enter personal username and password information. This is a "hacking" technique called "phishing." It basically tricks users into entering their usernames and passwords into a "fake" Website that will transmit that data to the hacker in question. Making sure that no one inserts HTML in your pages is a good first step to avoid this problem. In short, you must do thorough testing in all code that asks the user for data, using things like regular expressions, or even PHP functions such as *strip_tags* to annihilate any tags that could have been inserted.

If your script allows users to upload data to the server, be sure to test the data sent (there is an upload script in the appendixes), and keep your brain functioning to find new ways to break your code. You should spend much time in this phase, since the Internet is populated with malicious users who will attempt to break your pages.

Step 8—Presentation

The last important step after you are sure that you have produced the best Website ever is to present it to the program sponsors (the people who paid for it) and make sure that they like it. You probably think this is the easiest step, but unfortunately project sponsors always want new features in their sites, so be prepared for criticism, and other remarks on things that should be included that you did not work on. It is also a good chance to get some input that might help you do nice updates on the site. The approach I would recommend is to start explaining your project in general, discussing only the main features and then focusing a little more on details of the functionalities only if you are asked to. This is assuming that you are talking to a person with no Web programming knowledge. If you present to a fellow programmer, you might want to skip the "commercial talk" and go straight to the function-alities, emphasizing security features and administrator panel.

Step 9—Publication

After the project has been approved, it is time to release it. Upload it to the Web server of your choice, and make sure that everything is set up properly. All pages should be accessible, all include files should be in secured folders, all the links and images should be working, and the page should be accessible by anyone in the world. If you did the previous steps properly, this should not take long.

Step 10—Celebration ☺ (and Maintenance)

This is by far my favorite step of a Web development cycle! After you have tested absolutely every single step in the project, it is time to take your favorite brew from the cooler and celebrate with the people who helped you create your Website.

Unfortunately, this step is not long enough, since once the project is published you will need to maintain the project. This means fixing things that could have slipped through the cracks during all your testing, upgrading features, adding functionalities, or simply (in our example) adding all video-games that are announced.

WHAT LANGUAGE TO USE?

You finally know how to go step by step from a single idea to a full project, but you still might have a very important question, namely: "What language should I use?" Most Web programming books concentrate on a single approach and a maximum of one or two technologies, yet here we have talked about four programming languages as well as a database management tool, so how should you combine all these languages?

First, you should familiarize yourself with PhpMyAdmin. Since the creation of the database should be one of the first development steps on the project, you should use this tool to set everything up before writing a single line of code.

For scripts such as login procedures, logout, session handling, and anything that requires extracting information from the database and creating dynamic pages, you should use PHP combined with HTML for the layout. Of course, any query to gather information from the database should be done in MySQL syntax, but submitted to the database through PHP scripts. All the information gathered should be retrieved from PHP.

Actually PHP is probably the language that you will use for about three-quarters of your project as it is the backbone of your project, and handles every minute detail on things that need to get done for the user to see a nice output.

JavaScript should be used for enhancements, such as, for example, form verification. Many people want to check the forms in PHP, but that means that all the data are sent from your form to PHP, then verified, and, in case of problems, the user is redirected to the same first form. This takes time as you need to communicate several times with the server. Handling forms in JavaScript is an excellent idea for things like required fields that cannot be empty, valid email addresses, and other basic checks that should be done before sending any data to the processing PHP script. Here is where you should practice all those regular expressions in JavaScript and keep the user in the form (remember to return false) as long as there are one or more problems in the form. Once JavaScript verifies that all the required data are there and formatted as required, you may allow the form to send its data to PHP (return true) and have PHP run a second series of tests. I always recommend a two-phase verification to get rid of as many possible errors and security holes as possible. My JavaScript side takes care of required fields and formatting, and PHP will verify things like compatibility with the values in the database, user level, and so on.

JavaScript is also very useful in providing some visual enhancements such as dropdown menus or rollover buttons. The most basic rollovers you could do would be to change an image with *onmouseover* and *onmouseout* if you are using images for your menu items. You can otherwise change a text style.

In a nutshell, HTML will organize the output layout, PHP will populate the page with the appropriate data, and JavaScript will make it all look nicer, as well as verify that the user enters the required information. MySQL will be the tool used by PHP to manipulate the database.

Well, I hope this book will help you understand the ins and outs of Web programming, the folklore, and good and poor design, and I hope that creating Websites will be as gratifying for you as it is for me. I wish you all the best!

Appendix A

Special Characters

Name Code	Glyph	Description
‘	'	left single quote
’	'	right single quote
‚	‚	single low-9 quote
“	"	left double quote
”	"	right double quote
„	„	double low-9 quote
†	†	dagger
‡	‡	double dagger
‰	‰	per mill sign
‹	‹	single left-pointing angle quote
›	›	single right-pointing angle quote
♠	♠	black spade suit
♣	♣	black club suit
♥	♥	black heart suit
♦	♦	black diamond suit
‾	‾	overline, = spacing overscore
←	←	leftward arrow
↑	↑	upward arrow
→	→	rightward arrow
↓	↓	downward arrow
™	™	trademark sign
"	"	double quotation mark
&	&	ampersand
⁄	/	slash
<	<	less-than sign

Web Application Design and Implementation: Apache 2, PHP5, MySQL, JavaScript, and Linux/UNIX, by Steven A. Gabarró
Copyright © 2007 by John Wiley & Sons, Inc.

Name Code	Glyph	Description
&gt;	>	greater-than sign
&ndash;	–	en dash
&mdash;	—	em dash
		nonbreaking space
&iexcl;	¡	inverted exclamation
&cent;	¢	cent sign
&pound;	£	pound sterling
&curren;	¤	general currency sign
&yen;	¥	yen sign
¦ or &brkbar;	¦	broken vertical bar
&sect;	§	section sign
¨ or ¨	¨	umlaut
&copy;	©	copyright
&ordf;	ª	feminine ordinal
&laquo;	«	left-angle quote
&not;	¬	not sign
&shy;	-	soft hyphen
&reg;	®	registered trademark
¯ or &hibar;	¯	macron accent
&deg;	°	degree sign
&plusmn;	±	plus or minus
&sup2;	²	superscript two
&sup3;	³	superscript three
&acute;	´	acute accent
&micro;	µ	micro sign
&para;	¶	paragraph sign
&middot;	·	middle dot
&cedil;	¸	cedilla
&sup1;	¹	superscript one
&ordm;	º	masculine ordinal
&raquo;	»	right-angle quote
&frac14;	¼	one-fourth
&frac12;	½	one-half
&frac34;	¾	three-fourths
&iquest;	¿	inverted question mark
&Agrave;	À	uppercase A, grave accent
&Aacute;	Á	uppercase A, acute accent
&Acirc;	Â	uppercase A, circumflex accent
&Atilde;	Ã	uppercase A, tilde
&Auml;	Ä	uppercase A, umlaut
&Aring;	Å	uppercase A, ring
&AElig;	Æ	uppercase AE (diphthong)
&Ccedil;	Ç	uppercase C, cedilla
&Egrave;	È	uppercase E, grave accent
&Eacute;	É	uppercase E, acute accent
&Ecirc;	Ê	uppercase E, circumflex accent
&Euml;	Ë	uppercase E, umlaut
&Igrave;	Ì	uppercase I, grave accent
&Iacute;	Í	uppercase I, acute accent
&Icirc;	Î	uppercase I, circumflex accent
&Iuml;	Ï	uppercase I, umlaut
&ETH;	Ð	uppercase Eth, Icelandic

Name Code	Glyph	Description
&Ntilde;	Ñ	uppercase N, tilde
&Ograve;	Ò	uppercase O, grave accent
&Oacute;	Ó	uppercase O, acute accent
&Ocirc;	Ô	uppercase O, circumflex accent
&Otilde;	Õ	uppercase O, tilde
&Ouml;	Ö	uppercase O, umlaut
&times;	×	multiplication sign
&Oslash;	Ø	uppercase O, slash
&Ugrave;	Ù	uppercase U, grave accent
&Uacute;	Ú	uppercase U, acute accent
&Ucirc;	Û	uppercase U, circumflex accent
&Uuml;	Ü	uppercase U, umlaut
&Yacute;	Ý	uppercase Y, acute accent
&THORN;	Þ	uppercase THORN, Icelandic
&szlig;	ß	lowercase sharps, German
&agrave;	à	lowercase a, grave accent
&aacute;	á	lowercase a, acute accent
&acirc;	â	lowercase a, circumflex accent
&atilde;	ã	lowercase a, tilde
&auml;	ä	lowercase a, umlaut
&aring;	å	lowercase a, ring
&aelig;	æ	lowercase ae (diphthong)
&ccedil;	ç	lowercase c, cedilla
&egrave;	è	lowercase e, grave accent
&eacute;	é	lowercase e, acute accent
&ecirc;	ê	lowercase e, circumflex accent
&euml;	ë	lowercase e, umlaut
&igrave;	ì	lowercase i, grave accent
&iacute;	í	lowercase i, acute accent
&icirc;	î	lowercase i, circumflex accent
&iuml;	ï	lowercase i, umlaut
&eth;	ð	lowercase eth, Icelandic
&ntilde;	ñ	lowercase n, tilde
&ograve;	ò	lowercase o, grave accent
&oacute;	ó	lowercase o, acute accent
&ocirc;	ô	lowercase o, circumflex accent
&otilde;	õ	lowercase o, tilde
&ouml;	ö	lowercase o, umlaut
&divide;	÷	division sign
&oslash;	ø	lowercase o, slash
&ugrave;	ù	lowercase u, grave accent
&uacute;	ú	lowercase u, acute accent
&ucirc;	û	lowercase u, circumflex accent
&uuml;	ü	lowercase u, umlaut
&yacute;	ý	lowercase y, acute accent
&thorn;	þ	lowercase thorn, Icelandic
&yuml;	ÿ	lowercase y, umlaut

Installing on UNIX

OVERVIEW

In most cases, your UNIX distribution will install everything for you, but if you are one of the unlucky UNIX users who have to install everything manually, follow these directives on Apache, PHP, and MySQL installation. This just reflects installation steps, as the configuration is pretty much the same as when installing on a Windows-based computer. I will assume that you have *root* access in your UNIX server, since you will need it on many of the steps. If you do not know what *root* access is, I advise you to contact your system administrators and have them install everything for you. This should spare you some headaches, and your system administrators will be much happier as they will make sure that everything is done properly. The installation steps will assume that you are using default configuration options. For more advanced options, check www.apache.org, www.php.net, and www.mysql.com. I will not explain how to install phpBB or phpMyAdmin, as it is the same as a Windows installation.

INSTALLING Apache AND PHP

Download the most recent version of Apache 2.2 and a fitting PHP version from the abovementioned places. This quick guide covers only the basics to get you started with Apache 2.0 and PHP. For more information, read the Apache documentation. The version numbers have been omitted here, to

Web Application Design and Implementation: Apache 2, PHP5, MySQL, JavaScript, and Linux/UNIX, by Steven A. Gabarró
Copyright © 2007 by John Wiley & Sons, Inc.

ensure that the instructions are not incorrect. You will need to replace the "NN" here with the correct values from your files. (*Note*: The following guidelines were excepted directly from the PHP online manual.)

1. gzip -d httpd-2_2_NN.tar.gz
2. tar xvf httpd-2_2_NN.tar
3. gunzip php-NN.tar.gz
4. tar -xvf php-NN.tar
5. cd httpd-2_2_NN
6. ./configure --enable-so
7. make
8. make install

   Now you have Apache 2.2.NN available under /usr/local/apache2, configured with loadable module support and the standard MPM prefork. To test the installation use your normal procedure for starting the Apache server, e.g.:

   /usr/local/apache2/bin/apachectl start
   and stop the server to go on with the configuration for PHP:
   /usr/local/apache2/bin/apachectl stop.

9. cd ../php-NN

10. Now, configure your PHP. This is where you customize your PHP with various options, like which extensions will be enabled. Do a ./configure –help for a list of available options. In our example we'll do a simple configure with Apache 2 and MySQL support. Your path to apxs may differ, in fact, the binary may even be named apxs2 on your system.

    ./configure --with-apxs2=/usr/local/apache2/bin/apxs --with-mysql

11. make
12. make install

    If you decide to change your configure options after installation, you only need to repeat the last three steps. You only need to restart apache for the new module to take effect. A recompile of Apache is not needed.

    Note that unless told otherwise, "make install" will also install PEAR, various PHP tools such as phpize, install the PHP CLI, and more.

13. Setup your php.ini

    cp php.ini-dist /usr/local/lib/php.ini

    You may edit your .ini file to set PHP options. If you prefer having php.ini in another location, use --with-config-file-path=/some/path in step 10.

    If you instead choose php.ini-recommended, be certain to read the list of changes within, as they affect how PHP behaves.

14. Edit your httpd.conf to load the PHP module. The path on the right hand side of the LoadModule statement must point to the path of the PHP module on your system. The make install from above may have already added this for you, but be sure to check.

   For PHP 5:

   LoadModule php5_module modules/libphp5.so

15. Tell Apache to parse certain extensions as PHP. For example, let's have Apache parse the .php extension as PHP. You could have any extension(s) parse as PHP by simply adding more, with each separated by a space. We'll add .phtml to demonstrate.

   AddType application/x-httpd-php .php .phtml

   It's also common to setup the .phps extension to show highlighted PHP source, this can be done with:

   AddType application/x-httpd-php-source .phps

16. Use your normal procedure for starting the Apache server, e.g.:

   s/usr/local/apache2/bin/apachectl start

INSTALLING MySQL

(*Note:* The following notes are quoted directly from the online reference manual of MySQL.)

   The recommended way to install MySQL on Linux is by using the RPM packages. The MySQL RPMs are currently built on a SuSE Linux 7.3 system, but should work on most versions of Linux that support **rpm** and use glibc.

   MySQL AB does provide some platform-specific RPMs; the difference between a platform-specific RPM and a generic RPM is that a platform-specific RPM is built on the targeted platform and is linked dynamically whereas a generic RPM is linked statically with LinuxThreads.

   Note: RPM distributions of MySQL often are provided by other vendors. Be aware that they may differ in features and capabilities from those built by MySQL AB, and that the instructions in this manual do not necessarily apply to installing them. The vendor's instructions should be consulted instead.

   In most cases, you need to install only the MySQL-server and MySQL-client packages to get a functional MySQL installation. The other packages are not required for a standard installation.

If you get a dependency failure when trying to install MySQL packages (for example, `error: removing these packages would break dependencies: libmysqlclient.so.10 is needed by...`), you should also install the MySQL-shared-compat package, which includes both the shared libraries for backward compatibility (`libmysqlclient.so.12` for MySQL 4.0 and `libmysqlclient.so.10` for MySQL 3.23).

Some Linux distributions still ship with MySQL 3.23 and they usually link applications dynamically to save disk space. If these shared libraries are in a separate package (for example, `MySQL-shared`), it is sufficient to simply leave this package installed and just upgrade the MySQL server and client packages (which are statically linked and do not depend on the shared libraries). For distributions that include the shared libraries in the same package as the MySQL server (for example, Red Hat Linux), you could either install our 3.23 `MySQL-shared` RPM, or use the `MySQL-shared-compat` package instead.

The following RPM packages are available:

- `MySQL-server-VERSION.i386.rpm`

The MySQL server. You need this unless you only want to connect to a MySQL server running on another machine.

Note: Server RPM files were called `MySQL-VERSION.i386.rpm` before MySQL 4.0.10. That is, they did not have `-server` in the name.

- `MySQL-Max-VERSION.i386.rpm`

  The MySQL-Max server. This server has additional capabilities that the one provided in the `MySQL-server` RPM does not. You must install the `MySQL-server` RPM first, because the `MySQL-Max` RPM depends on it.

- `MySQL-client-VERSION.i386.rpm`

  The standard MySQL client programs. You probably always want to install this package.

- `MySQL-bench-VERSION.i386.rpm`

  Tests and benchmarks. Requires Perl and the `DBI` and `DBD::mysql` modules.

- `MySQL-devel-VERSION.i386.rpm`

  The libraries and include files that are needed if you want to compile other MySQL clients, such as the Perl modules.

- `MySQL-shared-VERSION.i386.rpm`

  This package contains the shared libraries (`libmysqlclient.so*`) that certain languages and applications need to dynamically load and use MySQL.

- `MySQL-shared-compat-VERSION.i386.rpm`

  This package includes the shared libraries for both MySQL 3.23 and MySQL 4.0. Install this package instead of `MySQL-shared` if you have applications installed that are dynamically linked against MySQL 3.23 but you want to upgrade to MySQL 4.0 without breaking the library dependencies. This package has been available since MySQL 4.0.13.

- `MySQL-embedded-VERSION.i386.rpm`

  The embedded MySQL server library (available as of MySQL 4.0).

- `MySQL-VERSION.src.rpm`

  This contains the source code for all of the previous packages. It can also be used to rebuild the RPMs on other architectures (for example, Alpha or SPARC).

To see all files in an RPM package (for example, a `MySQL-server` RPM), run a commnd like this:

```
shell> rpm -qpl MySQL-server-VERSION.i386.rpm>
```

To perform a standard minimal installation, install the server and client RPMs:

```
shell> rpm -i MySQL-server-VERSION.i386.rpm
shell> rpm -i MySQL-client-VERSION.i386.rpm
```

To install only the client programs, install just the client RPM:

```
shell> rpm -i MySQL-client-VERSION.i386.rpm
```

The server RPM places data under the `/var/lib/mysql` directory. The RPM also creates a login account for a user named `mysql` (if one does not exist) to use for running the MySQL server, and creates the appropriate entries in `/etc/init.d/` to start the server automatically at boot time. (This means that if you have performed a previous installation and have made changes to its startup script, you may want to make a copy of the script so that you don't lose it when you install a newer RPM.)

If you want to install the MySQL RPM on older Linux distributions that do not support initialization scripts in `/etc/init.d` (directly or via a symlink), you should create a symbolic link that points to the location where your initialization scripts actually are installed. For example, if that location is `/etc/rc.d/init.d`, use these commands before installing the RPM to create `/etc/init.d` as a symbolic link that points there:

```
shell> cd /etc
shell> ln -s rc.d/init.d.
```

However, all current major Linux distributions should support the new directory layout that uses /etc/init.d, because it is required for LSB (Linux Standard Base) compliance.

If the RPM files that you install include MySQL-server, the **mysqld** server should be up and running after installation. You should be able to start using MySQL.

Note: The accounts that are listed in the MySQL grant tables initially have no passwords. After starting the server, you should set up passwords for them.

Appendix C

Advanced phpBB

If you followed the steps of Chapter 4, you should know how to create forums in phpBB as well as setting up its rights. Let us now see more advanced features!

The first thing we will do is set up groups. This allows a faster rights handling on who has access to different boards. Any board that should be hidden except for specific user groups should have its rights set to PRIVATE, MOD, or ADMIN. The PRIVATE right will block everyone from accessing the forum in question unless you manually add the user in question to the allowed list, or if that user is in a group with the proper rights. Using groups is much faster in the long run.

In the Admin panel, under "Group Admin," click on "Management"; this will show a dropdown menu with the current groups. Selecting a group and clicking on "Look up group" will take you to the group editing page. The button "create group" takes you to the same page, but for a new group. In there, select the group name, its description, and a moderator, who will have the right to add new users to the group. A group can be open, allowing anyone to join it, closed so that everyone can see it but may only be part of the group if added by the group moderator, or hidden; in which only the group members can see the existence of the group. Admin groups should be hidden; if you have a "Members" area, it should be closed, for example.

To add users to a group, you must be the group moderator or an administrator of the boards. On the main page, click on "Usergroups" (top menu)

Web Application Design and Implementation: Apache 2, PHP5, MySQL, JavaScript, and Linux/UNIX, by Steven A. Gabarró
Copyright © 2007 by John Wiley & Sons, Inc.

and select the group in which to add a member. Click on "View information," which will bring the list of all users of the group. Under the list you have a text area in which you can enter a member name; do so and click "Add member" to add the user to the group.

To change the forum access rights of a group, click on "Permissions" under "Group Admin" in the administrator page. Choosing a group will show all the forums in your database. In each line corresponding to a forum, you will see a "Moderator status" dropdown menu that will allow you to make (or not make) the group members moderators of a specific forum. In any forum that has one of its rights set to PRIVATE, you will have another option "Allowed Access" or "Disallowed Access," which will decide whether the group is part of the "private" group of the forum. If you wish to set up the same kind of rights for a specific user, click on "Permissions" under "User Admin."

There is a feature in phpBB that most users look forward to, called "ranks." A rank represents your notoriety in the forums and can be special or post-count-based. Click on "Ranks" under "User Admin" to access the current list of ranks. To add a new rank, click on "Add New Rank" and fill the form with this information: Rank Title is the string that will appear under the user's name to show that person's rank. Special rank (yes or no) distinguishes between fixed ranks (e.g., "moderator," "admin," "ruler of the world") and ranks based on the number of messages posted. Minimum Posts are used for nonspecial ranks, and signify the number of posts needed to reach the rank. Finally, the Rank Image should be an image path, relative to the forum's root. For example, to use "5stars.gif" as a rank image, assuming that it is inside an "images" folder on the root, you would write *./images/5starts.gif*. Rank images should be fairly small. Usually they are stars or other symbols associated with the forum's theme. The more stars, the more notoriety. Don't be afraid to create outrageous ranks needing thousands of messages, since, as sad as it may sound, if your forums become popular enough, you might have people with those numbers. For example, in the forums I use for my courses, I use the following ranks: n00b (0 posts), Visitor (10 posts), Frequent Visitor (25 posts), Known Face (50 posts), and Friendly Face (100 posts). I could have pushed it further with things like "Friend" (250 posts), "Family" (500 posts), "Are you stalking me?" (1000 posts), and "Get a life!" (2500 posts). Be original with the names, and lots of people will look forward to what their next rank will be (as sad as it may sound).

Another important thing to know how to use in phpBB is how to moderate forums. When you are an administrator or moderator of a specific board, you will have a link on the bottom right appearing when you visit a forum that reads "Moderate this forum." Clicking it will show the list of topics in the forum with a checkbox at the end of each name. Selecting one or more topics and using one of the four buttons will allow you to moderate entire topics. The options are "Delete," to delete the entire topic along with all its replies; "Move," to move the topic to a different forum (in which case you may leave a "shadow" of the topic, basically the name will appear but will link to the new location of the thread); "Lock," used to prevent nonadministrators and nonmoderators from writing in a topic; and "Unlock," to unlock a locked topic.

Clicking on a topic name in this section allows you to change the name of the topic or even split the posts in the topic as different topics.

Finally, it is possible to edit and delete any message as long as you are an administrator or a moderator of the forum containing the message. To do so, simply click on the small "x" next to the message to delete, or click the "edit" button.

There are more features in phpBB like styles, mass email, and others, but they are pretty straightforward to understand, so I shall stop writing about them right here.

Appendix D

class.FastTemplate.php

This is the code for my version of the class FastTemplate. It is very similar to the one found in www.webmasters.net with some minor changes to avoid notices with PHP5:

```
<?PHP
/*
  CVS Revision. 1.1.0 with modifications by Steven
Gabarró
*/
class FastTemplate {
  var $FILELIST = array(); // Holds the array of
                                  filehandles
                         // FILELIST[HANDLE] == "fileName"
  var $DYNAMIC = array(); // Holds the array of dynamic
                  // blocks, and the fileHandles they
                                          // live in.
  var $PARSEVARS = array(); // Holds the array of Variable
                                          // handles.
                         // PARSEVARS[HANDLE] == "value"
  var $LOADED = array(); // We only want to load a
                         template
```

Web Application Design and Implementation: Apache 2, PHP5, MySQL, JavaScript, and Linux/UNIX, by Steven A. Gabarró
Copyright © 2007 by John Wiley & Sons, Inc.

```
                            // once - when it's used.
                      // LOADED[FILEHANDLE] == 1 if loaded
                          // undefined if not loaded yet.
  var $HANDLE = array(); // Holds the handle names
                            assigned
                      // by a call to parse()
  var $ROOT = "";        // Holds path-to-templates
  var $WIN32 = true;     // Set to true if this is a
                            WIN32 server
  var $ERROR = "";       // Holds the last error message
  var $LAST = "";        // Holds the HANDLE to the last
                      // template parsed by parse()
  var $STRICT = true;    // Strict template checking.
                      // Unresolved vars in templates will
                      // generate a warning when found.
// ************************************************************
  function FastTemplate ($pathToTemplates = "")
  {
    global $php_errormsg;
    if(!empty($pathToTemplates))
    {
      $this->set_root($pathToTemplates);
    }
  } // end (new) FastTemplate ()
// ************************************************************
// All templates will be loaded from this "root"
directory
// Can be changed in mid-process by re-calling with a
new
// value.
  function set_root ($root)
  {
    $trailer = substr($root,-1);
    if(!$this->WIN32)
    {
      if( (ord($trailer)) != 47 )
      {
        $root = "$root". chr(47);
      }
      if(is_dir($root))
      {
        $this->ROOT = $root;
      }
      else
      {
        $this->ROOT = "";
```

```
    $this->error("Specified ROOT dir [$root] is not a
directory");
      }
    }
    else
    {
      // WIN32 box - no testing
      if( (ord($trailer)) != 92 )
      {
        $root = "$root" . chr(92);
      }
      $this->ROOT = $root;
    }
  } // End set_root()
// ****************************************************************
// Calculates current microtime
//  I throw this into all my classes for benchmarking
purposes
// It's not used by anything in this class and can be
removed
// if you don't need it.
  function utime ()
  {
    $time = explode( " ", microtime());
    $usec = (double)$time[0];
    $sec = (double)$time[1];
    return $sec + $usec;
}
// ****************************************************************
// Strict template checking, if true sends warnings to
STDOUT when
// parsing a template with undefined variable references
// Used for tracking down bugs-n-such. Use no_strict()
to disable.
  function strict ()
  {
    $this->STRICT = true;
  }
// ****************************************************************
// Silently discards (removes) undefined variable
references
// found in templates
  function no_strict ()
  {
    $this->STRICT = false;
  }
```

```
//   ************************************************************
//   A quick check of the template file before reading it.
//   This is -not- a reliable check, mostly due to
inconsistencies
//   in the way PHP determines if a file is readable.
  function is_safe ($filename)
  {
    if(!file_exists($filename))
    {
      $this->error("[$filename] does not exist",0);
      return false;
    }
    return true;
  }
//   ************************************************************
//   Grabs a template from the root dir and
//   reads it into a (potentially REALLY) big string
  function get_template ($template)
  {
    if(empty($this->ROOT))
    {
      $this->error("Cannot open template. Root not
valid.",1);
      return false;
    }
    $filename = "$this->ROOT"."$template";
    $contents = implode("",(@file($filename)));
    if( (!$contents) or (empty($contents)) )
    {
      $this->error("get_template() failure: [$filename]
$php_errormsg",1);
    }
    return $contents;
  } // end get_template
//   ************************************************************
//   Prints the warnings for unresolved variable
references
//   in template files. Used if STRICT is true
  function show_unknowns ($Line)
  {
    $unknown = array();
    if (ereg("({[A-Z0-9_]+})",$Line,$unknown))
    {
      $UnkVar = $unknown[1];
      if(!(empty($UnkVar)))
```

```
    {
        @error_log("[FastTemplate] Warning: no value found
for variable: $UnkVar ",0);
      }
    }
  } // end show_unknowns()
// ***********************************************************
// This routine get's called by parse() and does the
actual
// {VAR} to VALUE conversion within the template.
  function parse_template ($template, $tpl_array)
  {
    while ( list ($key,$val) = each ($tpl_array) )
    {
      if (!(empty($key)))
      {
        if(gettype($val) != "string")
        {
          settype($val,"string");
        }
         // php4 doesn't like '{$' combinations
        $key = '{'."$key".'}';
        $template =
ereg_replace("$key","$val","$template");
        //$template =
str_replace("$key","$val","$template");
      }
    }
    if(!$this->STRICT)
    {
      // Silently remove anything not already found
      $template = ereg_replace("{([A-Z0-9_]+)}","",$template);
    }
    else
    {
      // Warn about unresolved template variables
      if (ereg("({[A-Z0-9_]+})",$template))
      {
        $unknown = split("\n",$template);
        while (list ($Element,$Line) = each($unknown) )
        {
          $UnkVar = $Line;
          if(!(empty($UnkVar)))
          {
            $this->show_unknowns($UnkVar);
```

```
          }
        }
      }
    }
    return $template;
  } // end parse_template();
// *********************************************************
// The meat of the whole class. The magic happens here.
  function parse ( $ReturnVar, $FileTags )
  {
    $append = false;
    $this->LAST = $ReturnVar;
    $this->HANDLE[$ReturnVar] = 1;
    if (!isset($this->$ReturnVar))
      $this->$ReturnVar = "";

    if (gettype($FileTags) == "array")
    {
      unset($this->$ReturnVar); // Clear any previous data
      while ( list ( $key , $val ) = each ( $FileTags ) )
      {
        if ( (!isset($this->$val)) || (empty($this->$val)) )
        {
          $this->LOADED["$val"] = 1;
          if(isset($this->DYNAMIC["$val"]))
          {
            $this->parse_dynamic($val,$ReturnVar);
          }
          else
          {
            $fileName = $this->FILELIST["$val"];
            $this->$val = $this->get_template($fileName);
          }
        }
        // Array context implies overwrite
        $this->$ReturnVar =
$this->parse_template($this->$val,$this->PARSEVARS);
        // For recursive calls.
        $this->assign( array( $ReturnVar => $this-
>$ReturnVar ) );
      }
    } // end if FileTags is array()
    else
    {
      // FileTags is not an array
```

```
      $val = $FileTags;
      if( (substr($val,0,1)) == '.' )
      {
        // Append this template to a previous ReturnVar
        $append = true;
        $val = substr($val,1);
      }
      if ( (!isset($this->$val)) || (empty($this->$val)) )
      {
          $this->LOADED["$val"] = 1;
          if(isset($this->DYNAMIC["$val"]))
          {
            $this->parse_dynamic($val,$ReturnVar);
          }
          else
          {
            $fileName = $this->FILELIST["$val"];
            $this->$val = $this->get_template($fileName);
          }
      }
      if($append)
      {
        $this->$ReturnVar .= $this->parse_template
($this->$val,$this->PARSEVARS);
      }
      else
      {
        $this->$ReturnVar = $this->parse_template
($this->$val,$this->PARSEVARS);
      }
      // For recursive calls.
      $this->assign(array( $ReturnVar => $this->$ReturnVar) );
    }
    return;
  } // End parse()
// ************************************************************
  function FastPrint ( $template = "" )
  {
    if(empty($template))
    {
      $template = $this->LAST;
    }
    if( (!(isset($this->$template))) || (empty($this-
>$template)) )
    {
```

```
    $this->error("Nothing parsed, nothing printed",0);
    return;
  }
  else
  {
    print $this->$template;
  }
  return;
}
// *********************************************************
function fetch ( $template = "" )
{
  if(empty($template))
  {
    $template = $this->LAST;
  }
  if( (!(isset($this->$template))) || (empty($this-
>$template)) )
  {
    $this->error("Nothing parsed, nothing printed",0);
    return "";
  }
  return($this->$template);
}
// *********************************************************
function define_dynamic ($Macro, $ParentName)
{
  // A dynamic block lives inside another template file.
  // It will be stripped from the template when parsed
  // and replaced with the {$Tag}.
  $this->DYNAMIC["$Macro"] = $ParentName;
  return true;
}
// *********************************************************
function parse_dynamic ($Macro,$MacroName)
{
  // The file must already be in memory.
  $ParentTag = $this->DYNAMIC["$Macro"];
  if( (!$this->$ParentTag) or (empty($this->$ParentTag)) )
  {
    $fileName = $this->FILELIST[$ParentTag];
    $this->$ParentTag = $this->get_template($fileName);
    $this->LOADED[$ParentTag] = 1;
  }
  if($this->$ParentTag)
```

```
  {
    $template = $this->$ParentTag;
    $DataArray = split("\n",$template);
    $newMacro = "";
    $newParent = "";
    $outside = true;
    $start = false;
    $end = false;
    while ( list ($lineNum,$lineData) = each ($DataArray) )
    {
      $lineTest = trim($lineData);
      if("<!-- BEGIN DYNAMIC BLOCK: $Macro -->" == "$lineTest" )
      {
        $start = true;
        $end = false;
        $outside = false;
      }
      if("<!--" END DYNAMIC BLOCK: $Macro -->" == "$lineTest" )
      {
        $start = false;
        $end = true;
        $outside = true;
      }
      if( (!$outside) and (!$start) and (!$end) )
      {
        $newMacro .= "$lineData\n"; // Restore linebreaks
      }
      if( ($outside) and (!$start) and (!$end) )
      {
        $newParent .= "$lineData\n"; // Restore linebreaks
      }
      if($end)
      {
        $newParent .= '{'."$MacroName}\n";
      }
      // Next line please
      if($end) { $end = false; }
      if($start) { $start = false; }
    } // end While
    $this->$Macro = $newMacro;
    $this->$ParentTag = $newParent;
    return true;
  } // $ParentTag NOT loaded - MAJOR oopsie
  else
```

```
    {
      @error_log("ParentTag: [$ParentTag] not loaded!",0);
      $this->error("ParentTag: [$ParentTag] not loaded!",0);
    }
    return false;
  }
//  ***********************************************************
//  Strips a DYNAMIC BLOCK from a template.
    function clear_dynamic ($Macro="")
    {
    if(empty($Macro)) { return false; }
    // The file must already be in memory.
    $ParentTag = $this->DYNAMIC["$Macro"];
    if( (!$this->$ParentTag) or (empty($this->$ParentTag)) )
    {
      $fileName = $this->FILELIST[$ParentTag];
      $this->$ParentTag = $this->get_template($fileName);
      $this->LOADED[$ParentTag] = 1;
    }
    if($this->$ParentTag)
    {
      $template = $this->$ParentTag;
      $DataArray = split("\n",$template);
      $newParent = "";
      $outside = true;
      $start = false;
      $end = false;
      while ( list ($lineNum,$lineData) = each ($DataArray) )
      {
        $lineTest = trim($lineData);
        if("<!-- BEGIN DYNAMIC BLOCK: $Macro -->" ==
"$lineTest" )
        {
          $start = true;
          $end = false;
          $outside = false;
        }
        if("<!-- END DYNAMIC BLOCK: $Macro -->" == "$lineTest" )
        {
          $start = false;
          $end = true;
          $outside = true;
        }
        if( ($outside) and (!$start) and (!$end) )
        {
```

```
      $newParent .= "$lineData\n"; // Restore
linebreaks
        }
       // Next line please
       if($end) { $end = false; }
       if($start) { $start = false; }
     } // end While
     $this->$ParentTag = $newParent;
     return true;
   } // $ParentTag NOT loaded - MAJOR oopsie
   else
   {
     @error_log("ParentTag: [$ParentTag] not loaded!",0);
     $this->error("ParentTag: [$ParentTag] not loaded!",0);
   }
   return false;
  }
// ***********************************************************
  function define ($fileList)
  {
    while ( list ($FileTag,$FileName) = each ($fileList) )
    {
      $this->FILELIST["$FileTag"] = $FileName;
    }
    return true;
  }
// ***********************************************************
  function clear_parse ( $ReturnVar = "")
  {
    $this->clear($ReturnVar);
  }
// ***********************************************************
  function clear ( $ReturnVar = "" )
  {
    // Clears out hash created by call to parse()
    if(!empty($ReturnVar))
    {
      if( (gettype($ReturnVar)) != "array")
      {
        unset($this->$ReturnVar);
        return;
      }
      else
      {
        while ( list ($key,$val) = each ($ReturnVar) )
```

```
      {
        unset($this->$val);
      }
      return;
    }
  }
  // Empty - clear all of them
  while ( list ( $key,$val) = each ($this->HANDLE) )
  {
    $KEY = $key;
    unset($this->$KEY);
  }
  return;
} // end clear()
// ***********************************************************
function clear_all ()
{
  $this->clear();
  $this->clear_assign();
  $this->clear_define();
  $this->clear_tpl();
  return;
} // end clear_all
// ***********************************************************
function clear_tpl ($fileHandle = "")
{
  if(empty($this->LOADED))
  {
    // Nothing loaded, nothing to clear
    return true;
  }
  if(empty($fileHandle))
  {
    // Clear ALL fileHandles
    while ( list ($key, $val) = each ($this->LOADED) )
    {
      unset($this->$key);
    }
    unset($this->LOADED);
    return true;
  }
  else
  {
    if( (gettype($fileHandle)) != "array")
    {
```

```
      if( (isset($this->$fileHandle)) || (!empty($this-
>$fileHandle)) )
        {
          unset($this->LOADED[$fileHandle]);
          unset($this->$fileHandle);
          return true;
        }
      }
      else
      {
        while ( list ($Key, $Val) = each ($fileHandle) )
        {
          unset($this->LOADED[$Key]);
          unset($this->$Key);
        }
        return true;
      }
    }
    return false;
  } // end clear_tpl
// ***********************************************************
  function clear_define ( $FileTag = "" )
  {
    if(empty($FileTag))
    {
      unset($this->FILELIST);
      return;
    }
    if( (gettype($Files)) != "array")
    {
      unset($this->FILELIST[$FileTag]);
      return;
    }
    else
    {
      while ( list ( $Tag, $Val) = each ($FileTag) )
      {
        unset($this->FILELIST[$Tag]);
      }
      return;
    }
  }
// ***********************************************************
// Aliased function - used for compatibility with CGI::
FastTemplate
```

```
//  function clear_parse ()
//  {
//    $this->clear_assign();
//  }
//  ************************************************************
//  Clears all variables set by assign()
  function clear_assign ()
  {
    if(!(empty($this->PARSEVARS)))
    {
      while(list($Ref,$Val) = each ($this->PARSEVARS) )
      {
        unset($this->PARSEVARS["$Ref"]);
      }
    }
  }
//  ************************************************************
  function clear_href ($href)
  {
    if(!empty($href))
    {
      if( (gettype($href)) != "array")
      {
        unset($this->PARSEVARS[$href]);
        return;
      }
      else
      {
        while (list ($Ref,$val) = each ($href) )
        {
          unset($this->PARSEVARS[$Ref]);
        }
        return;
      }
    }
    else
    {
      // Empty - clear them all
      $this->clear_assign();
    }
    return;
  }
//  ************************************************************
  function assign ($tpl_array, $trailer="")
  {
```

```php
      if(gettype($tpl_array) == "array")
      {
        while ( list ($key,$val) = each ($tpl_array) )
        {
          if (!(empty($key)))
          {
            //  Empty values are allowed
            //  Empty Keys are NOT
            $this->PARSEVARS["$key"] = $val;
          }
        }
      }
      else
      {
        // Empty values are allowed in non-array context now.
        if (!empty($tpl_array))
        {
          $this->PARSEVARS["$tpl_array"] = $trailer;
        }
      }
    }
// ************************************************************
// Return the value of an assigned variable.
// Christian Brandel cbrandel@gmx.de
  function get_assigned($tpl_name = "")
  {
    if(empty($tpl_name)) { return false; }
    if(isset($this->PARSEVARS["$tpl_name"]))
    {
      return ($this->PARSEVARS["$tpl_name"]);
    }
    else
    {
      return false;
  }
  }
// ************************************************************
  function error ($errorMsg, $die = 0)
  {
    $this->ERROR = $errorMsg;
    echo "ERROR: $this->ERROR <BR> \n";
    if ($die == 1)
    {
      exit;
    }
```

```
    return;
  } // end error()
// **********************************************************
// **********************************************************
} // End class.FastTemplate.php3
?>
```

Appendix E

File Upload Script

Here is a little script for uploading a file to a server. There are two files: a form in which to enter all details of the file to be uploaded, and the PHP file that will process the uploading and place the file in the desired folder:

```html
<html>
  <head>
    <title> A Simple Form for Uploading a File </title>
  </head>
  <body>
    <h1>A simple form for uploading a file </h1>
    <form action="upload.php" method="post"
enctype="multipart/form-data">
      Enter file name: <Input type=file name=userfile><br>
      <input type=submit><br>
    </form>
  </body>
</html>
```

Web Application Design and Implementation: Apache 2, PHP5, MySQL, JavaScript, and Linux/UNIX, by Steven A. Gabarró
Copyright © 2007 by John Wiley & Sons, Inc.

```
<html>
  <head>
    <title>
      Upload File Example
    </title>
  </head>
  <body>
  <?php
  printf("<b>Uploaded File Details</b><br><br>");
  printf("Name: %s <br>", $_FILES["userfile"]["name"]);
  printf("Temporary Name: %s <br>",
      $_FILES["userfile"]["tmp_name"]);
  printf("Size: %s <br>", $_FILES["userfile"]["size"]);
  printf("Type: %s <br> <br>", $_FILES["userfile"]["type"]);
  if (move_uploaded_file($_FILES["userfile"]["tmp_name"],
    "D:/Web/UploadedFiles/".$_FILES["userfile"]["name"])) {
      printf("<b>File successfully copied</b>");
  } else {
      printf("<b>Error: failed to copy file</b>");
  }
?>
  </body>
</html>
```

Bibliography

Apache Installation Notes (included in the Apache installation files; used as guidelines on how to install an Apache server).

Bellis, Mary, *The History of Communication*, http://inventors.about.com/library/inventors/bl_history_of_communication.htm (a timeline of communication-related inventions; I used those dates in Chapter 1).

Bernstein, Lawrence, and C. M. Yuhas, *Trustworthy System through Quantitative Software Engineering*, Wiley, October 2005 (nice guide on software development and quantitative software engineering).

Cambridge Advanced Learner's Dictionary (used for the definitions of "cookie").

Classes and Objects (PHP5), chapter of the PHP online manual http://www.php.net/manual/en/language.oop5.php (used in Chapter 9 to explain the object-oriented programming principles, as well as to present basic examples).

Englander, Irv, *The Architecture of Computer Hardware and Systems Software: An Information Technology Approach*, 3rd ed., Wiley, January 2003 (I have used this book as a reference on the basics of TCP/IP and also in one of my courses; it has a nice easy approach to the technologies presented).

Internet Society, *A Brief History of the Internet*, http://www.isoc.org/internet/history/brief.shtml (a brief explanation of how the Internet developed to the point it has reached now).

Jacobs, Ian (Head of W3C Communications), *About W3C: History*, http://www.w3.org/Consortium/history (a description of how the World Wide Web concept originated, leading to the creation of the W3C).

MySQL Reference Manual, http://dev.mysql.com/doc/refman/5.1/en/index.html (used for MySQL syntax references).

MySQL 5.1 Reference Manual: 2.4 Installing MySQL on Linux, http://dev.mysql.com/doc/refman/5.1/en/linux-rpm.html (used in Appendix B for MySQL installation notes).

Original FastTemplate Class, www.thewebmasters.net/php/FastTemplate.phtml (personally modified to make it compatible with newer versions of PHP).

PHP Installation Notes (included in the PHP5 package; used as guidelines on how to install PHP5 on Windows).

PHP: Installation on Unix Systems—Manual, http://www.php.et/manual/en/install.unix.php (installation guide for UNIX systems, used in Appendix B).

PHP Online Manual, http://www.php.net/manual/en/ (used as functions reference to ensure accuracy of function prototypes).

phpBB Installation Notes (included in phpBB installation files; used to give the guidelines on installing phpBB).

phpMyAdmin Installation notes (included in phpMyAdmin installation files; used to give the guidelines for installing phpMyAdmin).

Stroustrup, Bjarne, *The Design and Evolution of C++*, Addison-Wesley, 1994 (recommended book on C++).

The W3C Website, http://www.w3c.org (used as quick reference on HTML tag syntax).

Webmonkey | Reference: Special Characters, http://www.webmonkey.com/webmonkey/reference/special_characters/ (reference cited in Appendix A).

Wikipedia (the free encyclopedia), *Web Browser Entry*, http://en.wikipedia.org/wiki/Web_browser (this page describes all there is to know about Web browsers; I used it as a reference on the order in which the browsers appeared).

Wilton, Paul, *Beginning JavaScript*, Wrox, June 2000 (I used this book to learn JavaScript; it gave me ideas for new examples and approaches).

Windows Server 2003 R2 Pricing, http://www.microsoft.com/windowsserver2003/howtobuy/licensing/pricing.mspx (pricing guide for MS Windows Server 2003 R2).

Index